9/10

51/50
{dates}   {weeks}

The **Magical** Adventures
of a **Single** Life

51/50

The **Magical** Adventures
of a **Single** Life

Kristen McGuiness

Soft Skull Press
New York

Library of Congress Cataloging-in-Publication Data is available.

ISBN 978-1-59376-413-5

Cover design by Candice Woo
Book design by Marti Lou Critchfield
Interior by Neuwirth & Associates, Inc.
Printed in the United States of America

Soft Skull Press
An Imprint of Counterpoint LLC
1919 Fifth Street
Berkeley, CA 94710

www.softskull.com
www.counterpointpress.com

Distributed by Publishers Group West

10 9 8 7 6 5 4 3 2 1

To mi famiglia

Table of Contents

Definition of 51/50

5150 is a section of the California Welfare and Institutions Code which allows a qualified officer or clinician to involuntarily confine a person deemed to have a mental disorder that makes the person a danger to himself or herself, and/or others.

It is also the name of a Van Halen album.

Introduction

I am single.

I am thirty.

I am an alcoholic.

And this was not supposed to be my life.

I admit to being an alcoholic once a day, on average. But I am much more than that.

I am a secretary with a fancy college degree and more books in my kitchen than cooking ability. I am the only child of an incarcerated drug smuggler and a woman who won't even steal pens from the office. I am the granddaughter of a woman who regularly insists I should just marry rich. I am the niece to two adoring uncles who never had children themselves. I am a transplanted Los Angeleno with a questioning belief in the great powers above and an awful sense that I have more solo Saturday night trips to Trader Joe's and Blockbuster in store.

Back when I still participated in drugs and alcohol, my need for a boyfriend had been fleeting. Cocaine was my boyfriend, and he was all I ever needed. Like Uma Thurman in *Pulp Fiction*, I would cut my coke on some bathroom sink, roll up my dollar bill, blow the line, and exhale, "Goddamn. God. Damn." I would watch the blacks of my eyes expand, feel that deep breath, the warm drip sliding down the back of my throat, and know that I was home. And though, at times, there were real men too, I would always end up back with cocaine.

Things had changed since then. Because long gone were the days when I saw that 115 pound wreck staring back at me in the mirror. I was now sober. I was now sane. I was now a most unfortunate twenty pounds heavier. And I thought it would all be different—that men would see me as an excellent candidate to be their wife, and love would come easy.

But it didn't.

It had been five years since a man told me he loved me. Three years since there was anyone close to a boyfriend. A year and a half since I last had sex. And after going on only three dates in the last two years, I knew something had to change. Because at a certain point, it stops being strange to be the last single woman on the block. It just begins to hurt.

So I figured it was time for a new kind of 51/50. I would go on 51 dates over the course of 50 weeks, and I would write about it, and I would finally get the life I thought was supposed to be mine. Because more than anything—more than a different job or a dashing boyfriend—I just want to be in love again. I want to hold someone's hand in the movie theater. I want to put their name down as my emergency contact at the doctor's office. I want to slow dance and cook dinner and have someone pull me deep into their chest after sex and tell me that I am beautiful.

I didn't get sober to watch myself shut down, stop waxing, and retire to eating ice cream sandwiches by myself. So I decided I would give the middle finger to fate. I would go out and find him myself, because I had very little faith that the universe was going to figure this one out for me. I had given it plenty of chances. I prayed and I meditated, and I did all the things we're supposed to do in order to let go of loneliness and fear. And all I found was more loneliness and fear.

They say that if you want to hear God laugh, tell Him your plan. But I am willing to risk it. I think this plan might be much better than the one destiny has been offering.

Because at the end of the day, though I might always be an alcoholic, I'm going to get me a shot of being someone's girl.

Date One: First Impressions

"Do you want a cookie?" Richard points to one of the delicious, decadent pieces of heaven sitting safely behind the glass case. I do want a cookie. Desperately. But I am playing someone else tonight. I am playing the girl who doesn't want a cookie, who doesn't gorge herself on sweets, who smiles instead, and says, "No, just tea for me, please."

Bullshit. I try to be normal. I try to be the type of woman I think Richard would like. And I have to say, I'm pretty good at it. I didn't think I was going to want Richard's attentions prior to going on the date with him. In fact, I had planned on getting a pretty massive piece of cake at the café where we had agreed to meet. It's outdoors. It serves coffee and wine. It also serves cakes, and cookies, and brownies, and I like those things. It's kind of romantic without being obtusely so. It's where white people with decent jobs and Priuses go on their first date.

Historically, I am not a dater. I went on my first date when I was twenty-six and only because my boss at the time set me up with a friend of hers, and I had no other choice. High-pitched Marcus was surprised by the fact that I had made it that long without a date, but I wasn't. At one point in my life, finding a boyfriend had been easy. I would just get drunk, have a one-night stand with one of my friends, and then never leave. In some instances, I would stay in their beds for a good year or two. Sure, there were fights and fun and family vacations, and all the conventional things that come with a relationship, but none of them had actually started conventionally. I took breaks in between, and though I worried about when the next guy would appear, within eighteen months, he invariably would. That is the beauty of one's early twenties. There are so many of us who are single and looking for the starter romance that it seems as though love is always around the corner. But then people start getting married, or they come out as gay, or they settle into a bachelorhood that becomes far more interesting than any relationship, and the numbers grow slimmer as the streets between this love and the next grow farther apart.

Richard came to me by way of former co-worker Katie, which takes us back to 2006. I relapsed in 2006. It was a short three-week jaunt into what I thought was my old party life, except the old life had once been kind of fun. Instead, my relapse felt more like a bunch of naps caught between boring lines of cocaine and me vomiting in a toilet. After three weeks I was done, and I went back to being sober, and looking for a new job. The temp agency called me with my first assignment on a Friday afternoon. It was one of those moments that never leave you. The sun burns brighter, sound becomes clearer, and everything slows down because life is about to change. I would be sent to a nonprofit downtown which, from what I could tell, helped low-income kids of Latino descent. I would be someone's secretary, and it would pay me enough to eat.

I met Katie on my first day. We were the same age, but Katie was a manager, and I was a temporary assistant. I normally would have hated her for this. But Katie was a good egg, which is why when we recently got together to catch up, and she asked me how the love life was going, I told her the truth.

Over the last year, I had gotten rather good at posturing to the question. Bragging about my adventures and experiences and all the things that filled my life because I didn't have a boyfriend. Generally, people ignored my buoyant optimism only to respond with a handful of platitudes that annoyed me. Things like, "All in good time," "The right man will come along," and my favorite, "It happens when you least expect it." This is why I had begun acting like I was choosing singlehood in the first place. I didn't want their condescension, their suggestions, their strange, sad smiles. Because really, I can't be told I should read *The Secret* one more time without wanting to hit someone. But Katie didn't respond with any such nonsense because Katie's a smart girl.

"I know the perfect man for you," she told me. Alas, Richard.

People should be more careful about the photos they use to introduce themselves. Because in the photo Richard sends me, he clearly has man boobs. This was disturbing. Enough so, that after showing it to a few friends in the office, his nickname became the incredibly original and possibly trademarked "Man boob." Not a good start.

So when I walk up to the Christmas light–strewn café, I'm not sure if the relatively good-looking guy waiting there is the man in question. I don't even move to say his name just in case.

"Kristen?" he asks. I quietly exhale my sigh of relief.

Richard looks nothing like his picture. With a decent head of brown hair, and the educated style of a Northeastern boy come west, he stands a strong few inches taller than me, and I like that. For some unexplained reason, and with great Napoleon effect, there are a lot of short guys who live in L.A. It's always nice when I meet someone with whom I can wear heels.

Richard and I get our respective teas, coffees, and sweet treats (for the sir, not the lady) and sit down. We talk about writing projects and poets and yoga and where we've lived and what we want to be. Richard is half Italian, half Irish. I'm half Italian, a quarter Irish, and a quarter Hungarian, which is where we differ. Because Gypsy blood is dangerous, and Irish/Italian just makes for a good appetite. I figure this is probably why he knows of the Hungarian restaurant in the Valley I have always wanted to try, and where he invites me for a second date. I say yes, and actually am beginning to feel like that normal woman I was trying so hard to be. The type who simply hungers and does not crave.

I feel quite comfortable sitting across from this man. It's been so long since I did this—since I got to know someone a bit, got to settle into the easy banter of a nice first date. I have only been on three dates since I first got sober, and all of them were with sober men who already knew my life story.

Recovered alcoholics are a funny bunch. We very rarely respond to the question "How are you?" with "Fine." It's more like a therapy session than small talk, which is why going out on dates with them isn't always this casual. There's a joke that we tell that goes, "How do you know when a first date between two alcoholics went well?" The punch line: "They move in with each other." I have barely even used a swear word, let alone told some dirty sex story, because Richard and I are keeping up our most honest, personable, and pleasant personas. Maybe that's all he has, but either way, I am appreciating it.

Our table is right next to the street, so we're in full view of the foot traffic. And then I see my friend Ward. I call him my friend only because I lack a better word. Ward and I have hung out several times, but he still calls me Blair. Ward and I go to meetings together for said sober people. Ward is twitchy and sort of looks like Dave Navarro, if Dave Navarro were homeless. I think Ward might have a real case of Tourettes because he has a tendency to shout things out and talk to himself, but then again, so do I. At the end of the day, he can also be a really sweet guy, which is why when he recognizes me, I wave and say hello. Ward weaves and bobs his way over to our table.

"Hi. Blair."

I introduce the two men and then tell Ward I'll see him on Tuesday because that's the night we both go to the same meeting. He just nods his head and walks off in mid-sentence, muttering to himself as he heads down the street. I get the feeling that the normal cover I was trying to front here just got blown. Because most upper-middle-class, private-school girls working in nonprofits with a Honda Civic don't hang out with men like Ward. I know this, and Richard knows this.

He turns to me and asks, "What's Tuesday?"

What's Tuesday, Richard? Oh, just the place where me and my other mutant sober-hero friends get together and talk about what it was like, what happened, and what it's like now. I am terrible with confidentiality clauses, and so I explain it to him in nice, friendly terms. But Richard does little more than shrug. And then it hits me. Maybe this means little to him. Maybe only I care about my past and my stories and my strange associates that I think would be such a flag to the different lives I am assuming Richard and I have led.

"Do you have a sponsor?" he asks.

I laugh, "Yes, I do. Everyone should."

I like him more for that. I see how he has the sleeves of his button-down rolled up just right—how his arms are respectable, covered with a healthy amount of Italian hair. He could probably manage a grill, keep up a good conversation with the parents, and be the type of man I could trust. And I wonder whether I am at the point yet where I can be attracted to that kind of guy; whether it isn't always me insisting I don't go for the wrong ones while I continually do. Or rather that Gypsy blood is too wild for barbeque arms and a compassionate responsibility. Whether I am trustworthy when I meet someone who is willing to trust.

But at that moment, I don't feel anything but happy sitting there in the light-strewn garden with all the other Prius- and Civic-driving liberals, sipping tea and laughing about the *New Yorker*, and beginning to think that this might be what I was missing. Richard and I walk to our cars and hug. We confirm the next date. And though there is no kiss, no major (or even minor) overture of romance, I am giddy. Because I met someone with whom I rather enjoyed sharing a table—someone I look forward to seeing again, and who looks forward to seeing me. Someone without man boobs.

Date Two: The Prince and the Talker

I fell in love with a prince when I was nineteen. This had been a dream of mine ever since I was five and read my first book, *The Donkey Prince*. Same story as the *Frog Prince*, except starring a donkey. I figured my chances were better with the ass because girls like me don't date real princes. Then again, my prince wasn't a real prince, but he was French royalty. Years after we dated, I Googled him, only to discover that he was in line to a number of long-dead titles and possibly even a throne. So I'm gonna say he was about as close to a prince as I'm ever going to get.

We called him "Frenchie" because that's what you call French people in college, and, I think, in general. I don't know what arrow struck him the day he hung out of his dorm room window and called down to me as though we were old friends. I had just become a nervous and regularly stoned sophomore at Hamilton College in upstate New York. I grew up in the better parts of Dallas, Texas, so wealth didn't necessarily intimidate me just because I didn't have it. But the wealth at Hamilton was different. There were last names that you found on buildings. And international kids with diplomatic immunity. And there was Frenchie. I met him the year before when he was dating a quiet and beautiful Turkish girl with a strange name and lots of cashmere. She graduated and upon the first week of our new year at school, I found myself looking up into the sun and seeing Frenchie calling down to me. I invited him to my birthday party that week, and we began a love affair reserved for handwritten love notes and first edition books of poetry and a relationship that ultimately took me to his family's castles in France and his mother's rather cold disapproval of the American commoner her son had dragged in.

But none of that mattered. All that mattered was that I had him. And for the first time, I understood why women take their partner's names because I wanted to be forever identified with him. I wanted to be wrapped in his orange wool turtleneck and his old French movies and the accordion he would play while riding through the hallways of his dorm on a unicycle. I loved being us. I loved being his.

Which is why when I met Phillipe on MySpace in 2004, I thought I might have found that same great French love again. From his photo, I could tell he had the same mess of curly hair as my first Frenchie, and the same big cow eyes, and that lovely pert nose that once had been such a seamless counterpart to my Italian boxer schnoz. Phillipe and I e-mailed for a bit, and then decided to take it to the phone. The conversation was the longest five minutes of my life. Phillipe had a tenuous grasp of the English language, and in the middle of the call he hurt his thumb so badly that the conversation went from awkward to irritated. I never spoke to him again, and we dropped whatever loose plans we had to meet.

When I decided to look Phillipe up again, I realized I had found myself in the Summer of Desperation 2007. After a very long and confusing volley about when and where we were going to meet, it was confirmed that we would get gelato together in the neighborhood. The phone call was no less irritating than the one we had years before, and so I quickly moved to be done with it, but Phillipe felt like talking. Phillipe liked to talk.

"So you are feeling better?" he asked.

I had been sick that week, so I replied, very slowly, because I remember in the conversation years prior, Phillipe commenting that I talk too fast.

"Yes… I came home… and went to… bed… early."

"Ah, yes, last night, I rejhnjkhf kjkheug f jkh iueyh (because I have no idea what was actually said), and I put zee key in zee door. With my backpack. And I zit down on zee couch. With my backpack, my pack is for my motorbike. And I close my eyes. And zee captain. You know, zee captain of zee sheep?"

I lay there on my bed wide-eyed. Did I miss something? Zee captain of what sheep? He lives on a sheep? Phillipe gets irritated that I am obviously not following his story. He can hear it in my silence.

"You know! Zee pirate. Zee pirate with zee sheep. Zee wheel, he stands, zee wheel, he drives zee sheep."

At this point, I am playing a silent game of charades in my head. Pirates of Penzanze! Pirates of the Caribbean! There's a pirate on TV! You're dreaming! There's a pirate in your house! But Phillipe has moved on.

"And zen, I open my eyes and it's 3:30. Zat doesn't always happen."

I don't know how to respond. I don't even know what's been said. I grasp, "You… must… have had… a long… day."

"Yes, a long day."

I hoped that it was just the phone. He is a French artist with a motorcycle and a cottage in Pasadena, and even beyond the Frenchie factor, man, do I want to be in that movie. Because ever since the *Donkey Prince*, even before the *Donkey Prince*, I have been addicted to romance. Romeo and Juliet. Tristan and Isolde. Frenchie and Kristen. These were stories I not only told myself, they were ones I was determined to live. I wanted to love at such an intensity it felt as though I might die because of it. I wanted Wagner in the background and rain on command. I wanted the great big handsome star to sweep me off my feet, to look deeply into my eyes, and tell me, "Get on zee back of my motorbike, and I will take you to zee cottage in zee woods."

After three years, and two horrible phone conversations, I show up for gelato, with my fair share of apprehension, and a little bit of hope. For the most part, Phillipe is what I expected. He is wearing a fleece because it's October now, which is kind of cold by Los Angeles standards. But under the fleece are a button-down and some sort of cravat, which looks like a bow tie meets an ascot. I dig that. I dig funky cravats, which is why I have the French fetish in the first place. Because the accent on its own can be a little annoying.

We sit down, and Phillipe begins talking. Who knew someone with such a basic understanding of English could speak so much. Phillipe is probably strange even in his own country. He is obviously a bit of a loner and, admittedly, is "emancipated" from his family.

"Do you like it in L.A?" I ask him.

"Ummm, let me see. I think it is…," he thinks for a bit, "a rape of human kind. Yes, a rape of human kind."

"Oh. That's, yeah, that's what a lot of people think. I guess I see it as much more than that. I think L.A.'s dark side is her sweetness, her quaint neighborhoods and her palm trees. The rest of it…"

Phillipe interrupts, "They are nice, but no, it is a rape of human kind."

I am not sure if Phillipe is simply uninterested in what I have to say, or whether he is just confused by what I am actually saying. He tells me, "You don't sound like a California girl. You sound like a New Yorker girl." When I finally do speak, he sits back, much like I do while watching Telemundo—interested if only I could understand. Then he changes the channel. Back to him.

The thing is for all of Phillipe's knowledge, he doesn't know how to laugh. Maybe he hasn't yet learned to tell jokes in English. Or maybe he's just not funny. Frenchie was hysterical. And perhaps that's what made our otherwise fantasy romance feel so real. Because for all the slow dancing and long romantic talks, he could also make me laugh. We stayed together for one year, and then Frenchie graduated. The following summer I was working at *High Times* as an intern, beginning my journey into alcohol-induced bad behavior and rushing to the mailbox every day to see if I had received another one of the fountain pen–scrawled letters that contained the words, "I cannot stop thinking about when I will have you in my arms again, feel you. When I do, I forget everything, I'm just happy. Past, future, everything disappears when I am with you, ma chere. J'attend, j'attend, j'attend."

I wait, I wait, I wait.

There are days when I still pull out those letters. They remind me that though it's been so long since romance held me close, at one point it did. At one point, I sat with that man on a porch in France. We read our books and breathed softly. As his foot rested on mine, I looked over to find him watching me, and I knew that this was all that love ever needed to be. And though ten years have gone by, and he lives in France with his wife, and in many ways, feels as though he was a movie I once saw and not a man I knew, those letters always remind me that he believed in who I was, and he loved me for it.

I was almost afraid that Phillipe would remind me of him. That some long-healed wound would feel fresh for a moment. But he didn't. He did remind me that my dating life since the first Frenchie has been a game of Goldilocks—always searching for the romantic perfection I found in some silly relationship that I had before I was even twenty. I hold them all up to that prince, and I judge. Too smart. Not smart enough. Too wild. Not wild enough. Too funny. Not funny enough. And it's not to say that I didn't fall in love again because I did. For the most part though, I find myself slowly shaking my head that this one just won't do. Never just right, like that man, who ten years ago held me on a Paris street and told me he would love me forever, then put me in a taxi and never saw me again.

When I look at it that way, I can feel the years of disappointment. And tonight, as the minutes drag by, as Phillipe launches from one story to the next, as I pretend to listen, I can feel the wound. And I know I need to let go of this fantasy. I can't keep thinking that it's only the romances that take place across daunting odds that are the ones worth having. It hasn't served me in years, if it ever did.

Phillipe doesn't seem to notice that I am making life-altering resolutions across the table from him. Instead, he leans back, cocks his head, and asks, "Do you know who you look like little? I hope you don't sink it's an insult. Zee woman with zee curly hair, and zee big eyes, she sings, 'I love you like a woman.'"

I don't know this song. He attempts to sing it, but I am even worse at that game. "Oh you know, she was in zee operas in zee seventies."

I smile, "Barbra Streisand?"

"YES!! YES!! Little bit. Barbra Streisand." I don't take it as an insult. Because I get that. Often. And I don't even look like her. But I kind of dress like her. Or rather her in the seventies. As my friend Siren says, "All sweatery boots and tight pants." I would have liked to have shared her brilliance with Phillipe, but it was terminology like "sweatery boots" that was making it easier for me just to stay silent.

"So would you like to get some food?" Phillipe asks.

I look at the time on my cell phone, "Oh well, it's getting kind of…"

Phillipe interrupts, "Of course, I should say, I do not have enough money on me for two people. You pay for you. I pay for me."

"Yeah, I really should be going," I say, standing up. Because as much as I like the image of dating a French artist with a motorcycle, I realize that in this case, it would only be another fantasy. A celluloid still from a silent film that always sounds interesting when you're scrolling through Netflix, but gets boring before you're halfway through. And I know that's not the movie I want to be in; it would only be a really bad sequel to the masterpiece I made years ago. Today, I think I'll let that film reel crackle into oblivion. I will kiss that Donkey Prince on the forehead, and I will leave him standing in the rearview mirror of my Parisian taxi, forever waving goodbye.

Date Three: Normies

I'm rather excited for my second date with Richard. I see him as a perfect opportunity to find romance in reality. I even get a little dressed up for the date and talk to my mom about him minutes before he arrives. We drive to the restaurant, and it hits me—Richard is a "normie."

Being a normie is not a bad thing. Most people would say it's rather good. A normie is the nickname we alcoholics give to non-alcoholics. They drink in good measure, they don't overspend, they might have done drugs, but they're by no means addicts. They're just people who for whatever reason didn't come out quite as crazy as the rest of us. They follow directions. They pay attention. They don't even have eating problems. Honestly, we try to be like them every day. Many of us not-so-normies even go on to marry them, and interbreed. But it can be hard. Because they want to do things the right way naturally, and we have to work at it all the time.

"It's gotta be here somewhere," Richard mutters as we walk up and down Ventura Boulevard, in search of the Hungarian restaurant where he made our reservation.

"Maybe Nancy fucked up," I suggest. I am trying to be funny because I am not as freaked out about the missing restaurant. Unfortunately, I think my stab at humor is just riding Richard's nerves. Richard drives a Prius, and Nancy is his OnStar navigator. I call all OnStars that because, well, it makes sense. Richard, however, trusts Nancy. Strike one against him. I know it's not fair of me. Maybe it's even downright bitchy, but I can't understand how people can't find their way without those things. And the restaurant in question was around the corner from an apartment building Richard had lived in for years. I have never lived in the Valley and actually find it to be a bit of Kryptonite to my otherwise heightened sense of direction, and even I could have gotten us to Ventura and Campo de Cahuenga without Nancy's soothing yet slightly irritated voice giving us the most boring route possible. I think Nancy is exhausted. She's just a burned-out phone sex operator who dispenses the easiest means possible to what could be a far more interesting journey.

"Richard, I think this is it." We are standing in front of an Indian restaurant with the same address as the Hungarian joint that once sat in its place.

"Well, they could have told me that when I made the reservation."

"I'm okay with Indian if you are."

"I guess. I don't really eat Indian, but if it's our only option," Richard pouts.

Of course, when Richard confesses to not knowing what Tikka Masala is, I realize "I don't really" means never. Strike two. I can't date someone who doesn't have an adventurous appetite. I just can't. I'll eat anything. The way I look at it, what's a little food poisoning that this mysterious human body can't handle? So we order, or rather I order. For us. Another strike. And we haven't even begun the second-date conversation. Richard started a new job this week. And they work a lot of hours. And the natives aren't entirely friendly. And apparently, he's having insomnia. The admission of which was in response to my describing the hell on earth that is a come-down from cocaine. That's when I find out Richard's never tried cocaine. And herein lies the difference between the normie and me. It is this gulf in decision-making and risk-taking that makes the normie gap so terrifyingly wide.

It all started when Richard asked if I had ever been to Good. Good is an awkward, gay-owned, gay-friendly restaurant with really bad food. The next thing I know, I am telling Richard about how when I first started getting sober, I had gone to Good to try to do some controlled drinking. I was three weeks out of the relationship that changed my life.

Years after Frenchie, Oliver became the one. He was the one to replace my first young love with my first adult love. He was the one who I thought would save me but ended up not being able to love me at my worst. He was the one whom I lost, whom I loved more than drinking and still couldn't quit to keep. So he quit me. The day after he sent me the e-mail ending our three-month affair, I found myself in my first meeting. And two weeks later, I found myself at Good, trying to do some controlled drinking. I ordered a pitcher of beer, and I allowed the control to commence.

"Wait, wait, you ordered a pitcher, and you thought that was controlled drinking?" Richard asks, confused. "Yes," I say. Deadpan if you will. "See, I figured that I would just have a glass or two out of the pitcher, and then…"

"Isn't that like saying you're going to do some controlled eating, and then go and order a huge chocolate cake?"

Richard might be a normie, but he's a smart one. I explain to him that by the time I was done, the restaurant was closed, and I was sitting there drinking by myself watching Cher's last tour on DVD. I remember I was crying a little so she must have been singing, "Believe." But who knows? I might have been crying because my heart was more broken than it had ever been before. Or I might have been drinking because Sonny Bono was dead.

"Had he just died?" Richard asks.

"No," I shrug. "But it's still sad."

The night before my date with Richard, I had gone bowling with some friends. The only problem with bowling is that I hate it. Thankfully, there was someone there whom I had been trying to meet for some time. Ben. Toxic, sober alcoholic, Ben. I had seen him around at my meetings for a while, so when a mutual friend brought him to the bowling alley, I began to think fate was shifting to my side. Ben is a balding writer, who appears to wear a T-shirt and shorts on any given occasion, but he handles a pool stick with all muscle and cock, and though I barely know him, he seems like the type of guy who is more intrigued by the journey than by anything else. This might also explain why Ben is forty and single.

Toxic Ben said last night, "The only problem with normies is there's just no heat there." Normies like Richard. They ask how a pitcher is controlled drinking. They ask why one would do cocaine to feel less drunk when it would be much easier to simply stop drinking. They ask Nancy for directions. And that's the thing. There is just no heat there.

I get up to use the ladies room. I don't look so good. I'm tired. I'm still a bit bummed out about Toxic Ben. We and a couple of other anti-bowlers had left the pins to start a renegade game of pool. Ben and I had been having a great time playing pool and lightly flirting until my friend Joan asked me, "How's your 51 dates going?"

There might as well have been a scratch on the record. Ben quickly looked up from his shot and asked, "What 51 dates?"

"I'm going on 51 dates in 50 weeks in order to find love," I pronounced. I smiled across the pool table at Ben. I was hoping he would ask to be one of my dates. I even tried to swing my hip to the right, the way someone with much better flirting skills might do.

Ben just looked at me, pool stick in hand, smirk on face. "Good luck with that," he snorted. And then I watched as Ben took his shot and sunk the ball. And then I watched as he turned his attentions to Joan.

Later as we were getting ready to leave, I got up the gusto and asked Ben, "You wanna be one of my 51 dates?"

"Naw, I don't want to be fodder for one of your stories."

I walked up ahead of him to the bowling ball counter with my shoes, trying to fight back the tears because I suffer rejection like a ten- year-old.

"Hey," I heard behind me. I turned around, and Ben was right there. Eye to eye. He stared in. And I felt it. Heat.

"I'd like to be your 51st date."

I laughed, "That's in like a year from now."

"So," he said, "I want to be the last one. I want to see what you found out."

I slip back into the booth across from Richard and ask, "You want to get gelato?"

"Sure," Richard says. He mentioned being slightly lactose intolerant before, but I really can't tolerate that. I told him I think I am too, but I love dairy too damn much to ever let it stop me. So we go to my favorite gelato place in Silver Lake. It is also the Supreme Court for all my final dates. Maybe it's the lighting. Or the general bonhomie of my neighborhood. Or my date's choice in gelato. But it is an amazing primary for one's personality, and my final judgment of it.

Richard and I go in, and though I find myself in conversation with the couple next to us, Richard stands silent. And while I sample four gelatos, Richard gets two scoops of the same flavor without even trying them out. We go outside and sit down under the lighting that acts like a chemistry thermometer, but the temperature's not reading.

I know I am not better than Richard. I am not brighter than Richard. I am not even that much more attractive than Richard. But I can find my own way in this world. I can take risks that might make me sick, might make my heart break like a bad Cher song, but I enjoy every second of it. I like eating the entire cake and having dairy even when it makes my stomach cramp. And I want someone who gets lost for fun and sits down under the lighting and beams. Beams so brightly, there's heat.

Date Four: God and Herpes

I hit bottom in 2005 when I was twenty-seven years old. I didn't plan on doing it. I never thought I was wild enough to have to enter a plea of alcoholism and call it quits. Even with all the attempts at controlled drinking, and the mornings spent wishing I could get at least ten minutes of sleep before going to work, I just figured I was a young, single-ish party girl living in L.A. I thought sobriety was for rock stars, junkies, and old men in trench coats with Vietnam-vet toenails. I, at least, had a day job.

After three years of trying to quit the party on my own, and the acceleration past heavy drinking into downright embarrassment, I moved home to Dallas to live with Uncle Tom. People generally move home when shit hits the fan, and my shit was all over the place. I started going to meetings where I was told that I needed to find this thing called God. I had believed in God before. I was raised Catholic and went to an all-girl parochial school. I even attempted to be confirmed, but my best friend Maggie and I spent most of our catechism classes smoking cigarettes and eating candy outside the 7-Eleven across the street from church. By the time my rampant sexuality and drug use were in full swing, God had been relegated to a few foxhole prayers made over a toilet bowl, and a lot more drunken rants against His existence.

Going home to Texas and finding a God of my own understanding was not how I had intended to live out the end of my twenties. As I knelt by my bed in my uncle's house, grasping desperately to the six weeks of sobriety I had somehow found, I knew I had no choice. I had no idea what God was, but somehow I was going to find a way to believe. I cried, and I begged, and I said aloud, "If you're there, please show me. Show me." Oh, the sign. How many times have we asked for it, for the clear, broad stroke in the sky that spells out, "I am here?" I called for it, and I waited. My uncle traveled most of that year, so it was just me in the house. And the silence that responded made me cry even more.

I got up and went into the bathroom. My uncle lives in one of the most sterile neighborhoods in Dallas. There is no brush, there is no humidity, there are no dark, dank corners for creepy little crawlies to hide in. Never had I seen anything close to a cockroach in his house or gated community. But when I snapped on the light to the bathroom, there He sat. The cockroach was glued to the wall. He didn't even move. He just waited. Waited for me to see that He was there in all forms. The oldest living creature on earth, the hardiest beast, and there He sat to remind me that something is here indeed. And if I were willing to call it God, I might just find some relief. I began to cry even harder because all my life I had wished for a sign. And now, here I stood with the closest vision of the infinite I had yet to see. I had found my God. And then I calmly took off my flip flop and I killed Him.

For the most part, that is about as sophisticated or organized as my belief has been since then. I asked for a sign, God gave me a cockroach. And from there was born some messy little thing called faith. I can't say that I can articulate it much more than that, and I certainly don't expect my random date with a man named Nic to show me anymore than I think I already know, but that's the funny thing about God, He sure does like to show up in surprising forms.

Saturday night, I went out with my friend Mimi to try to pick up a guy. Mimi is a hip fashion designer, and I always feel cooler just being with her. She's been sober for over five years and is about the closest thing to a married friend that I have. Her boyfriend Carty is a low-key Southern boy with about the same amount of sober time, extensive tattoos covering nearly every inch of him, and the best set of social graces I have seen in a man since I moved back from Texas. And I can't help but want for a man who would make the perfect fourth to our friendship. Mimi decided that since she doesn't have any men to set me up with, she would help me find one herself. So we sauntered sober into a bar where we both used to drink. We did a half-circle, and stopped. There were available men, lots of them. Mimi asked, "Do you see anything that you want here?"

And I did. Braden. I don't know him, but I know who he is. I met Braden over a year ago at a meeting. I had just come in off my three-week relapse, and he had sixty days sober and was in love with recovery. He looked a little dangerous, and I like that. I stopped going to that meeting, and so I had also stopped fantasizing about Braden. But suddenly I looked up, and there he was pouring some drunk little hipster girl a whiskey and coke, and I wished desperately that I could have one too.

Mimi practically had to shove me up to the bar, but once I got there, I found out that Braden is still sober and still a little dangerous. As the bar began to wind down at last call, I knew that I might not have the liquid courage of years past, but I still had an offer up my sleeve. I slipped him my number with the note, "Call me when you get off work," and I rushed home to clean my apartment, just in case he was on his way.

Three days later, I'm on my date with Nic. Braden still hasn't called. My friend Latoya set me up with Nic with the caveat, "I'll give you his number, but I doubt that you'll fall in love."

Nic is a jive-talking black dude from South Central who works as a medical orderly at Cedars-Sinai. He slopes when he walks like some kind of a baller, and when he pulls out his iPod to show me pictures, they're all of him dressed in brightly colored suits singing with his church choir. I really don't think we're going to have much to talk about, and I can tell he knows as much as I do that the romantic potential is lost on us.

When I called Nic to set up the date, he told me, "There is only one thing you can't make up for in this life, baby girl. See, you can go to Vegas. You can lose twenty grand, you can mortgage the house, but one day, one day, you'll fix all that shit. The one thing you can't get back is time…baby…time." So I explained to him my dating experiment because I certainly didn't want to waste his.

"Hmmm…51 dates, huh?" he snorted.

"That's right."

"Which one am I?"

"Four."

"Hmm…four. Okay."

Because talking about work or childhood or books or movies or music all seems out of the question, Nic leads the conversation to sex. Nic likes sex. He tells me that he spent his youth in India and learned the ways of Tantric before he was twelve. If he thinks I am going to fall for that, he picked the wrong white girl. I don't, and Nic sees I'm not going to, so he starts bitching about women these days. He tells me about the last five girls he tried to date.

"It's a pain in the ass, baby girl." Nic keeps calling me this, which makes me think he can't remember my name. But Nic continues, "First woman I was into, and she was hot, on the third date, she tells me, 'Herpes.' And then I move on to girl number two, 'Herpes.' Girl #3 got 'em. Girl #4. By the time Girl #5 tell me, I'm done."

It's set up for me. I point to myself, "Herpes."

It's true. Unfortunate, but true. And here is where Nic and I find a common denominator: STDs. I have one, he has none, but he's pissed and a little paranoid that everyone else seems to. I explain to Nic that I'm not psyched that I have it, but that maybe in protecting someone else from getting it, I've protected myself from getting something far worse.

I didn't get herpes from a one-night stand. I got it from a boyfriend, and though perhaps it sounds better that way when I am explaining it to a potential romantic partner, the truth is it took me many years not to be devastated by its occurrence. I got it the last time I had sex with my crackhead ex-boyfriend, who later went on to become a regular in San Quentin. But no matter that he was my boyfriend at the time, or that I loved him, it didn't make its discovery any easier. I will never forget driving home from the doctor's office the night I found out and thinking that no one would love me again because of it. I tell Nic this, and I am not quite sure how he'll respond. He just smiles.

"God's will," he says, so matter of fact that I don't know what to say, even if I agree.

"That's the thing, baby girl," Nic leans forward, "God knows what the chessboard looks like."

Holy shit. I nod blankly because he has just put my entire outlook on God into one statement.

"You don't know why the rook isn't being moved yet," Nic smiles. "Only God knows it's to protect the queen."

And I forget that I don't want to be on this date. I almost start to cry as I find myself telling Nic about Braden, about being single, about believing in something, but still feeling horribly, horribly alone. I tell Nic how no guys hit on me. How they will talk to the friend on my left and the friend on the right, but I get ignored. Nic narrows his eyes and leans forward. He pulls back the hair from behind my ear as though to picture me at my sexiest.

"It because you're too much, baby girl. For most guys, you're just too much."

I understand what he means. I can be that girl, but only part of the time. Because as much as I can be the ballsy blonde with courage to spare, I can also be the scared little girl kneeling by her bed with snot on her face and an STD that smacks of damaged goods. And I am not quite sure which one is going to come out at any given moment.

"I don't know, Nic." I look down because I am really afraid I might start sobbing right there.

"Baby, it's the chessboard. You know it. You can't always see what's happening six moves out, but you gotta have faith."

And I think Nic might be right. Though I might be sad that the one I want isn't calling, I have to remember that I am no good at chess. I can't tell you what it's going to look like six moves out, and other than a cockroach and a guy named Nic, I can't even say much by the way of God. Either way, I am interested in finding out.

25

1 2 3 4 **5** 6 7 8 9 10 11 12 13 14 15 16 17 18 19 20
21 22 23 24 25 26 27 28 29 30 31 32 33 34 35 36
37 38 39 40 41 42 43 44 45 46 47 48 49 50 51

Date Five: Dreaming in the Land of CHA

People always say what a big city Los Angeles is, but I think that's a misnomer. To me, L.A. is a collection of seventeen small towns, all working quietly next to one another. Each town is its own universe, with its own language and culture and people. Years ago, I lived in the town of Hollywood. There, I went to cool parties, met celebrities, and made out with Quentin Tarantino, all between bumps in the bathroom.

About six months before I moved home to Dallas to get sober, I left Hollywood and moved into another universe called Silver Lake. The West Coast Williamsburg had its fair share of kids with bangs and skinny jeans, but it also had an older group of liberal professionals with their Audi station wagons and later, in 2008, their ubiquitous Obama stickers. As much as streets like Sunset and Cahuenga and hotspots like the Standard and Chateau once called my name, I had begun to stay away from those places. I would disregard them as gross Hollywood hangouts infiltrated by the CHAs. Cheesy. Hollywood. Actors. If I could trademark that nickname I would. I have always felt that my mere invention of it should have destined me for greatness. I am still waiting.

Needless to say, Hollywood is filled with CHAs. They all have skinny bodies and big heads and probably none of them were into high school theater. Those kids are geeks who actually read Arthur Miller and Tennessee Williams and know all the words to *Mame*. No, the CHAs were sluts and football players and small town playboys before they came out here to work in some shitty bar near Vine and pray for that big break as the stepson on some CBS sitcom that never makes it past Season One. They do shorts, and thank You Tube, and wait until the day that their hair-gelled good looks fade into the hopes of becoming a character actor. Or they go home and get real jobs. Maybe some parlay that bit role on *King of Queens* into some part on *CSI*. Most of them never make it past head shots. And God bless them.

I expect that my date tonight will be such a CHA. From what I have been briefed, Doug is a forty-year-old bar manager who lives in the Valley, and already I can sense the failed attempt at the big time. Doug was sent to me by my friend Rachel. When I met Rachel, she was in the middle of a divorce, but now she is in love with someone else, and his best friend just happens to be Doug. I am used to this. In the time that I have been single, I have watched people meet, fall in love, marry, have children, divorce, fall in love again. And then they all try to set me up with their new boyfriend's best friend.

Doug and I meet in Silver Lake. It doesn't take long for us to start discussing who we are and where we have been. Doug explains that he started out as an actor but then he began managing a bar ten years ago.

"It's weird," he tells me. "I just started doing it, and I realized a few years ago that I loved it. I love taking care of people. So why stop?"

There is something so refreshing in that statement that Doug becomes more attractive by the confession. And Doug is relatively attractive. Although he is in the transition stage of going from a thin-haired man in his thirties to a bald man in his forties, he looks a bit like many of the soap opera stars on whom I had a crush when I was a kid. I can imagine being eight, watching daytime TV during summer vacation, and drooling over the likes of a young Doug.

Doug tells me that he was born and raised in L.A. He laughs, "I know. There are only a few of us."

People from L.A. always tell that to transplants like me. Mimi once told me that she and a guy named Phil Bower are the only native Los Angelenos in the city. But that is another Los Angeles myth because there is an enormous number of people who are born, raised, and never leave here. And I understand. When you have seventeen different universes all within the space of one city, why bother?

But the one thing we all ultimately do is leave Hollywood. The big dream. The song and the dance. The famous hookups and the belief that we could have been a star. Whether you were raised here or not, this might be a town of broken dreams, but at one point, we all had one that was alive and well.

I find out that acting isn't the only dream Doug has lost. As he gets quiet and explains that he is still taking care of the cats he ended up with from a divorce a few years back, I sense another stalled hope in Doug's story. I can see why giving up acting might not have seemed like such a sacrifice set against a happy marriage, and why now, in its failure, there is the feeling that much more was lost than just a relationship. Doug doesn't go into details, refers to the whole thing as back story, but I know what back story is. Back story is when the wife leaves you and the pets, and then you're a single dude with three cats.

He smiles sadly and says, "As much as I love them, I have to say, they're getting old. And I'm kinda looking forward to traveling freely without always having to find someone to take care of them."

I am sure in their passing, those cats will give him more than just physical freedom. I can see that it takes a long time for the wounds of divorce to heal, and even longer for the scar to fade. And though I might have watched women fall in love, marry, go through divorce, and fall in love again, maybe I've been lucky that I have been spared that pain. I so often think of marriage as the ultimate prize that I forget it's not necessarily permanent. And might not actually be the dream to which I have pinned so many hopes.

Doug and I have a nice enough dinner. It's a little loud in the restaurant, and he's kind of a low talker, and I am kind of a little deaf, this makes me nod and smile a lot. But maybe that's better. I tell him how one day I hope to be a writer—that I have loved books since before I could read.

"So, you're really smart, huh?" he asks.

I want to say: *Yes, I am*. And you have no idea what a pain in the ass that is. Back in 2002 when I moved to Hollywood, I once had my own starstruck dream. Long before I found myself answering phones at a nonprofit downtown, I thought I was going to make it big. I moved out to L.A. with one screenplay, half a novel, and a laptop. I thought that between the jacaranda trees and the Hollywood sign and the lights of the Sunset Strip that some kind of fame might be mine. After two years in Los Angeles, I met and fell in love with Oliver, a successful Hollywood producer who I thought would be the answer to that dream. I would write books and screenplays, and he would make them into movies, and I too would see my Hollywood star rise.

But that wasn't reality. At the time, I could barely pay my bills. I would go to the local gas station, and it would be me and a bunch of female CHAs in their convertible BMWs. For all I know, they might have had PhDs in nuclear physics, but I get the feeling that their M3s came more from modeling gigs and wealthy older boyfriends. And I hated them. I wanted so badly just to have their good highlights and small button noses, and then I wouldn't have to do anything more than ask for a light in order to find love. Though being well-read and asking the tough questions and being considered a challenge to the men I dated might have helped me feel better about myself, I would wonder whether it was all worth it. Whether the CHAs had this thing figured out with a lot less thinking and a lot less disappointment.

I don't know how to respond to Doug's question. So I cock my head to the side and say something to the effect of, "On good days," which makes no sense. As though on my bad days, I become a blithering moron. It's actually on the bad days when I am too smart, when I overthink and overdose my head with thoughts about who I am and where I am going and why some things just aren't meant to be.

We finish dinner, and I need to get going. I am picking up my friend Siren to go to a party at the Standard in Hollywood. Even though I don't live there anymore, even though a part of me has moved on since that dream, I still like to visit the universe next door from time to time. Doug and I leave the restaurant, and I am laughing. I feel totally comfortable.

And here is where the dilemma is revealed: Would I like to go out with Doug again?

Sure.

Would I like Doug to be my boyfriend?

No.

And why not?

I don't know.

For all my smarts, I know even less.

Date Six: Desperado

I hang up the phone with my father and stare dumbly at the porch of my friends' beach house in Oxnard. My friends John and Teresa stay in this house every winter. It is one of those Big Easy rentals that make real life feel very far away—an old wood cabin with wind whistling through its walls. We have to climb out a window to get to the backyard, but it's well worth it because the backyard is the roiling Pacific. We come home smelling like salt, and every November I look forward to this time with my friends, lounging in blankets on the cold, wet sand.

Though this weekend is technically not a date, it feels like it has pushed me closer to love than any encounter I have had so far, and I wonder whether that is all these dates might be: real experiences in the search for this thing called love.

If that's the case, then next week my visit to my dad will probably be one of the most important dates of my life. I will be face-to-face with him for the first time in years, and for the first time since I got sober, and though there is a part of me that wants to see him, that has dreamed of seeing him, there is also a part of me that is really, really scared.

My father was arrested when I was four. I don't remember it happening. He was in Panama City with his mistress at the time, and my mom and I were down in Ft. Lauderdale, staying with my grandmother because everyone, except for my father, could feel that the end was near. I should say it wasn't the first time my father had been arrested. Before I was born, he had spent time in Mexican prisons, escaped from every jail they had put him in, and by the time I came along, had graduated from small-time pot dealer to one of the biggest marijuana smugglers working in 1977. Certainly not a cottage industry then, if ever.

I am consistently told that I loved my daddy like no one else on earth. I could be balling my eyes out, but once I was up and in that man's arms, it was all I ever needed. To be cradled by his love. He would lift me up and my back would straighten, and, according to the uncles who later played my fathers, I would instantly become a preening Queen of Sheba. To some he might have just been a big-talking con, barking orders while coke fell out of his nose, but to me he was the King of Diamonds, my Ace of Spades. And later, when I too became a big-talking con, barking orders while coke fell out of my nose, I thought I might actually be him. I would imagine him standing at the head of some table, leading his men into the next job, and I would try desperately to feel him in me even when he was far away. I would look for him in the lines of blow, in the shots of whiskey, in the loose memories I had of him all before I was five.

After the big arrest in 1981, I remember the police coming and taking the car away from my young and confused mother. She was begging them not to leave us stranded, and then when they threatened to take the Hartmann suitcases and the Louis Vuitton carry-ons, she began to cry because we would be left in this motel parking lot, with no way home, with the last things we owned laying in a pile on the pavement. I remember running up a green, grassy slope because I just wanted to get away, I just wanted to put space between me and the pain that had been struck into our life. Everyone knew the odds, including my mother, but I know that they were also hoping that my father was being honest when he promised that he was bringing in the last big load. The one which would allow him to retire and invest in legitimate businesses, and those years in the illegal drug trade would become a dark, distant memory for us all. But things rarely go that way, and so instead, I remember the nice police officer leading me back to my mom as she watched the very shaky deck of cards that had been our life fall all around us in a motel parking lot in South Florida.

I know that I went to the hearing, though I don't remember much besides running off again and walking back in through the wrong door, positioning myself between the judge and the lawyers' tables. I remember people laughing and being led back to where my family sat. I'm not even sure if these are real memories. Or if somehow, I had fantasized it all at such a young age and still carry it as truth. This image of me standing innocently between the judge and my father, making some sort of stand about the injustice of it all.

My father was initially sentenced to sixty-six years with no parole because whatever one might be able to say about his success rate as a smuggler, he had been more than successful at pissing off every US Marshall, DEA, and FBI agent along the Eastern seaboard. Because the fact is, my daddy is a career criminal, a drug-smuggling con, an outlaw and a cowboy, and he isn't going to stand for anyone telling him what to do. And if you want to find an archetype that creates a romantic figure that forever leads you into impossible romances and irresponsible love, well, there you have him. When my dad was officially sent away, I would catch my mom crying while she drove me in her Buick Regal. She would hear some song like "Desperado" by the Eagles, and I'm sure she would wish that this man with whom she had naively fallen in love would come to his senses, would stop riding fences, would let someone love him, before it was too late. But it was too late, and he never came home again.

Twenty-six years later, my dad sits in yet another federal penitentiary. Lompoc. Danbury. Allenwood. I know them all. You wouldn't think to look at me that I would. It always comes as a surprise to people that an educated young woman with preppy clothes and a deceiving set of dimples could carry such baggage, but I do.

My dad still thinks the big load is on its way and that the only reason he wears an orange jumpsuit everyday is because the system fucked him. For a long time, I was on his side. I worked at *High Times* and wrote articles about legalization and the best head shops in the country. Whereas other young writers were out doing their internships at *Vogue* and *Vanity Fair*, I was celebrating 4:20, the international pot-smoking hour, with aging hippies and hemp dealers named Dolphin. I believed in the romanticism of drugs and the lifestyle we once led, before the cars were taken and the suitcases were emptied, and the only reason we survived was because my grandmother had the foresight to steal $20,000 my father had hidden in her couch during one of his drunken stupors. She was terrified to do it; she cringed every time he would come over and sit on that same couch, but she knew one day it would just be my mom and me, and no amount of half-hearted promises from a convicted felon would be able to pay our bills. Growing up I knew very little of the dark side of my father. All I knew was I wanted to be a Desperado too.

But things change. I went home to Dallas to cease my own drunken stupors, and I discovered that not all cowboys have to live on the range. Not all cowboys need to gamble their lives away in order to prove they have lived. Because by my second month in Dallas I met someone who showed me that true cowboys work hard to be there for their families; they fight hard to protect what they love, and live hard not because they don't care but because they care so damn much. By my second month I met Louise, and Louise changed everything.

Louise is the type of woman who traditionally would have intimidated me. She wore tall Tony Lama cowboy boots and wild fringe jackets and had a tattoo of the Virgin of Guadalupe covering her entire back. But I was so desperate for help, I was willing to sacrifice my fear, and so I complimented the belt she was wearing the first night I saw her at a meeting, and we became quick friends. Louise is fifteen years older than me and, at the time, had two years of sobriety, and I was willing to believe anything she said. She became my first sponsor, and when she told me that we could do anything as long as we were sober, I believed her.

Which is why, nearly three years and one crazy relapse later, I sit excitedly in the passenger seat of Siren's car, waiting at LAX to pick up the woman who meant so much to me. We are driving up to Oxnard to stay with Louise's oldest friends. Since the eighties, she has run with the same crowd, which still includes her friend Ivan, a former dope dealer, John Knight, a violent alcoholic/speed freak, and Teresa Tall, the quintessential restaurant-owning drunk. Within the space of two years, and all pretty close to their fortieth birthdays, they got sober and have been since.

When I first moved back to L.A., I was pretty much on my own. Sure, I had my old friends, but my old friends still stayed up until 10:00 a.m. in the morning, searching for their own lost fathers in unlimited booze and hazy talk. After my brief relapse with them, it just didn't mesh so well with sober life. So instead, I borrowed Louise's posse.

I turn around to where Louise sits in the backseat. "Someone I like is going to be there," I tell her.

"Who?" she asks with her slight Texan lilt.

"Maybe you know him. Jimmy Voltage?"

She thinks. Her nose slides up a bit because she does that when she thinks. "I think I've heard of him. He's some aging hipster from Silver Lake, right?"

I laugh, "Yeah, I guess. Except, he's not *that* old."

Jimmy Voltage is thirty-nine and an electrician, hence the nickname. He has been sober for three years and has a twenty-year-old son. Louise isn't wrong. He is a bit of a hipster, with his glitter motorcycle helmet and a studded belt that actually has the word "Voltage" beaded on the back. He is tall, with haunting shoulders, an easy laugh and an even easier smile.

I met him the previous summer at a moustache party. Moustache parties were all the rage in hipsterland that season, though it meant we all had to try to look our best with glued-on facial hair. I arrived at the loft Jimmy Voltage was renting at the time, looking a bit like Chris Cornell from when he was in Soundgarden. We had seen each other on and off at meetings since then, but never really had the chance to talk. Until now. Because as I stand in the warm glow of my friends at the Oxnard house, I know the moment Jimmy Voltage walks into the room, looks at me and smiles, that is about to change.

I don't typically go for the popular guy. I prefer the quirky loners and the class clowns and the curly-haired intellectuals, but something about Jimmy makes me forget all that. Over the next day, Jimmy's increasingly flirtatious attentions are making me feel like the high school girl who has spent the better part of the year writing bad poetry in the back of the library only to come out and be swept away by the prom king.

Later that night, we all sit around the beach bonfire. Jimmy keeps taking photos of me with my friends. "Oh, that's a good one," he says as he looks at the picture on his digital camera and then leans over toward me so I can look. My hair falls against the "Banana" tattoo written across his wrist, and I know we can both feel that primordial surge rush up our arms and down our spines. That thing that I search for all on all dates, in all men. That experience that means very little in terms of compatibility or likelihood of success but is the number one reason people fall in love. That thing called chemistry.

Nothing happens that night because we're both playing it cool and sober and really quite polite. The next morning, I wake up and go outside to smoke a cigarette. My phone rings, and I see it is my dad. He is currently serving out a one-year sentence from a parole break in 2006, and we confirm my visit for the following weekend. I tell him that I am at the beach, and I can hear the sadness in his silence. For years, we have spoken while I have been in exciting and adventurous locales across the world, and he has sat in the same public phone room with the hum of other inmates making similar calls. I hang up and breathe deep and join Jimmy where he sits in a lounge chair, staring out at the ocean. His smile is so warm and welcoming; I can tell he has been thinking about me too. It's a cloudy, cool day in Oxnard, and with all of our turtlenecks and wide-legged jeans, it feels like a day straight from the seventies, when my father was still riding fences and not hanging up the pay phone in prison.

Jimmy and I sit smoking, staring out at the ocean. I'm not sure if it's the fact that I am about to see my dad for the first time in three years, or if it's that I love telling people the wild, surprising story of my father, but I want so badly to open up to Jimmy about it. I want to tell him that my dad hasn't seen the ocean in twenty years; I want to tell him that I will be traveling many cold and snowy miles next weekend to get to his maximum security prison in Pennsylvania; I want to tell him that I think my dad would like him. Because Jimmy rides a motorcycle, and flies a helicopter, and is a capable man's man, and would be just the type of Desperado I figure my dad would want for me.

Jimmy tells me that his dad was an alcoholic. And I tell him that mine is too. He tells me about watching him die from cirrhosis, and speaking at his funeral, and getting the chance to be the type of dad to his son that his father never was to him. I get up to put out my cigarette and as I walk back, I pass his chair. And I don't know why I do, but I put my hands on his shoulders. He slides his own hands up my wrists. He smells my perfume, his face close against my palm. It has been such a long time since someone has touched me so softly and intimately. I stand there staring out at the gray waves with Jimmy's face pressed against my skin, and I don't want to move. Ever.

That night we all go out to dinner, and I sit with Jimmy. Though nothing has happened yet, I know something will. I can feel it in the way people are looking at us, in the light brush of his knee against mine, how he laughs at everything I say and watches me when I get up to go talk to Louise at the other end of the table. I need to get home as I have to work the next day. I am putting my bag in Siren's car when Jimmy comes outside. He pulls me in for a great deep hug, and I look up into his warm, tan face, and he smiles down at me, and I cannot believe that this friendly weekend trip has ignited more romance than I have seen in years.

"Have you ever been to the Observatory?" Jimmy asks me.

When I was twelve years old, living in Dallas, the hottest video running on MTV at the time was Paula Abdul's "Rush, Rush," a *Rebel Without a Cause*-inspired mini-movie starring Keanu Reeves. And I remember looking at them as they pretended to be Natalie Wood and James Dean and wanting to go to the Griffith Park Observatory. Unfortunately, during the three years when I lived here before, the landmark was under renovation the whole time. Ever since I moved back, it has been up there waiting for me, taunting me every night when I drive home, and at this one perfect crest, I see the entire, famous thing.

"Would you like to go to the Observatory?" he asks.

"I would love to," I say.

I think he is just going to hug me, but then his lips are against mine. His tongue lightly along my mouth, nervous systems flushing and popping, and I am melting into his arms. This is a kiss. And I go home that night more dreamy and beautiful than I have been in some time.

1 2 3 4 5 6 **7** 8 9 10 11 12 13 14 15 16 17 18 19 20
21 22 23 24 25 26 27 28 29 30 31 32 33 34 35 36
37 38 39 40 41 42 43 44 45 46 47 48 49 50 51

Date Seven: Pie Crust Promises

"Are you sure you want to do this?" my mom asks. My mom and I sit in a Budget Rent A Car on the Upper East Side in Manhattan. I don't know why mom even bothers to ask. I doubt I have much choice. I know my dad is waiting for me.

When I was a kid, my grandmother always accused the men in our lives of making what Mary Poppins calls, "pie crust promises." Easily made, easily broken. My father is the king of pie crust promises, and though I might have tried to emulate him in the past, today, I do not make such promises.

"Your car's here," the cranky woman behind the desk interrupts any sort of choice my mom thinks I might have. I look outside and there sits a Town & Country minivan.

"That's my car?" I ask the woman.

My mom and I crack up. She jokes, "Well, I guess if your dad wants to escape, you've got the van."

"Shit, I can take some of his friends too."

It almost makes it all worth it. My mom and I get inside the minivan, and I turn around to my imaginary kids in the back, "Billy. Sarah. Quit it!"

My mom laughs, and then she stops. She squeezes my hand as I try to figure out the heater. "I love you, K." She watches me, and I try not to add any more gravity to the moment as I put the car in gear. I look at her and smile, "I love you too, Mom."

The night before, I was in Los Angeles with plans to go out with Jimmy Voltage. We had already seen each other a couple of times because whatever happened in Oxnard followed us safely home to L.A. I love traveling with a new crush in mind. It somehow makes all journeys sweeter. I don't even notice the security lines, the weight of my bag, the delay in takeoff as I daydream about what it might look like to do this trip to New York with Jimmy one day.

Unfortunately, I am doing this trip with a vicious cold, which made me cancel my date with Jimmy the night before. His band was having a show, and I was going to play groupie for the first time ever.

Before he went to the show, Jimmy came over anyway. His arms. His eyes. The small scar above his brow. His hands. If there were few reasons to fall for this man, his hands could be enough. Strong, thick, tan, even his knuckles. He spread them across my body. I could feel the meat of his palm against my ribs. We talked and laughed and kissed. The time clicked by, but Jimmy was busy tracing the round of my belly. He looked up at me and smiled, "I guess this is how people miss shows."

And it is. It's how they miss so much. I walked him outside, I kissed him goodbye, and he left for his show. And I went inside to ready myself to see the man that quite literally started it all. The next day, I fly to New York and rent my minivan. I drop my mom at her apartment in Manhattan, and I drive three and half hours alone to the federal penitentiary in Allenwood, Pennsylvania. It's a recently renovated facility in the middle of an old farming town. It looks like a fancy high school in a suburban neighborhood, but when I get to my father's building, the innocuous sign which reads "Maximum Security" reminds me of where I am. I am processed by the guard, sent through two metal detectors, and then led through many gates, holding rooms, and hallways. The trip gets more surreal with every step.

Being here reminds me that as much as I tried to pretend I was just like my father, there is nothing about my life that speaks to this. I do not understand this world with its high small windows and endless walls. I do not belong walking behind this guard with his 9 mm and long baton hanging from his belt. And though I might have spent my whole life wishing and praying that my daddy would come home, I realize that this might have been more his style than the safe, suburban existence my mother worked so hard to give me.

The last time I saw my father was in Tallahassee in 2005. Before that, I had not seen him since I was ten years old. In 2003, my father was released from a Nevada prison after serving twenty-one years of his sixty-six year sentence. He was supposed to go into a halfway house in Florida. He never showed up. A year and a half later, they arrested him on escape charges. I had flown into Tallahassee on a Friday for his sentencing.

"DC Docket No. 03-0031. United States of America versus Daniel McGuiness."

My father turned around to look at me. He wore an orange jumpsuit. His wrists and ankles were shackled. A pair of sunglasses hung from his shirt collar because at fifty-nine years old, on the day he is being sentenced in front of his twenty-seven-year-old daughter, my dad still had to look cool.

I testified on his behalf because I was the only non-criminal character witness he had left. "I have not seen my father in seventeen years. I want him to be a part of my life. I want a chance to have a normal relationship. Through letters and phone calls, he has helped to make me who I am today, and if a man's worth is to be judged by anything, I believe it should be by the quality of his offspring."

I am not kidding. I said that. In front of the judge. It's a matter of public record. I am such an ass. And not only because I used the phrase, "the quality of his offspring," but because the quality of my father's offspring was not too stellar at the time. I tried to get in to visit my father that afternoon, but the sentencing had run too late, and the prison was closing. I was supposed to leave that night, but I booked a room at a local Comfort Inn and headed to the bar.

I started with two shots of Jaeger, and by the time I made it to my third beer, and fourth shot, I wanted some weed. I saw four gang-banging black dudes playing pool, and I figured they had to have a connection. As they left, I followed them to their car because this was how the tables were turned in my world. I lurched up to them in a Jaegered stupor, and they all froze, as though they were afraid of me.

"Hey guys, I am here visiting my dad in the federal pen," I slurred. "And I need to score some weed for the night."

They all looked at me like I had lost my mind. As I often did when I was drinking, I thought of my father's street cred as my own. But as I stood there in pink corduroys, ballet slippers, and a button-down shirt, I was a far cry from gangster. No one said anything at first, some of them began to get into their car, and then one guy smiled and said he could help me.

Later that night, after I added two bottles of wine and a couple more beers to the mix, I got in my rental car and drove drunk into the hood. One of the other guys came out to my car to sell me the weed. I tried to invite myself inside because I heard they were having a party, and I like parties, but the dude was already sketched out enough by this crazy honky and just told me to get home safe.

That was the last time I saw my dad. And now, I walk into the great, big visitors' room, sober but feeling more lost than I did years before.

"You look great!" my dad says as he sits down across from me. I am sitting at a table in the middle of the room. I can feel the winter outside.

"Thanks, Dad. So do you."

"No, I don't. I've gained twenty pounds in this place. They don't let us go outside enough, and the food is disgusting."

I smile because I don't know how to respond. It's funny how we can imagine a scenario in perfect detail. The emotions, the setting, what everyone is going to say. We can spend years picturing it, and getting ready, and thinking everything is going to go exactly as planned. And then you get there, and it all goes out the window because really you have no fucking clue what to say or do or even how you're supposed to feel. As I sit across the table from this white-haired old man with a nose that looks like it's been broken way too many times, wearing a pair of prison issued huaraches, I know that as much as I am his daughter, that in so many ways, I am not. I wish it were easier for me to reach out to him. To feel the bond that I always thought was so natural. He grabs my hand. He can't hold it for long, or the guards will say something, but I look down at it, and it is unrecognizable to me. As this strange old man sits there, looking at me expectantly, all I can do is cry.

"Oh Kris, don't do that," he says, looking away, and I wonder whether I look like a stranger to him too. I don't remember if I felt this way in Tallahassee. I feel like we had more of a bond there, some sort of mutual understanding about who we both were, but now I think we are just two very different people with very different lives. We don't know how to take care of one another like this: in this maximum security prison, with its cold, white linoleum floors and its other prison families and its hardened inmates who have all somehow found themselves lost from the people they once loved so much.

I get up to go into the bathroom to try to compose myself. I stand there in the empty visitors' restroom, holding rough tissue paper to my nose. I look like a child who just found out that Santa Claus isn't real. I look blown apart by this man who I thought would be able to put me back together. I don't know what this trip is for anymore because it's not a reunion, and as much as I wish I could offer my dad a solution, some vision of the better life that is out there for him, I do not make pie crust promises.

"I'm an old dog, K," my dad tells me. He is being released within the month, with no immediate plans to go straight. "And you know old dogs and new tricks."

"I know that," I say. I look away as I tell him that I don't know that I can still be his daughter if that is the lifestyle he is choosing. I wish that things had been different, but I also know they never could have been. He would have always been looking for the last big load, and had my daddy actually come home all the years I wished for him to, he would have turned our lives upside down.

"I love you so much, Kris. You have no idea," he says as he squeezes my hand. They are words I have heard before, and I understand. He never grew up, and never will. I just wish I could stop dating guys like him. I wish I could stop falling for the hopeless romantic who looks at me all starry-eyed and then disappears. As he tells me later, "I'm not coming back here, kid. If they get me again, I'll go out in a blaze of glory."

Underneath the bravado, lies an element of truth. I don't know if we'll ever see each other again. This might be it. And sadly, it might also be better that way. Because I just can't picture what our relationship would look like. I cannot see it in any kind of detail; I cannot place the setting, and I have no idea what we would say. I wish so badly that I felt differently. I wish this trip had been filled with laughter and inside jokes and hope for what the future might hold. But as my pockets bulge with used tissues, it has been filled with nothing but sadness for what we might have once had and what might never be there again—the innocent love between a little girl and her daddy.

He walks me to the edge of the visiting room, right to the line where it says, "No inmates past this point." The guard walks to the gate to lead me out. Dad and I have already hugged and kissed. I step over the line. And he's standing there in his prison garb, and he's too far away to touch now. And so I salute. And he salutes back. The guard leads me out down the long, sterile hallway, back through the metal gates, and I walk out into the cold Pennsylvania air. The tears freeze on my face as I return to this world of sunsets and snowfall and the great wide Pacific, and my father is left there behind a chain-link fence, with high small windows and guards who won't let us touch.

I get in my minivan, and later that night I cross the George Washington Bridge. I call Jimmy. I do not talk about my dad. I tell him about Manhattan, twinkling in the distance; I tell him about the beauty of the Poconos; I tell him all that I can without telling him the truth. That my heart is broken, that I can't figure out where my father fits in my story anymore, that I am afraid I will never see him again, and that I am so very tired of loving men I cannot trust.

Date Eight: The Way We Are

Everyone thinks their grandmother is special—filled with wise sayings and funny quips and the occasional horrific sexual comment. But if there were a market for quirky grandparents, my grandmother would pretty much take the cake. If she ate cake.

Nana, as she is known worldwide, has been a source of humor, anxiety, and love from as far back as I can remember. She's like any other one-named wonder: Madonna, Cher, Elton—a diva at her best, something else at her worst. When I was a baby, she was probably one of the hottest grandmothers around, with her Farrah Fawcett do, string bikini tops, and multiple long, gold necklaces. But then when my dad left, and she moved in, Nana just became the hippest grandma on the block.

Between her permed blonde hair and her CP Shades knits, her turquoise jewelry, and her Rolex watch, I idolized her as much as I hated her. Because for every time she hunted through the sales rack at Neiman Marcus so she could buy me a designer dress, she would also rip me down for not being cool enough, hip enough, in the know. I don't know what exactly I was supposed to know at eight, but apparently talking to myself and playing video games were not it. A firm believer in the ethos, "It doesn't matter if you are rich, so long as you dress it," Nana obsesses on how things look on the outside. She is like a narcissistic fashion designer, watching her looks walk down the red carpet, screaming at the models, the set designer, anyone who will listen, "Everything must be perfect!"

When I was little, there were three things Nana and I always agreed on: music (preferably Whitney Houston and Guns N' Roses), books (Danielle Steele and J.D. Salinger), and movies (anything starring Robert Redford or Gene Wilder). We watched *The Way We Were* as many times as we watched *Willy Wonka & the Chocolate Factory*. And I learned everything I needed to know about romance from Hubbell and Katie. And from Nana. Because it is Nana whose four marriages taught me that strong women have trouble settling down. It is Nana, whose greatest love was a married man fifteen years her junior, who showed me that more often than not, it is the ones we cannot have whom we love the most. At seventy–five, and as single as one can be, she now quips that men are only good for two things: breeding and heavy lifting.

And I learned everything I needed to know about family from Charlie and his Grandpa Joe. Because that, to me, was Nana. Although impossibly critical, she was my older pal, my wingman, taking me to school, dancing with me in the living room, and joining in my birthday parties as though she was one of the kids herself. Even today when she visits, we sleep in the same double bed, just like Grandpa Joe and the rest of the family. Nana taught me that even when the rest of the world deserts you, for better or worse, your family will always be there.

I return to L.A. from visiting my father, and Jimmy Voltage and I make plans for our first real date. He picks me up, and we go to a lovely restaurant up the street. We sit outside. We smoke. We talk. A little awkwardly. I still have a cold, and I blame it on that. I get up to use the restroom and discover this backroom with high ceilings and dim light and wide, cold walls.

I come back to the table and take my seat across from Jimmy. I tell him, "That backroom makes me want to dance."

"Really? Why?" he asks.

"I don't know. There was just something about it. It wanted to be danced in."

He stands up. "Show me."

I have been waiting years for someone to say that. *Show me*. I lead him to the room. And we slow dance. And he kisses me. I feel just like

Barbra Streisand in *The Way We Were*, with the cool guy sweeping me off my feet, acting as though he has never seen anything like me in his life. I laser the memory into my brain. Take the photo and develop it immediately. I know it will hurt someday so I burn it in deeper, just to be sure.

We go back to Jimmy's house to kiss more, but take a break to go outside to smoke. I know that Jimmy Voltage and I have the physical part down so I am not quite sure why we are having such trouble with talking. But then again, so did Hubbell and Katie. And like Hubbell, Jimmy is that all-American guy with the too-cool style and the sense that even in his darkest moments he has always been a golden boy. And I am the nervous, talkative nut who doesn't generally catch myself a Hubbell.

Maybe it's just that Jimmy and I come from different worlds. He likes rock music and westerns and motorcycles and has tattoos. He has lived his whole life in California, and fixes things, and reads biographies on Lee Marvin. I don't know rock music or westerns or motorcycles and only have one tattoo that no one can see. I have been many places, and don't fix things, and just learned who Lee Marvin is. But that didn't stop Hubbell and Katie, at least not at first. They were also from different worlds, and somehow, slow dancing was enough. Jimmy asks me if I've ever read *Newsweek*, and suddenly I am telling him how I was once obsessed with the conservative editorialist George Will. He just looks at me. I would like to say with rapt attention, but it's more like sleepy boredom. Sadly, this doesn't stop me. I continue, "I was really into Ayn Rand at the time. I even wrote George Will a letter about his take on Hillary Clinton's insurance reform."

Jimmy doesn't even blink. I don't know if I am showing off, or if I am just trying to make conversation, but it appears that he was trying to have another conversation.

He clears his throat and says, "Yeah, I was reading in there about corporate titans. I guess you forget what it's like to stand at the head of a business. You know, to really have that responsibility."

There is a strange pause, and I am beginning to feel like two actors who have incredible on-screen chemistry, but the minute the director yells "cut," have nothing to say to each other.

I shrug, "Yeah, it's not all about power and greed."

"I guess not." He sounds disappointed, but I have faith that it's simply a matter of settling into this thing, of finding the spaces where we do meet, like on the dance floor and in his bed. I put out my cigarette. I don't really know what else to say. I stand up, and Jimmy grabs me from behind, and that type of conversation is far more comfortable.

We sleep in our underwear. His strong arms wrap around me. My hands flit through his hair. And he smells so good that any awkward conversations are soon lost in this impossibly lovely thing that happens when the cameras are rolling. He drives me home the next morning, and I go to work. As I drive to pick up pastries for my boss's morning meeting, I realize that I am not in *The Way We Were*. Though this recent romance feels like it has broken open my year of peace and quiet and paid bills and boring meals, I have to remember that my life is real. And as Jimmy goes off to his day as an electrician, and I go off to mine as a secretary, I try to let go of these Robert Redford romances of the way we are, or one day, might be.

Date Nine: Cowboys and Peter Pan

Two days after my slumber party with Jimmy Voltage, he calls me at 7:50 a.m. on a Friday morning.

"What are you doing later?" Jimmy asks, and though I am still slightly asleep, his enthusiasm brings me to life.

"I don't know. I'm not even awake."

"You wanna go shoot some guns tonight?" I am groggy, but I like shooting guns, and I like Jimmy, and together it sounds dreamy.

Last year my mom bought me a book called *Cowgirls in English Saddles*, and if I had a band that would totally be its name. Because I got back into horses about a year ago. And guns? Well, I fell in love with guns in 2005.

I was visiting my uncle Vic in Florida and had about three months sober. Though I was living in Dallas as that point, my family decided, since I had managed to not get myself into trouble for ninety days, that I would be the perfect person to go save my uncle. My uncle Vic had always played a special role in my life. Gay, short, with a penchant for leather pants and fancy antiques, he taught me that it was beautiful to be different. But over the last few years, he has been going through a slow financial and psychological breakdown that I am sad to say still isn't over. Because we're Sicilian and Hungarian, I think there's an inherent "you're blood, go do something" policy that isn't always effective. So though I was in my own worst life crisis, and though I had recently gone through my own financial and psychological breakdown, off I went to Ft. Lauderdale to save the day.

I spent the next week on the Master Cleanse because I figured, if nothing else, I might as well lose weight while I was there. But after four days of sitting with my uncle in his flower shop (yes, he owned a flower shop), I had begun to get a little bored. I had been doing nothing but chain-smoking, drinking cayenne lemonade, and helping my uncle find naked men on manhunt.com. His shop was right next to a shooting range so one afternoon I decided to go shoot my first gun. And that's when I found out: I'm kind of a cowgirl. Maybe it's just an easy rush when my old easy rushes are no longer an option, but, man, do I love pulling that trigger. Feeling that blast. Watching as my awkward aim rips a hole in the target.

So when this new cowboy in my life invites me out for a night of shooting guns, I could not be happier. Someone takes a picture of me firing his shotgun that night, and I look so happy; I look like I have always wanted to look, in my tight, ripped jeans and my quickly slimming figure. The minute I introduce romance to my diet, I just don't need sugar as much, and so I have been watching as the weight drops off me. Jimmy and I don't spend the night together because we are still trying to take this quickly-paced romance slow. Instead, we meet the next morning for breakfast. Jimmy invites me to his family's house for Thanksgiving because we're both still alcoholics, and this is about as taking-it-slow as we get. We agree to go back up to John and Teresa's in Oxnard afterward for the rest of the weekend.

It all feels so perfect. Me and this cowboy rising above the social fray to create a romance of family dinners and road trips and sweet breakfasts in our shared neighborhood of Silver Lake. The fact that I was supposed to go on 51 dates in 50 weeks feels like a distant memory because I am getting exactly what I want in only eight. As I get dressed to go out with Jimmy that night, I feel like a lottery winner. Jimmy and I had planned to go to the Observatory on his motorcycle, but then one of our mutual friends was having an art show and that seemed to make more sense. I walk outside, and he stands waiting for me in front of his truck. And then I am in his arms, and he is telling me how beautiful I am, and I am in awe that after all this time, I finally won. I won. I won me a cowboy.

I sit across from him at the restaurant, and the magic continues. We talk about our fathers and God and sobriety and whatever awkwardness was there is quickly fading in the candlelight.

Jimmy tells me, "My dad was such a good man. Conservative as hell. But he was honest."

"Even when he was drunk?" I ask.

"Yeah, in a way. I mean I come from drinking men. It's what they do."

"Yeah, my dad isn't so much like that." I look around because my recent trip to visit my father is still raw. I want desperately to share all of this with Jimmy, but maybe this is where the awkwardness comes in. I am trying not to be the babbling, let-me-share-everything-with-you type of girl, but I don't really know what else to say in its place. Still, I think Jimmy understands.

"Don't get me wrong, Kristen. My dad was fucking miserable." He catches my eye, and we smile because we share this thing with our fathers, and though we don't say it, I know that we are both sober because we didn't want to end up like them. He comes and sits next to me on the booth during coffee, and it feels so nice leaning into him, making out in the back of the restaurant, believing in romance again.

We go to the art show, and if ever there was a coming-out party for us, this is it. Everyone we know is there, and I float around on his arm, feeling not like the nerdy girl I was so determined to make myself out to be, but like the cool, country girlfriend, glowing in the bask of my man. We are walking away from the party, and Jimmy keeps kissing me, so much so that we nearly trip over ourselves. I can see our silhouettes in the light, all tall and sexy and free.

He looks down into my eyes and says, "God, you're so refreshing."

I should know better right here. Oliver once called me that. Others have before. Like a tall glass of lemonade, I satisfy the thirst but am put down after a few quick gulps. That is what refreshing will get you. But in the moment, it works, and I want to be refreshing. I want to be so different from anything he has dated that he actually sticks around this time. Because I sense from the looks I get at the art show, and from the way his friends shake my hand, that there is often a new girl on Jimmy's arm and that many of them are here tonight. And I do not want to be just another stop on this cowboy's adventure.

We stop by my apartment so I can pick up some things, and I watch as he walks in front of me down the hallway of my building. There is nothing like Jimmy Voltage from behind: his shoulders, his arms, the way his jeans hang off his ass. I don't know that a man has ever actually made me go weak in the knees. But this one does. He can feel me watching, and he knows the effect. He shoots a glance behind him, cocky and innocent at the same time, and I know and he knows and everybody knows that we are going to have sex tonight.

I haven't had sex in a year and a half. Jimmy will be the fiftieth man with whom I've slept, if we're keeping score on those things. And so though Jimmy and I are still getting to know each other, and though I really just met him a few weeks prior, and though I have said I am not going to sleep with him yet, my hormones lurch and I do, that night, and it's beautiful. I tell him about having herpes, and he kisses my forehead, looks into my eyes, and says, "It's okay." And it is, it's all okay. Afterward, we talk in bed. It feels so safe and so right that I begin to relax. I begin to believe that this thing is real.

"So how could someone like you not be snatched up already?" Jimmy asks me as I lay cuddled in his arms.

"I don't know," I giggle as I kiss the tattoo on his wrist and pull myself in tighter. "I guess I've been focused on sobriety, but that's not all true. I've fallen for a couple of people. I tried to date someone, but he ended up being kind of mean."

Jimmy squeezes me as he kisses the back of my neck and whispers, "How could anyone be mean to you?"

I love hearing that. But again, it's not the first time. My mom was once walking down Third Avenue in New York when she heard a little boy ask his mother, "Mom, why are boys happy and girls so sad?" My mom and I laughed—it's because boys make girls sad. But at the moment, I am not sad. I am incredibly happy, and I am staying present with this man as I curl naked into his form.

And I forget that others have looked at me with the same intensity and lost it just as quickly. And I forget that sometimes we are mean to each other without meaning to be. And I forget that I don't know this man at all but am making hopeful assumptions about kindred spirits, and kind cowboys, and these kisses that finally feel like the destination to my very long search. As my eyelids begin to close, I look around this man's room because at thirty-nine, Jimmy is a man. I look at the stacked cans of tuna in his kitchenette, the motorcycle helmets on his armoire, the wooden horse beside his bed. I draw it all in with my last sleepy breath. And though it all screams Peter Pan, I am Wendy Darling, and I have been waiting sometime for this trip to Neverland.

Date Ten: And the RAD Played On

I am beginning to wonder if there might be something wrong with me. If I were, in fact, born with a very rude pheromonal magnet that pulls my instincts in the wrong direction, or worse, that I have simply lost the ability to make people *stay*.

A year ago I met a man who was mean to me; the one I told Jimmy about. I had ten days sober when Sunshine sauntered into my life. Now, I should have known right then. The name Sunshine was pretty much a dead giveaway.

Sunshine kept telling me that he couldn't date me; that we needed to take it slow, because I was just newly sober again, and he didn't feel it was right for us to be in a relationship.

Since I was working under the pretense that I wanted a man named Sunshine in my life, I went with it. I went with it when he failed to call me for weeks at a time. I went with it when I got the feeling he was hitting on my friends. And I went with it when he looked me deep in the eyes and told me that we had a spiritual connection that would last forever. I leaned over the emergency brake in his car, and I showed him just how spiritual I could be, and that was the last time I saw him.

I walked away from that brief but not so sunny romance telling myself I would never need to learn this lesson again. And the lesson is this: Don't take candy from strangers. Because the kind words, the generous offers of romance, the moony, starstruck eyes are all wonderful, but if you don't know who is giving them to you, then I wouldn't advise getting in their truck. But only a year later, I end up in Jimmy's truck.

I know the minute Jimmy closes the trunk of my car that something is, in fact, different. Perhaps it's in the way he tosses his bag in my car, or his distracted embrace upon greeting me, or maybe it's that he doesn't kiss me or tell me I look pretty or even really smile when he walks up and sees me. I try to pretend that he is just going through something, busy worrying about work or his family or anything that has nothing to do with me.

Two nights before, Jimmy had come over to spend the night at my apartment. This was huge because every man I have ever dated has had an aversion to staying at my place. For some reason, the idea of waking up in my bed has always caused an anxiety apparently too great for any man to sleep anywhere but his own home. I made Jimmy tea, and I offered him pie, and I attempted to show him my world in one night. I tried desperately to find my favorite quote by Salman Rushdie in my worn-out copy of *Midnight's Children*, "To understand just one life, you have to swallow the world." But I couldn't, and so I aimlessly rooted around the book searching for the page. This has been a bad habit of mine since cocaine. I was well-known to spend a good hour of a party sitting in a corner, searching through *The Norton Shakespeare* anthology, all for one line from one play I read in college years before. It typically drove everyone crazy, but thankfully, there would be enough people around that they could just ignore me, until I shouted out, "Here it is!" And then forced them to listen to whatever passage I had been so desperate to find.

"It's okay, Kristen. I can hear the quote some other time," Jimmy said as he tried to get me to put the book down.

"Just a second, I think it's in this chapter."

I wanted him to know; I wanted him to hear it; I wanted him to believe like I do that "to understand just one life, you have to swallow the world." Because I believe that though Jimmy and I might not always share the most comfortable conversation, we share this. This bold zest for living, this power and intensity that I think might be the bond that makes what we have feel real. Jimmy went to the bathroom, and when he returned, I was still sitting in the kitchen, searching for the quote.

"Oh my God, put it down," he said.

I laughed, and I thought that Jimmy would too, but he seemed more annoyed than loving when he took the book from my hands and led me into the bedroom. Then he unzipped my dress, and my lips were against his, and I forgot all about Salman Rushdie and men named Sunshine and the fear that there is something missing from this very powerful thing.

When I awoke in the morning, my heart lurched, and I didn't know why. His head was buried into my chest, and my lips were pressed into his forehead, and we fit together perfectly. He murmured into my skin and kissed my breast, and as we drifted back into sleep I thought, "I will be sad if this ends."

Two days later he closes the door to my trunk, and we drive to his family's house for Thanksgiving dinner, and though he is nice, and introduces me to everybody, I can tell, as he stands across the room playing with his little niece, that there is an estrangement here where before there was none.

His sister and her husband are cordial, but once again I get the feeling they've met many before me. They ask some cursory questions but only in the way that they don't really expect to see me again. When Jimmy's brother-in-law jokes while passing the turkey that I'm "a quick one," I go back to feeling like Katie in *The Way We Were*. The random, "quick one" Hubbell dates before going back to his more unrefreshing type.

As we drive to Oxnard that night to spend the weekend with John and Teresa, I know, without words, without any obvious action, there is a hiccup in our chemistry. Though we do our best to make conversation, though Jimmy's hand cups the back of my neck, and I get to relax a little, though we are laughing and listening to music and pretending that everything is okay, something has changed. And those kinds of changes are never good.

I make it through the first two days. Jimmy's hugs are infrequent and far away, but I have been here before. We all have. Wanting so badly for the affection we thought was ours and feeling all the more awkward and insecure as the object of that affection crawls into itself and away from us. I try to be cool about it, and I try not to cry when Jimmy doesn't follow me to bed that first night, when he stays up in the living room watching a Lee Marvin movie by himself.

The next day I leave for a while to work at the stables where I ride. I go into my favorite horse's stall, and I hug that great big animal, and I cry and I cry and I cry. Because I thought it was real this time and that the candy was only going to lead to more candy. I believed that the kind words and the generous offers of romance were all just the beginning and not the end.

I get back to the beach house that night. Jimmy is friendlier. When I yawn and get up and go to bed, he comes in soon after me. At first, we begin to make out, but then I stop it. I may not know what to say, but I know I need to say something. Though I may have found myself in this same place a year ago, I don't have to react the same. I can ask why. I pull away from Jimmy, and I can see him brace himself for what he surely knows is coming. I tell him I have felt a shift. And I ask him. Why?

And that's when I find out.

That is when the greatest revelation in my thirty years is revealed. That is when Jimmy tells me about RAD.

RAD stands for "Relationship Anxiety Disorder" and apparently Jimmy has a bad case of it. I feel like the scientist who discovered the cellular engineering of polio. The doctor who broke the riddle of AIDS. The girl who found out why so many of the men she has ever fallen for have left as quickly as they came.

"I've been working with my sponsor on it," Jimmy tells me.

I am trying desperately not to laugh because Jimmy is taking this all very, very seriously.

He looks like he might cry, and I almost begin to feel bad that this nearly forty-year-old man still needs to make up acronyms for his inability to commit. Because RAD? I mean, come on. Who doesn't have that? It could be on the cover of *Newsweek*. In fact, I'm pretty sure I've got a decent dose of it too. I haven't been in a relationship in three years; in fact, at this point, I don't even know what a relationship is. So though he might have anxiety over the whole deal, I can't even tell you what the deal looks like. Does he think I'm on the verge of wearing his letterman jacket, his class ring, changing my relationship status on Facebook?

"I just think we should take it slow," he says.

And the smile on my face slides into sadness because I know what that means. I've heard about *slow* before. It wasn't long after Sunshine that my own sponsor and I discussed my habit of falling for what we call Counterfeit Romeos. Like Sunshine, like Jimmy, like that man I call Dad, they tell me all the things I want to hear, but they can't actually be there in any real way. They have things like RAD or a prison sentence that prevent them from putting action behind all that powerful romance.

I silently fight back the tears that have begun to surface, and I take his hand in mine, "Okay, hey. All I ask is that you're honest with me. Because otherwise, well, it's just a waste of our time."

"I don't believe that anything is a waste of time," he says.

"You're right. I guess it's our romantic foibles that really show us what it means to be human."

"That's good," Jimmy tells me. "You should use it in one of your books."

So I do. Right here. That one is for you.

Jimmy and I try to enjoy our last day in Oxnard, but the jig is up. There is nothing like watching a three-week relationship with all its hope and possibility die in the same place it blossomed. It's awkward, it's uncomfortable, and it breaks my little heart. I wanted so badly for this man to be my boyfriend. As I sit on the other side of the living room from him, both of us pretending to care about the football game that is on TV, I feel like I want to throw up right there. But I don't. I get up, and I offer him tea, and I pretend that we are just friends, that we've always been just friends, and I secretly hope that his kind smile means that there might still be a chance for more.

But then Jimmy doesn't call for days, and whatever hope I had that RAD was just a forty-eight-hour bug quickly begins to fade. For Jimmy, RAD is something far more chronic. I don't know why this keeps happening to me, but when Jimmy sees me at a meeting and says he'll call and he doesn't, I know that I don't have to let it. I can't keep falling for these Counterfeit Romeos with their California heartbreak names and their easy compliments. I break up with Jimmy via voice mail, and I thank him for the good time. I say I just see us as friends, and he leaves a voice mail in turn.

"God, Kristen, thanks so much for your message. Wow, you're such a fucking gem."

I couldn't have written the line better myself. Though in some alternate reality we might have shot guns and rode horses and zipped through the night on yet another motorcycle I never got to ride, that was not our reality. The reality was that Jimmy has RAD, and I have a bad sense of direction when it comes to cowboys. I lie alone once again in my bed, and I begin to cry. Because I know I can't keep taking candy from strangers and not expect to find myself hurt and used in the back of their trucks. After a while, I can't even blame them.

61

1 2 3 4 5 6 7 8 9 10 **11** 12 13 14 15 16 17 18 19 20 21 22 23 24 25 26 27 28 29 30 31 32 33 34 35 36 37 38 39 40 41 42 43 44 45 46 47 48 49 50 51

Date Eleven: Finding Faith in Chatsworth

I was sitting across from Noelle when she asked me, "So what qualifies as a date then?" She found me crying in my office and because she is a boss who cares, she sat me down to find out what was going on. Before I knew it, I had told her about my visit to my dad, my fling with Jimmy, and my fear that this whole idea of 51 dates in 50 weeks was a pointless attempt for me to change an unchangeable situation.

"I have someone for you," Noelle offers.

Noelle and I have never discussed men before. We talk about work and our families, and though I know she is divorced, she seems to have evolved past the point where needing a man is part of her life. She is everything I want to be, and fear I never will. Whereas I can never wake up in time to put on makeup or blow dry my hair, Noelle comes in every day looking like she's been hand-painted. Her soft voice, her warm green eyes, her perfect auburn hair speak of a femininity that I can only imagine has won her a number of suitors.

When she tells me that she has someone for me, I think she is referring to a guy. I begin to decline, but she stops me, "No, I think you might need some spiritual work."

I nod and begin to cry again because I do. I do very, very badly. Noelle is the first female boss I have ever been able to trust. In my years in books and film, I worked for a slew of notorious female executives. Most of them came up in the wild and rowdy seventies when to make it as a woman you either fucked the boss or were mean as hell. I generally worked for the latter. When I landed on Noelle's desk, I had just moved back to L.A. after six months working for the most notorious boss in book publishing. She was my best friend one minute, taking me to movie sets and fancy restaurants and introducing me to celebrities like I too was someone important. But then, like all look good megalomaniacs, she turned, and she not only made it impossible for me to be her friend, she made it impossible to be her employee.

I had returned to L.A. with her company in 2006 after first getting sober. I had so many hopes and dreams about what my life would be. I was going to be a famous book editor under her tutelage. I was sure that once I saw Oliver, the movie producer ex who I thought would change it all, we would reunite, and life would be what I had been waiting and hoping and staying sober for it to be.

The minute I arrived back in L.A. with the publisher, I texted Oliver. We had broken up a good six months before I had moved back home to Dallas, and though we didn't talk at first, we started reaching out to each other again after I left. And then I came back. It had been two years since Oliver and I were together. Two years since we fell apart. And I knew so fully, like I had never known anything before in my life, that we would get back together. Because I was sober now. I had been fixed. And there was nothing to stop him from loving me.

He picked me up at the fancy Sunset Boulevard hotel where I was staying with the notorious publisher and took me to a restaurant near his house. He looked at me all starry-eyed and overwhelmed like he did when we first met. He told me how he had been working with a shaman, that the spiritual work had been teaching him about healing and wholeness and making right all the things that had been wronged. He said he would love to take me sometime. I wanted to reply, "Yes, yes, please take me. Take me wherever you're going, and I will gladly follow." But I didn't. I might have tried to smile, but I was scared. I didn't want to ever stop sitting across that table from him. I wanted that invite to stay there extended forever. And so the conversation stopped because I just couldn't find the words to keep it going.

"You know what's always confused me about you, Kristen?" he asked. I came back to him. "What?"

"You're so smart, and yet, why do I sometimes feel like I am hanging out with a teenager?"

It was a mean comment, but I didn't have the strength or esteem to give it a proper response. "I don't know, Oliver." And I didn't know. I still don't.

We drove back to his house, listening to Mozart. We sat in his driveway, and I smiled as I said, "He was just a child. Can't you hear him? He's playing with the music."

And Oliver looked at me as he picked up my hand, his eyes filling with love. He whispered, "I knew you got it, sweetheart."

We went into his house, and he put on Fellini's *8 ½*. We lay down on his bed as the opening sequence began. We had barely kissed or touched or even held each other, and then Oliver was asleep. Two years apart, so much had changed, and finally we were together again in the same bed that had once meant so much. And he falls asleep? I looked down at him just as I had done years before when we were actually dating, and I realized that even though I lay there sober and sane, for some reason, there was still a bridge between us that we just couldn't cross together. He dropped me off at the hotel the next day, and though I didn't want to admit it, I knew it was finally over.

And so, as with most of the men in my life, I didn't get what I wanted or expected at all. The fancy job, the romantic boyfriend, the big, bad, beautiful life I thought was almost mine—it was taken away just as quickly as it was offered. Two weeks afterward I quit the job with the publisher, relapsed, and a month later found myself working as a secretary for Noelle, who today sends me to get some spiritual work.

I drive out to Chatsworth for the appointment. Previously, I have only known Chatsworth to be horse country and the capital of the porn industry, but apparently it is also home to a large shamanic community, which includes the woman I am meeting today. Lidia is a therapist, but she has been trained by spiritual leaders throughout the Native Americas. She is also Jewish, and I like the idea of a Jewish Shaman. It's like having the power of the two oldest tribes harnessed into the body of one woman.

When we spoke on the phone a couple of weeks back, she asked me to write down any interesting dreams I had before I came to meet her. Oliver used to say, "If you want to lose anyone's attention, start your sentence with, 'last night I dreamed…'" So last night, I dreamed I was still dating Oliver, and we are out to dinner with two of my current friends, Nat and Reggie, who happen to be engaged, both in the dream and in real life. In real life, I am the bridesmaid in their wedding, so the bridesmaid/bride cliché is fully in play here. In the dream, however, it is Oliver who pulls out the diamond ring. He looks at me in full earnestness. And I look down, and I realize that he has gotten me some tacky modern number from the local mall jeweler.

"Will you marry me?" he asks.

I am upset that this man who I thought knew me so well has gotten me such an ugly ring. I want to say yes, but I am also in shock. He knows what kind of ring I would want. And the fact that he has gotten me something that I know even he would think is ugly tells me he really doesn't care about this. Reggie and Nat eagerly await my response. But again, I can't say anything. I am caught between everything I want and my fear that it's not real, that it's not going as planned, that if I say something, it might go away altogether. And so I sit there, frozen, until I wake up and wish desperately that I could go back.

"It's a good dream, huh?" I ask Lidia, whom I like immediately. She is small, toned, with yoga arms and graying blonde hair. She sits opposite me in a chair, sipping tea in a pair of loose white pants and a white tunic. But she uses the word "fuck" enough to throw off the stereotype.

She nods, "You got a lot trapped in there, don't you?" Like that perfect bolt of truth, it hits. I do have a lot trapped in there. And I can talk, and I can write, and I can do all the things we're taught to do to get it out, but when I am forced to really speak, to really say the things I think, I just sit there staring dumbly at the person across the table from me.

I am told to choose a stone out of the twelve sacred rocks she lays out on the ground. I want to choose the big, shiny, round ones that look like crystal balls. But I always want the big, shiny, round ones that look like crystal balls.

Instead, I choose a grayish quartz that feels safe in my hand.

"Good choice," Lidia tells me. The entire time I am going through "the ceremony" as Lidia calls it, I wonder why it was a good choice.

I lay still on the floor. I don't cry. I barely emote at all. Lidia puts the stone on my sacrum. I can feel the tension flowing there before she even decides where to place the stone. She whistles, she blows, she passes magic wands over my body. I cannot help but hear the Woody Allen that lives somewhere in my psyche thinking, "So, it's come to this." I am becoming the California loony I always thought I'd be. But I let go of Woody Allen. I let go of daddies, and mommies, and being a secretary, and not having anyone, and all the bullshit that I like to wallow in to feel sorry for myself. I let the energy pulse through my body.

And I feel something in me pulse back.

Years ago, jacked up on booze and coke, I walked outside into a rainstorm and believed that there was so much energy in me that I could create balls of fire in the palms of my hands. The thing is, I still kind of feel that way. And as Lidia guides me with her stones and her blessings to the ancestors, and asks of the earth and sky and mountains to lead us through, down this path, I feel that energy course down my arms and into my palms once again. I feel spheres of power and hope, and I know that my path is so much bigger than RAD or Jimmy or Oliver or any who came before them. I know that my path is larger than 51 dates. I know that I understand very little and that all my words and alliterations and pretty poetry are just translations of a much larger source. And though that source feels deeply hidden, it's there. And it's real. And it's what I need when I am sitting across from love, and I am terrified to respond.

And then Lidia puts away her stones and opens the blinds, and we are back in her house in Chatsworth, home to horses and porn stars and this strange magical woman sitting across from me.

Date Twelve: Love Is a Lot like Basketball

I've never actually seen a game of basketball, so I might be off on this, but I believe a rebound is when the ball is sent flying toward the hoop, with the hope and/or expectation that it is going to go in, only to bounce back out and return to play. In my life, rebound is just the easiest way to get over someone. And since my recent expected slam dunk with Jimmy Voltage wasn't meant to be, I hope that my date tonight with Peter will put me back in the game.

I was complaining to my friend Ivan the other day that I was having trouble finding dates when he told me that he had been going out on almost a date a day by using the Internet. The Internet. Why didn't I think of that? Here I had been trying to meet people the good, old-fashioned way, and all it was getting me was a bunch of my friends with their faces twisted up, thinking, until they say, "Yeah. I don't know anyone that you would like." I try to explain that I would prefer to make that decision on my own, but apparently it's not even worth the risk.

Ivan is the friend who one would expect to become my perfect boyfriend at the end of this journey. We can talk about anything, we crack each other up, he's there for me unconditionally, and we're both sober. Unfortunately, there are just some men who will never be more than your friend.

Outside of Ivan, however, I am beginning to wonder whether I might be willing to date anyone. Anyone who can take my mind off the strapping electrician with whom I spend way too much of my time having imaginary conversations. I am a big fan of the imaginary conversation. I could claim it as one of my hobbies—a bit like talking to yourself but on steroids, mixed with a healthy dose of chardonnay.

A few years back, I once got so enraptured by my brilliant parting shot, my Oscar worthy speech to the mirror, that I forgot I was in my own apartment, alone. I walked dramatically across the length of my studio apartment, put my hand on the knob of the front door, and then stopped. I woke up from the fantasy and realized, "Holy shit. I'm storming out on myself." To add insult to insanity, I was about to enter the hallway of my apartment building in a great big huff, wearing only a T-shirt and underwear. But that's fantasy for you: it's dangerous at its worst, downright embarrassing at its best. So I do what any self-respecting woman with a habit for talking to herself does. I go online, and I find Peter.

I've never dated a Peter before. The name is cute enough. Peter is an attorney from outside of Boston. He spent the last fourteen years in Chicago until last summer when he moved to L.A. for a job in Business Affairs at Fox. I don't think people move halfway across the country at the age of thirty-seven without being prompted by something, and though he doesn't say it, and I don't ask, I'm going to assume it was a very serious breakup. She's probably still bitching him out in the mirror.

Peter and I meet at a local coffee shop because we're not sure how long this date is going to last. The holidays are coming, and the place is decorated with just the right amount of red and green and depressing all over.

"It's hard to feel like it's Christmas when it's still seventy degrees outside," Peter comments.

"How long you been here, again?" I ask.

"Eight months."

"Oh, yeah. It still sucks at eight months. Give it two years. It takes two years."

"In two years, will it still be seventy degrees in December?"

I feel for him, because coming out here with not much to hold on to, and an apparent taste for cold weather, was bold and brave, if not a little stupid. Peter looks like Clark Kent. He has a delicate nose, a sturdy jaw, and beautiful hazel eyes with thick dark lashes. He wears glasses and looks good in them too. Just like Clark Kent. And he's hilarious. I don't even think about what I would say to Jimmy if he walked through the door right now because I am too busy laughing. And then I remember the power of the rebound and that I have been here before.

When Oliver and I first broke up, I already had someone lined up to take his place. I didn't mean for it to happen that way, but in the midst of my movie-star love for that man I met someone else who caught my eye. Sabbath was tall and lovely, with rich black skin that seemed to warm itself from the inside out. His parents were from Côte D'Ivoire, and unfortunately for Sabbath, had never heard of the Ozzy Osbourne band when they named their only son after the Lord's Day. Sabbath was a fashion designer at a downtown studio and was good friends with my neighbor. I still remember watching him walk up to me and my friends at a party and not being able to take my eyes off this too-cool man with his Christian Dior glasses and his friendly smile. When Oliver ended it, my neighbor made the call, and I learned the power of rebound.

Sabbath fell in love with me. But I was too wrapped up in my alcoholism and my sad, sad sorrow over losing the greatest love of my life, so I failed to see who this rebound really was. I failed to see that Sabbath was one of the good ones. About two months into our relationship, Sabbath tried, like Oliver before him, to get me to quit cocaine. New Year's had just passed, and though we were all on ecstasy, though Sabbath had joined us in the cocaine that night, I noticed that he had stopped doing it around 3:00 a.m. and by 4:00 a.m., he was ready to leave.

We returned to his house, and as I started doing some addict mathematics I realized that Sabbath was the last one holding the bag and that he should have more on him. I begged, I cried, and finally, I slipped into bed with him, shaking and whimpering as I did when coming down from cocaine. He pulled me into his chest. "Sweetheart, I'm sorry. I didn't know."

"Didn't know what?" I choked.

"That you had a problem. I thought we were just having fun. I'm so sorry. We'll never do that again. I don't ever want to do coke with you again."

"Okay," I murmured into his chest. Because at that moment I didn't ever want to do it again either.

But four days later I was doing it again. I went over to Sabbath's house the next day, and he didn't even need to ask. He could see it in my swollen nose, my bloodshot eyes, the way I cringed to even move. He didn't say anything. He just got up and went to his bookshelf.

"I was going to throw this away," he told me as he pulled out a CD.

"Huh?" I asked. I was hurting too much to really pay attention. And then I watched as he dumped a gram of coke on top of the CD cover.

"It's yours," he said. He pulled out a dollar bill from his wallet, rolled it up, and offered it to me. "But I don't want to see you anymore if you do it."

This was too big of a challenge for me on any night, let alone a night where I had woken up thirty minutes prior.

"You wanna keep partying, fine. But I don't want a part of it, Kristen."

I couldn't move my eyes from the cocaine. It begged for me; it called my name; it knew me so much better than this man. I didn't know what was more confusing: that I was being asked to fulfill some sort of ultimatum, or that Sabbath lied on New Year's, and I could have done more blow that night. The fact that he was able to keep it without doing any was, at this point, staggering to me.

"What do you want?" he asked.

I wished I could say that I wanted him. That I wanted him so much more than the cocaine. But I didn't. I wanted the coke. And there it sat, the answer to all my problems. To all my pain. So easy. And so free. My favorite kind.

"Keep thinking about it," he sneered as he walked outside to smoke a cigarette.

To make such a clear decision, I knew, was dangerous. I was a good addict. I avoided any major moves that would have resulted in a loss of job or home or anything which might have harkened the dreaded process known as "intervention." And though I wasn't quite clear on why I needed to get up and go outside to join Sabbath, I knew that if I chose the line of coke right then, it would take that addict label Sabbath had given me and broadcast it across my life like the Goodyear blimp.

When I walked outside, he pulled me into a great big hug and kissed my head and told me that he would help me. And I knew he would. But I didn't want it. He flushed the gram that night, but it didn't take long before he was once again going home from parties alone. And he would cajole me and ask me again to stop when I would slip into his bed many hours later. Ultimately, he let me go when I moved home to Dallas to get sober.

When I came back to L.A., I stopped by his apartment, and we had a cigarette.

"I thought maybe there might be some hope for us again," he offered. But I was hoping there might be hope between me and Oliver, and so I told him, "We'll see." I walked away, knowing it was now me who would disappear from someone else's life. And so I did, and I never called, and he moved to New York, and we never saw each other again.

Peter sits across the table from me, making me laugh. I like his honest demeanor, the way he readily admits to "being a little alone in this town." And I can't help but think, while he's telling me about his most recent road trip to the Salton Sea, that I wouldn't mind exploring California with him. We could go on trips to Big Sur together and laugh on the drive up about a misspelled traffic sign. We could drive to Joshua Tree and pretend to spot meth labs. We could visit my friends Jenny and Phil in San Diego and play video games, and everyone would get along great.

Peter and I shut down the coffee shop. We keep talking as they clean up around us, and I realize that for all his MVP status, Jimmy Voltage and I never had this. We didn't sit and laugh with ease.

Peter walks me to my car. I am hoping he will surprise me and kiss me passionately. I am hoping that after all the laughter and easy conversation he will kick in a firework for the sake of romance. Instead, Peter hugs me awkwardly and then shuffles around as he asks me out for a second date. I want to say that I feel empathy for him, for all men who have to make that offer and pray the girl accepts.

So I say yes.

I don't know if Peter will be my new Sabbath. Because that was the thing, Sabbath wasn't afraid. There was nothing I could do to scare that man. And though I was too busy thinking about the one I had lost, I can't help but think today that I lost again when I refused to give Sabbath the chance he so deserved. And I don't want to make that mistake again.

Date Thirteen: New Beginnings

It's raining in L.A. tonight. The way it sometimes does. In huge gushing blows. As though the heavens have opened, and God lets loose on our otherwise drought-worn city. The New Year began this week. What a loaded holiday. "Auld Lang Syne". The search for a pair of lips at midnight. And new beginnings. I'm pretty sure it's all about new beginnings.

Ivan and I decide to throw a party at his house to celebrate 2008. I am on my way home from Smart & Final with a trunk full of Red Bull, cookies, and cheese for the party because that's just how the sober folk roll. My phone rings, and though I can't identify the number, I have become used to these calls. It is my dad, and he has started his own new beginning. In the middle of December, he was released from prison in Pennsylvania and sent once again to Northern Florida to serve out his probation. This time, he went. Begrudgingly, but he went.

"I'm no rat, K," he explains to me over the phone. I can hear the heaviness in his voice, and I know he has been drinking.

"Then don't rat, Daddy."

"But I figure I'll give them enough," he continues. "Enough, and they'll get me out of this hellhole."

The FBI has offered my father a longer leash if he provides them with information about things he learned on the inside of federal prison. He begins telling me about a terrorist plot, but I stop him.

"Dad, please. I don't want to know this stuff."

"Yeah, I guess." He sounds disappointed. He sounds like he was hoping he could win some cool points with me by telling me as much.

"Oh, K, I can't stay here. You know that, right? I can't stay here."

My father refers to the halfway house he has been paroled to as a homeless shelter.

"I don't get it, Daddy. You've been in prison for almost thirty years, how bad can it be?"

But I do get it. The nonprofit where I work is situated in a relatively unknown ghetto in Los Angeles. We're between downtown and a major hospital, and there can't be much worse of a pedestrian highway than that. Around the corner sits a halfway house for recently released convicts. It is called "New Beginnings." I see it every day. I see the men sitting outside, smoking cigarettes. I see the broken-down alcoholism in their faces. I see my father. And I know that it was actually so much better in prison for him and for all these men, who lost their new beginnings long ago.

In prison, they're all the same. The same jumpsuits and haircuts and makeshift huaraches. On the outside, my dad is a middle-class guy with high-class tastes sitting in front of a halfway house in Northern Florida, squinting at the sun. But he wasn't always there. He once wore Ralph Lauren. He once lived next door to Ralph Lauren. Back in the late seventies, we shared an East Hampton compound with him and a magazine czar. My dad would get the magazine czar and some of the *Saturday Night Live* guys from the late seventies high. We had the biggest house in the compound; we even had the pool, and my father would play host to the fancy people on Egypt Road, and for a moment, everyone thought that the great, big dream was coming true.

He tells me on the phone, "K, this isn't me. This isn't me."

And again, I get it. I get living a life that feels so much smaller than the one you once had and the one you think you deserve. My heart breaks for him. And it breaks for me too. I am beginning to fear that I will continue to go on consecutive aimless dates with no real love in sight. That I will be stuck answering Noelle's phones and scheduling her meetings, never fulfilling my own potential. I am afraid that these new beginnings are only teases about life actually changing, becoming something different, when really they're just halfway houses for our dreams.

I tell my dad I love him; I wish him a happy New Year, and we both agree that next year we'll be celebrating it together. But we've been saying that since I was four.

I go home to change myself into something hot. I get my hair cut with Brigitte Bardot bangs, squeeze into my 1920s prom dress from high school, and am surprised by how good I look. For all intents and purposes, I am in my prime. God love heartbreak.

I pick up my friend Siren. Siren's mother still tells people that she named her daughter Rene, Siren's real name, because she looks like Rene Russo. This drives Siren nuts, but her mom is right. Siren does look eerily like Rene Russo, with her thick red hair and long, lanky limbs. I've had a crush on her since the moment we met, when I had just come back into sobriety after my relapse, and she was one of the only women at the meetings to ask for my number and actually call.

Since then, we have become each other's diaries—reporting almost every day to one another on our thoughts, fears, brilliant plans for the future. And tonight, when I need her most, she gets over her social anxieties to join me for a New Year's night out. We go to the party, we drink Red Bull, we play Spin the Bottle, and we hit the dance floor.

The DJ is spinning "Beast of Burden," and there I rock in my vintage gown and my red Chucks and my bright red lipstick. I look toward the door for the seventh time in the last half hour. Because without realizing it, I have also staged a great potential reunion landscape for Jimmy Voltage and me. And I wait for his tall build to saunter in, grab me up in his arms, and kiss me torrentially.

But he doesn't.

I want to invoke the "It's my party, and I can cry if I want to" rule, but it doesn't play as well at thirty, if ever. Instead, I stay poised. I dance until the last guest leaves. I clean up Ivan's house like a good host. I drive Siren home. And I wake up the next morning with an emotional hangover that keeps me in bed for the better part of the next two days.

On the second day, I receive a text message from a number I had almost forgotten. Oliver. All it said was, "Happy New Year," but that was almost too much. When it ended, I had felt that there was an unspoken agreement between us that such trivialities were too dangerous for two people who would always be caught in a game of cat and mouse. And so I don't respond because I know that if this year is to be a new beginning, that means taking new actions, creating new behaviors, and not continuing to respond to the same old call.

The following Monday, I go into work, and I tell Noelle that I can no longer be her assistant. At first, she sits back and glares at me. I am afraid she will become just like the notorious publisher and turn on me. I am afraid she will tell me she can't help me. I swallow the lump in my throat and keep going.

"I nnnn-eed something more, Noelle." I don't know where the stutter came from, but I'm not very good at asking for promotions. This is one of the reasons why I am a thirty-year-old assistant. "I wwww-ant to stay here," I continue, "bbbb-ut I, I, I need something more."

I wait. And then she smiles. "Yes, you do."

She doesn't know what it is yet, she tells me, but we will find something. We will get something where I use more of my talents than answering phones and scheduling meetings. She asks me to go back to school, and I agree. I enroll in a night course that day. I do these small, silly things that years ago I would have laughed at. Because years ago, I was just like my father, always believing that I was something more than I was. Always thinking I deserved a certain life, but never being willing to change to make that life happen.

That night, I leave my office building in the rain, the one right around the corner from that halfway house. As I carry boxes that are too big for me, struggling against the large metal gates that lock up our nonprofit in the hood, I am scared that though I might be willing change for the new beginnings, no one will change for me. And I am tired of doing this alone. I am tired of having no one to help me carry this load. The boxes, the gates, my father. I ache for a partner who will steady me through it, and I fear that I will run out of faith before he gets here.

77

1 2 3 4 5 6 7 8 9 10 11 12 13 **14** 15 16 17 18 19 20
21 22 23 24 25 26 27 28 29 30 31 32 33 34 35 36
37 38 39 40 41 42 43 44 45 46 47 48 49 50 51

Date Fourteen: Gay Uncles
Give Good Heart

All girls should have a gay uncle. And for those who weren't fortunate enough to have been born into a family where the gay gene is prevalent, I highly recommend finding a surrogate. My gay uncle is named Vic. He was one of Southern Florida's premier florists until he hit fifty and went through what appears to be a national phenomenon best called "gay menopause." Gay menopause pretty much skips the hot flashes and memory loss and instead focuses all of its energies on making its host body completely, entirely insane. It's sad but true. Not that my uncle Vic hasn't always been crazy; it's what made him my dearest uncle in the first place. Sure, my uncle Tommy was cute and young and came to all the school dances, but my uncle Vic took me shopping for Gaultier.

I remember first questioning my mom and Nana on Vic's gay-ness when I was eight. We were vacationing in Ft. Lauderdale and staying at my uncle's house. I had noticed that he and his "roommate" Paul slept in the same bed, even though they had a three-bedroom house. And then there was the issue of the word "honey." My uncle always called Paul "honey" or some other term of endearment and that too seemed suspicious. Because of the AIDS epidemic and the subsequent letter that was sent to every household in America, I had gotten wind of this "gay" thing and had begun to think that my uncle might be one.

I knew better then to just come out with it. This was still the eighties, after all. My mom, Nana, and I were getting into our rented car when I decided to pop the question. "Mom, why does Uncle Vic call Paul 'honey'?" I saw my mother and Nana pause; they both shot each other a look over the roof of the car, and then my mom began, "Um, well, you know Uncle Vic, he..."

But Nana stepped in, "He calls everyone honey. Your grandpa did the same thing." My grandfather is a very rarely mentioned figure in my family, so bringing him up at all almost threw me off my game, but then I remembered that Vic and Paul shared a bed and decided I would try that tack. As though she could see me formulating it, Nana turned her steely-eyed glare on me and ordered, "Get in the car." The glare didn't always get me to obey, but this time it did. I got in the car and decided it was better not to bring it up. Yet.

Years later, Nana and I were vacationing at Vic's house again. I was watching TV while Nana talked on the phone behind me. I decided to see what was in the VHS machine because it was summer, and I was bored. The next thing I knew I was watching a man get fucked in more ways than I knew was possible. In fact, more ways than I still know is possible. I tried to turn it off but the battery in the remote control wasn't working, I banged the damn thing a couple of times, but it just kept going. Nana's back was away from the TV, but she could turn at any moment. I flew up, leaped over the coffee table, slammed my ankle into the side of it, and hit the "off" button on the TV.

Nana swiveled around. "What are you doing?"

"Nothing," I said, rubbing my ankle as I limped backward out the front door. Then I turned around and ran. I ran fast and hard, as though if I got far enough away from the video, Nana wouldn't dare see it. I got to the end of the block, and then I began to smile. Because I was right; I was right! Vic was indeed gay. Very gay.

Vic calls me the other day because he has been speaking with Nana and has some concerns about my recent attempts at dating.

"Nana says it's that neighborhood you're living in," he tells me.

"What? Silver Lake?"

"Such a good name," he sighs.

"What is Nana talking about? She likes Silver Lake. I mean, I know she would prefer Beverly Hills, but she thinks it's charming."

"Yeah. But she says there are no professionals in the neighborhood. That they're all artists. K, believe me, stay away from artists."

My uncle and I both share a vision of the big dream. His was to become a top florist and mine is to become a famous writer, and we both know that big dreams can come with steep prices. My mom and Uncle Tom believe in nice things and decent jobs, but they're no artists. They pay their bills. They do their taxes. They vote Republican. And so I understand why Vic warns me against the artist. He is warning me against our kind. He is also, without saying it, warning me against Jimmy Voltage. I should have never told Nana about him.

"I go out with professionals, Vic. I just went out with a professional last night."

"Really? How did it go?"

I don't really know how to respond to that. How did it go?

Peter and I met last night at a local Mexican restaurant for our second date. Because of the holidays, it has been a long and lackluster break since the first time we met. We had sent a bunch of funny e-mails, but after date number one, I was pretty convinced on the "he makes me laugh" front, so it didn't really add much to our already humorous rapport. I don't dread our second date, but there is no daydreaming involved. No thinking about my outfit ahead of time. No dancing around before the time of departure. I simply shower, dry my hair, put on makeup, throw on jeans and a sweater from the night before, and meet him at a restaurant up the street. And I think that this is what people do all the time and call it romance. It's just I'm used to a little more spit in my fire. I know that life would probably be cushy with Peter. There would be paid-for travel and big meals we would cook at home together and sailing lessons. And this sounds a lot like what I first wrote about Peter, but ultimately it's the same concern as I had on the first date. The same concerns I had with Sabbath years before. That for all our similarities, we're very different people, and I'm still looking for my kind.

We sit down at the restaurant, we order drinks, and we launch into long and storied talk before we even look at the menu. We talk a lot.

"I can't believe you got to study abroad in South Africa," Peter says. He seems genuinely excited about my five months in Durban. And I like that. I loved my five months in Durban.

"Well, it's not like you're not well traveled."

"I guess, but really only to Europe. Although my friends and I did once go to Normandy. We went swimming there."

"Really? Wow...I bet that was eerie."

"Yeah, it was. It's crazy to think how many people died in those waters."

We talk about his job, and I can tell he's been waiting for a woman with whom he can share his work concerns. The first phone call. Bad day: call her. Good day: call her. And I know as I listen and ask questions and offer supportive thoughts and cheer that I am making for a good her. Peter is also a good him.

"But no spark, huh?" Vic asks me.

"I don't know, Uncle Vic. I just feel like, is that all it's supposed to be? Is life just supposed to be comfortable?"

Vic sighs, "You're so much like me, it's scary, you know?"

I am and it is.

He continues, "K, some people just want to live life with their hearts. They don't care that they'll be broken; they're not afraid to lose. They just know that they have to go wherever their hearts take them. Even if it's really hard."

I don't want this to come down to the emotional girl versus the safe guy. I have never wanted to play Dharma to anyone's Greg. And so as I sit across from Peter as he analyzes the check and figures out exactly how much he should be tipping the waitress, I decide that I should try again. And I hope that it's not simply a generational problem. That the men in our world today go swimming off of Normandy, and have long forgotten what it means to fight for it.

Date Fifteen: Arrow

Mimi is concerned about me. I can tell by her newfound determination to see me meet someone. Whereas before she found my mission entertaining, if not slightly ludicrous, she has now officially jumped on board the "Find Kristen a Boyfriend" cause célèbre. To her credit, she has been experiencing a significant spike in phone calls from me where I sound like I have been crying. All the same, I know that Mimi takes my dramatic tantrums a bit more seriously than I do. That's the unfortunate nature of a tantrum thrower. Everyone else worries about you long past the point of you actually feeling bad.

"I can't imagine there's not anyone for you on that site," she questions me one night.

"My God, Mimi, I'm searching *The Onion* every day. Thank God people at work can't see my computer screen. They'd fire me if they knew that's all I was doing." *The Onion* Web site shares a personals database of eligible men and women with a handful of other online magazines, and they do a good job of pooling all the single, literary, liberal modernists of our fair city into one giant meat market. Ivan got me started, and I have to admit it's a pretty impressive selection.

"What happened with Peter?" Mimi asks.

"We're going out again in a couple of weeks. He's in London."

"London's good."

"I know, but I'm just not sure. I'm afraid he's just another normie. And more importantly, he still hasn't kissed me."

"That's not good."

"I know," I say. I'm beginning to think that my uncle is wrong. That I need my kind. I want someone who gets me, the way I thought Jimmy did. Maybe that's the problem. I'm still thinking about Jimmy Voltage.

"Hmmm," Mimi mulls this one over. "You need a sober alcoholic."

"Jimmy was sober," I offer, but my friends have been getting pretty good at ignoring his name these days.

"Have you looked to see if there is a dating Web site for sober people?"

"Goddamn, you're brilliant, Mimi." Since I don't have Internet at home, Mimi does the research for me, and she finds a number of sites.

"Aha," she exclaims while doing some preliminary prospecting, "I found him." Him is a tennis pro with an MBA. Him is from New York and has been sober for four years. And by his picture, Him looks hot and yet still sweet-natured.

I sign up for the site and e-mail Him. Him turns out to be a guy named Micah. We e-mail back and forth, and though his e-mails are curt, and slightly uninterested, I decide he is just a man of few written words. So when he asks me what I am doing tonight, and my genuine response is "laundry and a viewing of *Dial M for Murder*," I am a little surprised that he asks me to bring the movie to his part of town.

I call him and explain, "I do not go to strange men's apartments bearing Hitchcock films as a general rule, sir."

"Okay, then," Micah offers. "Let's get coffee."

It's Saturday night, and I don't have any other plans, but it still feels a little wild and clumsy nonetheless. Most Saturdays, I am pretty exhausted from working at the stables.

A year ago, I returned to my childhood passion of riding horses. I was the little girl with a collection of plastic Breyer ponies and pictures of horses on my walls. I rode Arabians and was jumping at thirteen. But then I met boys. And getting up at 7:00 a.m. on Saturday mornings when I could be sleeping over at a slumber party after sneaking out with them, just didn't sound like too much fun anymore. So I chose boys over horses. When I turned twenty-nine, I decided to go back to the horses. It had been a dream of mine for years. About a month before I moved home to Dallas to get sober, I went to the Equestrian Center in Burbank. I walked around and pet the ponies and promised myself that one day when I had my shit together, I'd come back here and would learn again to ride. And I did.

Whenever I think that nothing has changed in my life, the stables always remind me things are entirely, wonderfully different. I used to sleep every Saturday until five or six in the evening. I would try to fall asleep against the chirping of birds and the sound of waking life, and I would want to die. Now, today, I am a part of waking life. And I get up early every Saturday, and I go to a morning meeting in the Valley, and I see my sponsor, and I have a cup of coffee and a cigarette, and I drive to work at the stables, knowing how much my life has changed.

My favorite horse at the stable is a thoroughbred named Arrow. If Arrow were human, he would be exactly what I am looking for. I went into his stable today, and he leaned his chestnut head against my body, and I wished so desperately that I could find a man who does the same. Arrow fights with all the horses around him. He is, in fact, a bad boy, and he has the scars all over his face to prove it, marring his otherwise perfect thoroughbred beauty, and yet, he stops fighting almost every time I enter his stall to come and tell me that he loves me.

"He is my unicorn," I told my mom recently.

My family has gotten to know so much about this horse that they ask about him as though he were my boyfriend. And I know all the Catherine the Great jokes that can be told, but the truth is that horse gives me love like no other. When Jimmy Voltage disappeared, it was Arrow whose shoulder I cried on. When I got my new job, it was Arrow who bit my ponytail when I told him. And today, when I said hello, he rested his head in my hand and let his lids slide closed, and we stood there—me holding this sleeping horse in the palm of my hand and having no doubt what kind of love I have in my life. I looked out past Arrow, out onto the San Bernardino Mountains: the sun played against the shadows of the hills, the perfect breeze of a seventy-degree day in January whistled through the barn and through my hair. I leaned into Arrow's neck. Griffith Park surrounded us with its burned-out brush and its wild coyotes and its rough and ready horse trails veiled in oak trees and the scent of eucalyptus. And I knew that I could not love more. And that is what sobriety has given me.

I need to meet someone who is also sober and could understand that moment. Who could understand the path that I have walked to get here. Well, that's a good someone. As Mimi says, Micah is an albino. At first, I retort that he has brown hair, but then she reminds my blonde brain that he is like an albino because he is rare. So I drive to Micah's side of town at a moment's notice because I've been looking for an albino.

There is a chance, and a relatively good one, that Micah was just not attracted to me. I might be too blonde, or not blonde enough. I might be too tall, or short, or skinny, or fat. I might be too overdressed or underdressed, or not sexy enough, or too sexy. In other words, I might not be his cup of tea. Or he might just be incredibly, painfully dull. Because I discover that Micah is not just a man of few written words, he is a man of few words. Period. This does not make for an easy first date. I end up sitting in my chair, legs crossed, hand under chin, like some hackneyed version of Barbara Walters. Not even. More like Tyra. I ask questions. I elaborate on the questions. I respond to my own questions. I try to go deep. I try to stay shallow. I do anything to get him to talk.

Kristen: So, where're you from in New York?

Micah (in a mumbling, barely audible baritone): Mm, around... (pause) Riverdale.

Kristen (really trying): And you moved straight out to L.A. from there?

Micah: (looks at me, yay, then he stops, boo) No. (Thinks some more) Miami.

Kristen (with my usual enthusiasm for all places warm and sunny): Oh, you lived in Miami. I love Miami!

Micah (hold it, hold it; his eyes glaze; he looks like he is about to fall asleep): Me too.

If he weren't sober, I would have suspected pills. Really. Strong. Pills. But that's not the case. Micah is just bored, though I'm not sure with me, with him, or with life. And it's funny because in some alternate universe, I think Micah and I might have had something.

He was nice looking enough—with the brown curly hair, big brown eyes, and the pert nose that I normally find to be such a kicker. Had he been magnanimous, I would have gladly been magnanimous in turn. We had plenty in common. He grew up in New York City. My mom lives there. He had time sober, relapsed for two weeks, came back in and has been sober since. I relapsed for three weeks and did the same.

Micah tells me, "It didn't take me long to figure out that I didn't want to drink anymore, that I needed sobriety."

"Me too. I just wanted to go home." I think we might be having a moment, but Micah's focus is back to over my shoulder, like he's waiting for somebody else to walk in. I turn around because I'm kind of hoping someone will. Please. Anyone. Take my fucking seat. I want the date to end. But that is awkward too. Because what do you say? Well, outside of the fact that we have a lot in common, and we're both sober, and we're sitting at a Coffee Bean in the middle of West Hollywood on a Saturday night, I've got to go because, quite frankly, this is the worst date of my life.

Micah doesn't really laugh, so I can't even make a joke to break the long silences. Instead, I just take the opportunity of one of the tumbleweeds blowing through our conversation to say how tired I am and that I should probably get going. He readily agrees, and I can tell he has been dying for me to shoot this one in the head. And within the space of an hour, the most entertaining prospect on the table ends not with a bang, as I think Micah might have initially hoped, but with an interminably awkward mumble.

But I do not drive home sad. I do not miss that sober guy I recently dated whose name shall not be uttered. I do not feel anything but the same joy I felt looking out at the San Bernardino Mountains. Because tonight, I'm going back to horses.

87

1 2 3 4 5 6 7 8 9 10 11 12 13 14 15 **16** 17 18 19 20
21 22 23 24 25 26 27 28 29 30 31 32 33 34 35 36
37 38 39 40 41 42 43 44 45 46 47 48 49 50 51

Date Sixteen: Jakes of All Trades

"Yeah, I got laid off about two months ago," Jake tells me as he sips a beer.

Jake is a struggling writer. Jake lives above the bar where we are now meeting in a small studio that he has been in for the last ten years. Jake just went through a major breakup last year. Jake is depressed. And though Jake looks at me with the bored resolve that he knows I won't date him, my guess is he'll probably still try to invite me upstairs by the end of the night.

I had more hopes for Jake when we found each other online. When you're e-mailing, it seems like everyone is funnier, more successful, and definitely more optimistic about the state of their life. But as I sit next to Jake at the old Korean bar below his apartment, I know there is little here between us but a memory of a Jake I knew years before.

My first Jake, who henceforth shall be named Jake One, was a mother's worst nightmare. Definitely my mother's worst nightmare. He was a drug dealer. An ex-con. He drove a motorcycle. If only I had had a pink shiny jacket, we could have formed a gang and started a musical. Sadly, Jake One was also the one to give me herpes. So although it might always be entertaining to make fun of him, part of that joke still stings.

Jake Two doesn't hold a candle to Jake One. He has neither the charisma nor the chutzpah nor the je ne sais quoi to pull the wool over my eyes the way Jake One did. I met Jake One when I was twenty-three. I had been trying for two years to be a good girl. To go to work and collect my check. To only do drugs at concerts and on the weekends, to prove to myself and my family that the degree I had just earned would be put to good use in the rat race of New York City. I rode the F train every morning, and so what if I jumped a turnstile or two on weeks where I had blown my paycheck. I wore enough Club Monaco to make up for it, and for all intents and purposes, it looked like my shit was together. And then I met Jake.

I can still remember watching him play pool for the first time. He would aim the cue and take down shot after shot, knowing how his actions would cause a reaction. Knowing how the game was to be played out. Jake was like any drug, wonderfully seductive on the outside and incredibly abusive once you were hooked. And I was hooked. If Oliver was my cocaine, Sabbath my relaxing spliff, Frenchie, a lovely glass of Beaujolais, Jake One was nothing but pure crack rock.

"The reason why you two love each other so much is because you bring out the rogues in one another," Nana warned me at the outset. She was partially right. He brought out the rogue in me, but that's all he was. Jake One was trying to get over his crack addiction when we met, and after two years of fronting like I was normal, I was heading back into my addiction for coke. So we met halfway, and we fueled the relationship with cocaine, whiskey, roast beef sandwiches, and sex. There would be nights when it would just be him and me on the streets of the East Village, making out in phone booths, doing bumps off each other's body parts and singing through the streets because we were in L-O-O-O-O-V-E.

But like all relationships fueled by cocaine, whiskey, roast beef sandwiches, and sex, ultimately, we also began to fight. Big fights. Though I had always prided myself on not being a codependent lover, I discovered the most powerful drug I had ever done in Jake One. With his scent, his cock, his arms around me in the moments when it was good, I found everything I had ever wanted. The bad boy I had spent my whole life waiting to come home, finally did. And instead of it being in the form of my dad, it came in a close approximation of him. It came in the form of Jake One.

One night I was standing in the vestibule of my apartment on 5th and A in Manhattan. The pizza box Jake had just thrown at me lay on the floor between us. The line in the sand so to speak.

"I cannot believe you fucking just did that," I screamed amidst my tears.

"Fuck you!" Jake yelled at me across the hallway.

"You don't throw things at me."

"Sorry, little Miss Princess. You're such a righteous bitch. Go do some more lines."

"Fuck you. Go smoke some more crack."

We stood there. Pizza scattered all over the floor. Jake looked down, and I could see a smile begin to form. I began to feel one spreading across my own face.

I laughed, "I can't believe you just threw away your favorite pizza."

"I know. That was dumb."

And we went about our way upstairs to more codependent sex and fighting. And that is the heart of addiction—of all addictions. I don't know if I was born with this sad, fat hole in the middle of my being, or if it grew through the years from a daddy who wouldn't come home and a mommy who worked too much and all my fears that I would never be or get or have enough. But that hole is there, and it's real. At first, Jake One filled it up. But then he tried to take it away, and I couldn't have that. In a matter of months, I went from being the bright, boisterous blonde who wanted to play Bonnie and Clyde to a shrunken fearful replica of myself. Even when the fights began to get physical, it was like any drug—the longer you stay hooked, the lower you're willing to drop the bar.

Eight months into the relationship, I moved to L.A. Many of my friends thought I ran to California to get away from him, and maybe I did, but they didn't understand the power of addiction. I was a wreck within eleven hours of leaving his side. And within a month, he had moved to Oakland, where he lived on a sinking sailboat, and we took our battles to the Bay.

One of the last fights we had, we had gotten into an argument at a bar because I had talked to someone while having a cigarette outside, and Jake accused me of flirting. This is what our relationship had become. Brief glimmers of lightness and laughter, but more often than not, it was me living in the fear that he would turn at any moment. We couldn't find cocaine in the Bay area, the drinking had only gotten worse, and when Nana told me that Jake had become a "cancer on my soul," I understood because he had. He was rotting me away from the inside, and all my good parts had become eroded by the fear that I was going to lose him.

The night he accused me of making a play on a man who had simply asked me for a light, I reacted the only way I knew how: I punched Jake in the face. I knew I was going to get it, and by the look in his eyes, I knew I had better run and fast. I took off down the street and somehow found the sailboat on which we had sailed to the bar. He found me there, and the fight escalated. The next thing I knew I was backed up against the v-berth, Jake's hands around my throat. I think I was screaming, but between the booze and Jake's grip, my vision was sliding dark, and then I saw them. The classic sign that for all my good breeding, my fine education, my carefully taught lessons about respect and decency, I was becoming someone I was not raised to be. Red and blue lights flashed outside the boat. Two policemen boarded the deck, and I watched as Jake backed away from me with hatred in his eyes.

We tried to patch things up; we tried to make nice. We spoke of buying a house together and growing tomatoes, as only crazy people would think they could do at that point. What really happened is that Jake stole a thousand dollars from me, started sleeping with a meth-head he met in Oakland, and gave me herpes. I broke up with him and went through three tortuous months coming off one of my strongest drugs of choice. Recently, I had to send him an amends letter. I could not do it in person because Jake One has spent the better part of the last four years in San Quentin.

Jake Two would not know what to do with a woman who has lived that life. As I talk about the horses and my work at the nonprofit and my writing and my funny uncles and my kooky grandma, I know that I am not for this man. I am too much of a story, and he only writes them. Jake One used to say that I was better at pretending to live my life than actually living it. And though he was an asshole, he also wasn't entirely wrong. I know I can lose myself in who I think I am. But Jake One never really knew who that was either. He just saw a scared and angry girl desperate for his love. And though initially my brightness attracted him, he refused to see that there was real light in it. He hasn't been the first to make that mistake, and he certainly wasn't the last. But the Jake I am sitting with tonight won't be the next.

Date Seventeen: Cadillacs and the Two-Headed Snake

I am getting ready for work when my phone rings. Once again, it is a number I don't recognize.

"Hi, Dad," I answer.

I haven't spoken to him in weeks. The last time we talked, he was still in Tallahassee, still in the halfway house, still threatening to run. I had received some missed calls from various unidentifiable numbers, but whenever I called back, I would always hit an out-of-service message or a motel clerk who had never heard of Dan McGuiness.

"Kris, you shouldn't mention my name to people."

"To motel receptionists?"

"To anyone. I don't use my real name anyway but just in case." He continues on, telling me that he has been traveling along the East Coast. Telling me what an amazing world it is that we live in, telling me how you have to squeeze every drop out of this life. How it is so precious and so beautiful, and that he is living it. I understand the sentiment. Not a day goes by that I don't think those exact same words, making me ever more his daughter, but I also know that his way of living it is very different from mine. In fact, it's illegal.

I don't want to ask; everything in me says it's better not to ask, but when he starts complaining about the Cadillac he's driving having too many gadgets, I can't help it. The last time my dad was arrested after bailing on a halfway house in Florida was in a Cadillac, and the mere mention of the car creates an instinctual kick in me so strong I want to vomit.

"Dad, where are you right now? What are you doing?"

"Nothing, K. Just visiting friends upstate."

He is referring to upstate New York, and I know from the last stint what that means. He once told me how they had buried a thousand pounds of pot in a van outside of Poughkeepsie. That they were waiting for his next release to sell it. He told me that they were going to make a fortune. And as much as I hope I am wrong, I cannot help but question, "What kind of friends?"

"Oh, Kris, don't ask, don't tell, please."

The next thing I know I am screaming in the middle of my kitchen. I am issuing ultimatums ("I will not be your daughter anymore if you do this"), I am threatening jail time ("You know where you'll be by the end of the year if you keep this up"), and I am begging ("Please, Daddy, please try to do the right thing. Please."). My dad tries to issue some half-hearted explanation, like covering a gunshot wound with a Band-Aid. He tells me, "K, I am working with the Feds. I'm all covered. I gave them enough information to get here, and now I have a chance to make some real money. The kind of money that will buy us a boat. We can sail away. Anywhere in the world, we can sail away."

I don't know if my father has any sense left, or if the "sail away" escape plan is so embedded in the mind of all prisoners, it is pointless to argue. I wonder whether they play *Shawshank Redemption* on rerun in there, fighting over who gets the latest maritime news, waiting, waiting for the day that they all get to sail away, leaving behind the disappointed children and the angry ex-wives and the worlds of pie crust promises they have created in their wake.

I try to breathe, "Dad, I don't want to sail away. I just want you to be normal. I want us to have a normal life."

"K, a normal life?" he moans. "Oh God, what's happened to you?"

I sniff my last sob and try with all my strength to say, "I grew up, Daddy. So should you."

My Shaman Lidia sits across from me, and I think she might be slightly stunned.

"Wow."

"I know," I agree. This is my second date with Lidia today. And like all second dates, I find myself much more at ease.

She smiles at me, "Although you do know, right? You know there is no such thing as a normal life?"

"I know, Lidia, but there's got to be one where my dad isn't playing the FBI so that he can smuggle drugs on the side. I mean there's got to be something out there more normal than that."

Lidia agrees, but as she explains, my father might not know how to find it. In recovery, we have a tendency to be wary of therapy because it allows for almost too much self-analysis. And self-analysis can easily lead to self-pity, which is next door to despair and pretty much in earshot of fucking shit up. My experience with therapists is that they were no better than mental prostitutes. I paid them to listen to my shit. They nodded and made me feel that all of my problems were of the world's making, and I would leave feeling more righteous in my mistakes but not necessarily better and certainly not different.

I think Lidia might be well worth her $120 an hour. Because instead of telling me that I am right, instead of telling me about how I probably suffer from one disorder or another and that my father is a sociopath and my mother is a codependent, instead of telling me all the things I have heard before from people with fancy degrees on their walls and much more formal clothing, Lidia tells me about Sach'amama—the great two-headed snake that the Incan shamans believe is the Goddess of the Jungle. Sach'amama, Lidia explains, is our great god spirit of the South. She is the guide who shows us how to shed our skins, how to learn new ways, how to find a different path in the jungle when the old one no longer serves us.

"It sounds like, by the way you stood up to your father, you have already met her," Lidia says and smiles. I have. I know that. I know that as confused as my last month has been, as painful as it has been, I feel like I am on a new path, even if I'm not quite sure where it is going. Lidia stands up and removes the small glasses from her face. The long skin of a dead snake decorates her walls, along with many pictures of a large black cat. She pulls her hair into a ponytail, and I watch her strong arms as she moves the pillows off the couch to create a place for me to lie on the floor. I want to help her, but I don't know how. I don't quite know where I fit in this space yet.

The night before I had a dream that I was twelve again. I was at the house of a friend that I had during that time. Her name was Beth, and I always had a crush on her older brother. In the dream, I have just hooked up with that brother in their parents' bed, and all I remember is seeing his face as he stands up and backs away from me.

"Because up until that moment, he had thought I was his age," I explain. "And then he sees that I am a child, and I can see the fear and shame and horror on his face."

Lidia is laying out her sacred stones as she asks, "And what were you thinking?"

"That I have seen that same confused look on so many of the men I have dated. It's like they think they're getting a woman, and then they wake up the next morning only to find this twelve-year-old child lying there."

"Scared," Lidia says.

"Terrified."

"You fucking bet," she replies. This is only our second date, and I know I am in love with this woman.

I lie down, and Lidia tells me to call to that great snake and ask her to lead me where I need to go. And she does, and we do, and I go find that twelve-year-old girl inside. The one who couldn't create real honesty with Jimmy, the one who didn't know how to respond when Oliver told me I talked like a teenager, the one who deferred to Jake One because she was too scared to stand up for herself.

I reach out to her, and I don't even know where I am. Somewhere between imagination and dream, but I see her. I see me. I am twelve years old, and I am the disappointed child waiting on the shore. Waiting for the man I love so much to come and get me, to sail me away to a brighter place. But when I fear he isn't going to show up for me, I hide that bright place because I cannot trust anyone with it, most especially me. And then I am sucking the light back in, trapping it inside, and all that is left is that wounded twelve-year-old girl wondering why they're backing away from me.

We are closing up the session. I lie there, my body slack, the energy between my heart and hands, still very much alive.

"Will you do something for me?" Lidia asks.

"Of course," I reply.

"Do you feel the energy coming from your hands into your heart right now?"

I do.

"Okay, I want you to start holding that heart every day for five minutes and think that you're holding that little girl. If you give her love, you will have the chance to become one with her, and then you cannot hide from her, just as she cannot hide from you."

"Okay."

"And remember, now that you've started this work, some of your biggest challenges will come into play. You have asked for an adventure of the spirit. That isn't always easy."

"I don't have a choice, Lidia." And I don't. Because that little girl is the innocence and the vulnerability, and ultimately, she is the great gatekeeper for the light. And I kind of want her on my side; I kind of need her there. I don't know that calling this great snake guide my God will lead me any closer, but I also know that I need to shed some skins. Even if it hurts, even if it's awkward and uncomfortable, and I just want to hiss and bite as it all falls away, I think I might owe myself that much. And if that means I need to hold my raw and soft-shelled heart every morning for five minutes to help me grow, to help me become the woman I want to be, then just as willingness has served me before, I will pray to Sach'amama that it will serve me again.

Date Eighteen: The Well

I met Oliver over four years ago. It was my twenty-sixth birthday, and I was on a job interview. I sat in the reception area of a Westside production company, waiting to meet with the assistant that I was interviewing to replace. She was running late, and I had no clue what was about to happen. I still wonder whether things might be different today had I not found myself on that chair, in that lobby, reading that *Variety* when Oliver walked in. He wore a sweater vest and a button-down shirt, and I want to say corduroys but maybe that's just because it seems to fit with the rest of the outfit. And I looked up.

I looked up, and the world slowed. The sun came in from behind him, and though I wasn't actually around in the time of Christ, I kind of imagine that he had a similar effect because without knowing it or understanding it, my savior had just walked into the room. And apparently, my savior was a Hollywood producer with a sweater vest and brown curly hair.

And Oliver? He looked confused, lost, thrown, as though he knew where he was going, but then he saw me and something flew out. The ground between us shrinking, and all I could think was, "Who? Is? That?" Little did I know, but he was actually the guy with whom I was interviewing, but the job got put on hold, and I never became his assistant. Months later, when I had moved into a new position at another film company in town, we met for drink at a Hollywood bar called The Well, where tonight, I go to meet Rob.

Rob is a new man, provided once again by the incredible menu that is *The Onion* personals. I stand outside awkwardly waiting for my date, much like I sat in that lobby years before. As with Oliver, I have already been able to tell that my date is fatally smart. With multiple degrees and a cutting sense of his own intelligence, I actually look forward to sparring with this one. Plus, he's late. And I kind of like it when they're late. I text him to tell him where he can find me because I understand the pains of searching for someone you've never met before. It's pretty much the motto of my romantic state.

I receive a text in response, "Has anyone hit on you yet?" I begin typing in my reply as a man backs up to stand next to me. I can tell this is Rob. He waits, staring at his phone looking for my text to come through. He doesn't say anything but he doesn't need to. I like him immediately.

Rob is an organic nutritionist, which might be kind of tough for me, and for him, considering I am probably the only professional in Los Angeles who still eats McDonald's. But that's just his most recent profession. Rob actually has a PhD in political theory from Cornell but gave up being a professor at a small Ohio college to come west and teach rich people how to eat. I walk us through the bar, past the corner where Oliver and I met years ago, and I try desperately not to feel the pang of memory that I know will hit. But for some reason, the energy of the man walking behind me keeps the sensation at bay, and I almost forget. I almost forget how I once walked into that bar four years before and found Oliver standing at the jukebox waiting for me.

"You know some people take being late as an insult." Oliver turned around from the music he was selecting to begin what would become a tradition of snarky criticisms.

"Are you insulted?" I threw back because as I stood there in my three-inch heels I was slightly taller than him, and it felt good. I tossed my recently highlighted hair behind my shoulder. I could feel him inhale. And as I smiled at him, my eyes going soft, I knew that he was going to be mine.

But as I walk with Rob, my date for tonight, I almost don't think about that. I think about the heat coming off of him as he leads us over to the small section available for us to sit.

"What do you want to drink?" Rob asks.

"I don't drink." I'm still not particularly skilled at informing people of this small detail.

"At all?" he asks. "Not even water?"

"I drink Red Bull."

"You got it."

Rob gets back from the bar, and I have made more room on the small booth we are forced to share. Normally, I find that my dates are either too intimidated or insecure or uninterested to get close to me off the bat, but Rob isn't like that. He's confident and cool and moves right in next to me. His hand falls on my leg accidentally, but he lets it linger and makes fun of himself for grabbing a thigh grope so quickly. He laughs at himself a lot, and at me. And I like him all the more.

He explains his change in profession (breakup, mid-life crisis, father dying) and how much feeding his body right has shown him everything he hoped to once figure out through academia. "It's always about systems of movement," he explains. "The economics of nutrition. What keeps us healthy, societies healthy, and what poisons us from within, it's all the same."

My secret dream in life is to run away to grad school and study political systems, so what Rob is describing is akin to intellectual porn for me. We begin to look around us, and we both laugh at the desperate scene in which so many of us single folk are forced to participate. These rituals of standing at the bar, making small talk with friends while our eyes slide to check out what's walking by. We laugh at all the porkpie hats that guys are sporting these days, and the women standing around in the awkward hopes that they might be asked to dance. But we don't dance anymore, and it's too hard to go up to anyone without assuming it's just for sex. Because that's normally all you're going to find on a Friday night in Hollywood. Rob has their number, and he also has mine, which means I can only be myself. And it feels nice.

I sit back and try to decide if I find Rob attractive. He has a good body, strong forearms, and sexy hands, and though he's forty, he has a nice, solid face, with just the right type of wrinkles. Ones that make him look sweet and almost endearingly younger than his age.

He is also wearing the right shoes. Pull-up suede boots. He's not that tall, but his personality is, and when he moves closer to me, he feels warm and sturdy next to me. God, I love that feeling. Of the human form against my own. Rob puts his arm around the back of the bench so that it graces my shoulders.

"We should just start spooning right here," he jokes.

I love games like this, making up stories. "We could just lie down on the booth and pretend we're watching TV."

Rob refers to the meat market we have been observing, "We are watching TV. It's perfect. I would breathe in your shampoo, the smell of your neck…"

I like that Rob knows the feeling so well that he can reference it here on this first date with ease. And I remember what that feels like. It's been years since I spooned on a couch with a guy watching TV. Years. And I think I might visibly wince because just the thought of being able to do that with someone again makes me wish with all my heart that it will happen soon.

I have to work at the stables in the morning, so I cut the date short. I look back around at all the single people on the make, and I feel for us. All of us alone and just wanting someone to lie on the couch with on rainy nights like this one. Some partner to call our own.

I turn to Rob and say, "Aren't humans funny?"

And without missing a beat, he says, "Yes, they are."

And that's why I like him, because I had begun to think that men didn't see it anymore. That they had stopped observing how much our world has changed and how lost we all seem to be in this modern life.

We walk out, and as I look to the corner where I shared three martinis and the beginning of love with Oliver, I feel that pang I had done so well to forget, and I remember that night quite clearly.

As I sat across from Oliver, caught in his gaze, I remember thinking that I would never have to go hunting in a bar again. As we veered from one important conversation to the next, completing each other's sentences, laughing at the same jokes, I saw, as clearly as the martini glass in front of me, the future that we would share.

I saw us becoming creative as well as romantic partners. I saw our bright, sunny house in the hills filled with laughter and art and bowls of fresh fruit on our kitchen table. I saw us getting ready for one soiree or another—him pushing back a stray hair, me standing a sexy inch taller in my heels, and him telling me how much he loved me. I saw us at the Academy Awards because ever since I was eight, I saw myself there. I am accepting a screenwriting award for the film he produced, and I am smiling out at him as he sits in the audience, and I say, "I just want to thank my wonderful love, my savior, my beautiful Oliver. Thank you for finding me. Thank you." Our friends and family cry at the moment because they know how hard we fought to make it there.

"What are you looking for in a man?" Oliver asked me that night.

"What we're all looking for. Ourselves, of course." I am young and naive and incredibly bold. Oliver looked past martini number two and straight into my being, and I knew he saw in me a brief flicker of his own reflection. I remember our hands brushing past one another, not knowing at the time that he was living with another woman, and feeling so much energy, it felt we might set the place on fire. I remember telling everything we could about ourselves and as the vodka settled in and over us, me relaxing into a state of love and discovery because I had found my reflection.

I pull back as I see Rob leading the way out, and I shake the vision off. I am no longer that girl. I probably couldn't tell you now what I wore on my date with Rob, and I long stopped putting myself in a wedding dress the minute I meet someone of interest. And if asked now what I am looking for in a man, well, I don't think it would be my own reflection.

Rob and I run across the street to my car, dodging traffic and laughing, my hand caught in his. And though I feel the heat, it's not the A-bomb that exploded at that same bar when I was twenty-six and found my savior.

Rob leans against my car and smiles, "Now's the part where I try to kiss you."

And as much as I have enjoyed the evening, I can't. I don't know why. I don't know if it's that I'm still looking for a nuclear reaction or if I just want to get to know people a little more before I begin handing pieces of myself over to what we can be.

I try to joke, "Don't, Rob. I will just have to fend you off, and it will be embarrassing, and we've had such a lovely evening."

"So why wouldn't we end with a kiss?" he asks.

"Maybe we will next time." A car pulls up to take the parking spot I am about to vacate, interrupting the conversation.

"Okay, fine," he relents. "But I will call you tomorrow." And I know he will. I get in my car, and I drive away, and I do not think of Oliver, or even Rob. I just turn on the windshield wipers, light a cigarette, and go home.

Date Nineteen: Ladies Angeles

And just like that, my friend Siren announces that she is leaving
L.A. She is leaving me. My closest single friend, my confidante, my
Siren. And here she is nonchalantly breaking the news that she is giving
up on the Hollywood dream and going home. The great irony of my
dear friend is that for as much as we both make fun of CHAs (Cheesy
Hollywood Actors), Siren has been trying to become one for the better
part of the last decade. And though there have been a few hopeful
moments of a national commercial or the part of a waitress in a major
motion picture, the fame train just ain't showing up at her door.

"I'm tired of waiting, Kristen," she tells me, and I understand. I
would be too. Siren's family is a bunch of loud, drunk Greeks back in
Philadelphia, and I know that leaving here and going home is not an
easy choice.

"I want to get my master's degree. I want it more than an Oscar.
And I've tried to do it here. You know that. But if I go home, I can live
for free; I can focus on school. I just can't do the CHA race anymore,"
she explains to me one night on the phone.

Siren is one of the few people with whom I can share my Academy
Award–winning dream without feeling like a complete ass. And I
wonder whether at some point, an advanced degree will be all I want
too. Maybe the Hollywood dream comes to a close for all of us who still
haven't made it by thirty, and we realize that the pie in the sky doesn't
taste very good anyway.

Siren tells me that before she leaves L.A., she wants to visit
Marilyn Monroe's tomb and see the house in which Marilyn died. I

think that's a great idea and add that we should do so dressed up in 1960s funeral attire. So we do just that. I go to her house in the afternoon, and we do our makeup together in her bathroom. I am standing next to her in her dingy Hollywood boudoir, watching her curl her hair in the mirror.

"It's so weird we've never done this before," I tell her.

"Do what?" Siren asks.

"Get ready together. I guess we don't really get ready with friends at this age anymore. I mean it's not like high school."

"That's true."

"But doesn't it feel like we've been friends since high school?"

Siren's reflection smiles at me, "It does."

Because the better part of our relationship has taken place in the two-hour phone conversations we have many nights a week, I realize that in a way it's like we're already in a long distance relationship, and this is just one of our rare in-person visits. Siren and I look beautiful. Her with her thick red hair and me with my big blonde bun, and we head down Sunset Boulevard in her car, listening to Frank Sinatra. I go to slide the CD in when she tells me, "Oh don't bother, the CD player hasn't worked in years."

But the disc is in, and Frank is singing.

We get to the cemetery, and the day is perfect. It feels like spring, though it's just the beginning of February. Marilyn's tomb is set in a small memorial in Westwood. Dean Martin, Natalie Wood, and Merv Griffin are also buried there. Merv's headstone reads, "We will not be back after these messages," and you gotta love a man who takes the joke into eternity. It's a special place because the patron saint of our dear town holds court over all of them.

We go to the catacomb and take out the camera. We pose as though Marilyn has just been enshrined, and we are at the service. We look sad, we look confused, we pretend that Bobby Kennedy is standing in the distance, and we look reservedly flirtatious. We hold the camera out and take pictures of the two of us together. We make funny faces, and if not for the fine lines, we could be any two high school kids up to some sort of merry mischief. We apply our lipstick doubly thick, and we press our lips against her tomb, and we let her know that though we might have never known her, we understand. Because we too have sold so much of who we are to get the things we want, and we too have paid a price. And we have found ourselves at alternating points in our lives, lying naked by the pool, wishing for it to end. But unlike our legend, we got out.

We get in Siren's car and drive to Brentwood—to the house where the candle burned out and to the neighborhood where women like Marilyn and Nicole Simpson met their fates. It is a neighborhood filled with charming homes and good schools and BMW SUVs, and by the looks of it, you would never know celebrity blood had been shed there. Siren and I drive down Wilshire, and we watch as the clean-cut, well-educated, high-salaried residents go for their evening runs. We sit, stopped at a light, and Siren says, "I don't think I could ever be one of them."

She's right. Siren has the edgy style and the Greek attitude and a love for vintage that might never make this feel quite like home, but I have posed here before. I have enough J. Crew, Ralph Lauren, and Tiffany's in my closet to pull it off on command. I know the restaurants and vacation spots and what series of German vehicle one should get, in order to seem as though I have always had it. But the truth is, it would be just as big of a lie for me as it would be for Siren.

I love Silver Lake. I like going to the Food for Less, where I am the only white person in the market. And I like that though I might be more preppy than most on my side of town, my quirks are easily accepted and completely understood. Whenever I am with people of the Westside mentality, I always find that they look at me much like the kids did growing up, replying to my sense of humor with the statement, "You're so funny," but really, what they're saying is, "You're so weird." On my side of town, they just all agree or laugh, and not at me, with me. Because that's the thing, though we might want the perks of the Hollywood dream, neither Siren nor I are capable of fitting into the Brentwood life.

We leave and drive home down Santa Monica Boulevard. As much as this day has been about Siren, it has also been about the city in which we live—our great, beautiful Lady Angeles. I look out at the sun setting in my passenger side window, at the hills in the distance, and I roll down my window, and I whisper, "I love you, Los Angeles."

Siren follows suit, except she yells it, and then I am yelling it, and so we go in our 1960s funeral garb, driving through Century City, hollering into Beverly Hills, hollering so that others can hear us, hollering so that L.A. knows, "We love you, Los Angeles!"

We love you, Los Angeles.

We are driving through West Hollywood when Siren asks me if we can go to the Normandy Room. The Normandy Room was the lesbian bar where I drank for my last two years in L.A. It was filled with butch dykes and the gay men who were my best friends at the time, and when there were probably few places in the city where disaster wasn't around my every corner, the Normandy Room was the safest place I knew. I went home with my gay friends every night. I played pool with the lesbians. The coke dealer felt safe meeting us there. Every good alcoholic needs a place like that.

Siren and I walk up to the bar, and Madonna is blasting from within. We smile at each other. Fucking perfect. We order our Red Bull and Cran mocktails, and I lean over and kiss Siren on the cheek. "This is my best date yet."

She returns the kiss. "It's not forever you know. I'll be back."

"Before I moved to Dallas," I tell her, "I used to say L.A. was trying to kick me out, but I don't feel that way anymore. I think she likes me here."

Siren thinks about it before saying, "I actually don't feel like L.A. is kicking me out. Maybe in the past, but not now. I kinda feel like she is giving me a chance to date other people, knowing that I need that freedom right now. I need something more than what she can give me."

I watch Siren as she sips her mocktail and wonder whether she will. I wonder sometimes how long I will stay with Lady Angeles. Because as much as I love her, I fear we might only live once, and I need to see more than just Los Angeles. I am afraid I can't commit like that, no matter how beautiful I might find her—her hills so lovely, her people so strange and lost and found. The town where I found Siren, and now, the one she must lose.

Date Twenty: If It Fits

I talk to William on the phone for an hour and a half before we meet. I try to avoid this with most of my dates because I don't want us using up all of our material before we're actually mano a mano. And I find that most people feel the same way. But somehow William and I start talking, and the conversation doesn't end. And that's how I find out that William builds things—with his hands.

"Like what things?" I worry I might be coming off as annoying, but I am truly interested, and William seems to like talking about his work. William works for two very famous artists, managing the design and construction of their large-scale art installations. He also built a tree house in Massachusetts in which he once lived. William grew up outside of Boston and went to a small liberal arts college like mine. He lives in Eagle Rock, which is a burgeoning artistic neighborhood near my established artistic neighborhood. He's funny, and we make jokes about going out to eat at some horrible corporate establishment like Chili's or Friday's or Applebee's. But then we realize we live in L.A.

I laugh. "L.A. is too cool for Chili's. There is a Grand Lux though."

"Would that work?"

I think about it. "Naw, not really, too upscale."

Instead, we agree to go see a midnight showing of *Cool as Ice*, the early nineties film starring Vanilla himself. I spent the better part of my freshman year in high school watching that film with my best friends at the time. We memorized every line and then repeated them back to each other ad nauseam through fits of adolescent laughter. So when William asks if I'd be interested, I tell him immediately, "I'm in," because though it is only a movie, going to see a midnight show on a first date still feels slightly adventurous.

I was at Ivan's house the other night for one of our bimonthly game nights when my friend John showed up. John is the man who introduced me to Jimmy Voltage when we were in Oxnard. He finds my dating adventures hysterical and is always asking for full reports on the men I have gone out with.

"So have you begun to categorize them?" he questioned me over our game of Cranium.

I thought about it and fear I might be. There are definitely types that I can spot off the bat, and those fall into four categories:

1. We will be attracted to each other.
2. He will be attracted to me with no reciprocation.
3. I will be attracted to him with no reciprocation.
4. We will both fail at attraction mutually.

William and I fall into this last category. I walk into the restaurant and know this immediately. And I can see on his face that so does he. The Williams of the world and the Kristens of the world were not meant for each other. I've never been able to figure out why, until William starts talking about how much he hates Sandra Bullock. She's an easy target, but William takes her much more personally.

William is pretty laid-back, so I am rather surprised by the venom in his eyes when he tells me, "I was watching her in an interview once, and just her voice. Oh my God, that voice. She is so fucking obnoxious. I kept wanting to turn the TV off, but I hated her so much I just kept watching."

Wow. As I think about it I realize that I am probably pretty darn close to a Sandra Bullock in his mind. My voice is too loud, my laugh too incessant, and my need to explain, divulge, and carry on, annoying.

Ivan's other friend Ric was also at the party. Months ago, I went to brunch with Ric, Ivan, and Ric's two-year-old son Nathan. I fell in love with Nathan instantly. And when halfway through the brunch, he slid his hand up my arm, looked me in the eye and said, "Mommy," I was sold.

Ric is in an unhappy marriage and started calling me his second wife. I let him because he's hot. And sober. And with a full tattoo covering his back, kind of dangerous. I drew the line, however, when we were walking down the Venice boardwalk, each holding one of Nathan's hands, swinging him into the air, and Ric referred to me as Nathan's second mommy. I don't know Ric's wife, but I can promise that I would not want the father of my children assigning the title of "Mommy" to any other woman but me.

So when I walked into the party, and the first person I saw was Ric, something in me lurched. Nathan was also there, but I tried to keep my distance from both of them. Even when Ric pulled me into his lap, and I noticed he wasn't wearing his ring, I knew it wasn't right and wasn't good, and I'm done being interested in men who do those sorts of things. I made sure that I was not on Ric's team for the board game and sat across the table to give myself distance. That didn't stop Ric from sliding his hand across my shoulder blades when he walked behind my chair to go to the kitchen. And it didn't stop me from being a little wistful that I want a Nathan of my own as I watched him quiet and observant as the adults laughed and acted silly and cooed in his direction.

"I fear that you are going to hate men by the end of this book," John said as he leaned over while the other team argued about their Word Worm question.

"Really, John? God, I think it's going to be quite the opposite." And I do. I am beginning to see that attraction isn't about the other person, it's about us. I don't take William's lack of interest personally. And I doubt he takes mine as that. We just know what we like. As he waxes on about house music and the clothing line he once did and as I wax on about living in South Africa and 1980s country music, it's okay that we don't find a common bond. We take up the time talking as two humans can and do.

And I wonder, what kind of fit am I looking for? Because if neither the artist (#20), the electrician (#6), the TV writer (#1), the medical technician (#4), the bar manager (#5), nor the tennis pro (#15) will do, what will? Should I find another intellectual movie producer like Oliver or lovable fashionista like Sabbath or goofball prince like Frenchie? Because though I might have loved them all, I am not sure if any of them fit, either. That the illusions about what my life would have been like with those men are actually delusions is another silly fantasy I torture myself with as entertainment.

William and I finish dinner. If I could have broken the second part of our date, I would have. But in the end, I am really glad I didn't. Because *Cool as Ice* has aged like a fine fucking wine. And I am truly grateful to William for taking me out. Because without that date, I don't think either of us would have seen it. And when he tells me how I can find furniture-making classes in Los Angeles and how to upholster a couch, I know that this was a Saturday night well spent. So John is wrong to think I will hate men because I am learning an enormous amount from them. I am learning what I like, and what I don't like. Whom I should get closer to, and whom I should stay the hell away from. And I am learning a lot from each man himself. As I get out of William's car, I know we won't see each other again, but I don't leave with any hard feelings.

At Ivan's house, I said goodbye to Ric just as coolly. I knelt down and gave my true love, my little Nathan, a hug. He hugged back, which is odd for Nathan. I think he respected the fact that I stayed away from his dad, but he's only two, and I don't think he is that observational yet. Earlier in the night, Ric had remarked when I showed him the peach tart that I made, "How are you not married?" For a long time, I thought it was about me. That I was missing something. But I am beginning to think that's it actually about them—about these men I am having the chance to meet and date and get to know. And I am just going to have to go through a lot of different patterns before I find the one that fits.

113

1 2 3 4 5 6 7 8 9 10 11 12 13 14 15 16 17 18 19 20
21 22 23 24 25 26 27 28 29 30 31 32 33 34 35 36
37 38 39 40 41 42 43 44 45 46 47 48 49 50 51

Date Twenty-One: The Sparkling Ribbon of Time, Act I

The Griffith Observatory was first unveiled to the Los Angeles public in 1935. It was the same year they founded the program that keeps me sober. In 2002, right before I moved to L.A., they closed the Observatory for renovations. And so I remember being at numerous rooftop parties during those years, staring up at the crest-line dome and asking repeatedly because I was typically drunk at rooftop parties, "When do we get to go?" Oliver had promised to take me once it reopened, but by the time it did in 2006, Oliver and I were a long-extinct planet.

When I came to L.A., I didn't have many preconceived notions or images about the city. Sure, I had seen the Hollywood sign and some vague pictures of Malibu, but most of my expectations came from years of watching *MTV Raps* and *Boys in the Hood*. I thought the whole place was going to look like South Central. But the one image I did carry, the one glimmer that this town was about more than movie stars and boob jobs and Ice Cube, was the fact that somewhere in that city I had never seen, sat the Observatory.

Like all things I deem special in my life, I decided the scene had to be just right for my first visit. The perfect date to take me up to Mount Hollywood on his motorcycle, the vintage dress I could wear, and the air of romance that I was determined would be felt like an earthquake up at that great, looming building I saw every night as I drove home from work. When Jimmy Voltage invited me there, it was as though he knew about my lifelong fantasy, and I felt like it was a sign from God that he had chosen the locale. Whoever would think to invite me to the Observatory, one of Los Angeles's most popular landmarks, but my soul mate?

But we never made it, and I think the sign from God was, "Not yet, Kristen. Not this way."

I wasn't sure what I was expecting to find once I got there. Stars, Los Angeles, Keanu Reeves? But I always knew it would mean something. It was the grand evidence that my city was built on poetry, not pimps.

The weekend before Siren left, we went up to the Observatory for my first time, and though we hiked instead of going by motorcycle, and though I wore leggings and Nikes and not the vintage dress, and though the only romance we felt was the one we share for life, the scene couldn't have been written any better. Because it was my last weekend with my friend, I didn't think about Jimmy or Oliver or what's missing from my life. I just knew, like a rock of solid truth, that I was exactly where I was supposed to be.

Which is why I confuse myself when Superman Peter asks me if I want to go hiking, and I suggest the Observatory. Again? I was just there, the memory with Siren still potent, and though I might have an addictive personality, good luck explaining an obsession with a seventy-year-old building to anyone. Also, by our third date, I think both Peter and I know this isn't going anywhere. After he returned from London, it took us nearly three weeks to set up the date, and apparently the only time either of us was willing to sacrifice was during the day. Peter picks me up in his Volvo station wagon, and it fits his careful lawyer personality to a T. He explains he got the car so that he could go on bike trips. He hadn't mentioned this yet, and so I ask, "Oh, do you go biking often?"

Peter shrugs. "Not really."

It's funny, but I have begun to notice this trait in men. When they first meet you and are excited, they are enthusiastic about everything: the coffee, their hobbies, work, life, the moon. Once they decide they're not interested, everything ends in a shrug. I take Peter on the trail that leads through Griffith Park up to the Observatory, and we relax into the easy banter of two friends going for a walk.

Peter has never been to the Observatory, and I get excited as we turn the corner, and I get ready to show him the startling white view that greets you at the top of Mount Hollywood. But Peter doesn't say a word.

"Isn't it great?" I ask.

He looks around at the Asian tourists, people taking pictures. "Sure. It's like the Empire State Building."

I want to scream, "No it's not! It's the Observatory!" But I don't because that would just be weird. I lead us inside, and I am quickly engrossed by all the exhibits and illustrations that break my heart. Like the fact that we are made of stars and that one day our sun will die and that we will never know the end of the world because it's too far for us to see, and no amount of human willpower can get us there anyway. We walk from exhibit to exhibit telling light-hearted jokes, and I wish we were able to engage in these lessons of the solar system on a more romantic level. Instead, we start going our separate ways through the museum, and I am suddenly overwhelmed by the greatest sense of loneliness. How I wish I was with someone who was as wowed by this world as me. How I wish I could walk hand in hand with some man who looked around and asked questions and felt the same pressing mortality that I do when I realize that we are so, so finite.

Peter and I walk downstairs to what is quickly becoming my favorite exhibit at the museum. During the renovations, a woman named Kara Knack donated over 2,200 pendants, brooches, earrings, and other costume jewelry to what the Observatory calls, "The Sparkling Ribbon of Time." Each little gem stands for another era in the creation of the universe. From the big bang to the present, it shows us how long it has taken us to get here and how very short of a time we all get to stay.

The Wednesday before, my boss Noelle called me into her office. Recently a manager position in our fundraising department had opened up, and I got the feeling by all her dropped hints that it might be mine.

"How hard are you willing to work?" she asked me.

"Noelle, you know how hard I can work. I'm already taking classes in fundraising. This job is for me." I didn't stutter. I didn't doubt myself.

Just as fate brought me to our wonderful organization so many years before, so fate created the perfect job into which for me to move.

Noelle took my hand in hers and smiled. "It's yours."

Later that day I accompanied her on my first fundraising tour of our Charter School. We showed the prospective donors our incredible classrooms, our children, our belief that we are all made of stars and deserve the chance to sparkle. I never would have expected that this work could bring me such joy. As I watched our kids run up to Noelle, looking up at her as their hero, this woman who has brought them opportunity as much as hope, I wanted to hug her too. Because she did the same thing for me. And now I stand on the verge of that opportunity. As the children I know came up and gave me hugs too, as one of my favorite students handed me a heart she drew for me, as Noelle smiled over to where I knelt, talking with a little boy about his art project, I knew that though I might be willing to do the work, something else quite powerful actually got me here.

And if I could identify that new God, it would be the Sparkling Ribbon of Time. It would be that great mass of energy that got those molecules moshing up against each other in the first place. It would be the hazy clusters of life and movement that keep our earth spinning, that make the mountains form, that show us that we can't do it on our own. And for every pendant in our own life, for every Jimmy, for every Siren, for every Noelle and new job, there will be another sparkling gem soon on its heels, showing us that we are cared for. Even when we feel absolutely alone while walking through the Griffith Park Observatory, we are cared for.

"That's a ridiculous illustration," Peter scoffs. He is standing next to me, staring at the jewelry. He shakes his head, disappointed. "Fucking L.A."

He wanders off, and I smile. Because he's right. You could only find such an illustration of God made out of costume jewelry in L.A. And I'm okay with the fact that Peter isn't for me. In fact, I'm a little excited. Because I wonder what my next gem will look like. I wonder whether he'll be the bright diamond brooch, or the pearl ring, or the turquoise pendant. I wonder who he will be.

We finish the tour and grab lunch at the museum café. We sit outside and look at the incredible view of Los Angeles, and though we have been able to talk easily on all the dates thus far, we're a little quiet now. We know we won't go out again. We sit under a beautiful tree in the shade as the city, in all its hazy glory, spreads out before us.

119

1 2 3 4 5 6 7 8 9 10 11 12 13 14 15 16 17 18 19 20 21 **22** 23 24 25 26 27 28 29 30 31 32 33 34 35 36 37 38 39 40 41 42 43 44 45 46 47 48 49 50 51

Date Twenty-Two: The Schmoos

I walk up to my Tuesday night meeting for sober people who want to stay that way and have to pause to catch my breath. Jimmy Voltage stands there talking with some small little hipster girl with her tattoos and fringe bag and old fake riding boots. I can hear her giggling half a block away, and I cringe. I try to casually take the last drag off my cigarette, crushing it out with the toe of my work shoe. This was not the night to run into Jimmy. I am not wearing makeup; I am wearing argyle and Banana Republic slacks. There is nothing cool or fringe or cowgirl about me. I look like any other conservative professional, with my hair in a bun and my work bag hanging limply from my shoulder. Jimmy looks up and sees me. He smiles warmly, and so I breathe it in, walk up, and say "hello." He instantly grabs me in a hug for which I am wholly unprepared, making me practically trip into his embrace. But it is warm and comfortable, and I am sad when he pulls away. The schmoo to whom he was talking still stands there, staring at her competition, and I can tell she is relatively confused as to why Jimmy is hugging the yuppie.

The term "schmoo" is Siren's claim to fame. It doesn't stand for anything, except that it does. It stands for the easy girls, and we don't mean sluts. No, the schmoos are what my gay friend Tommy refers to as "Ikea girlfriends" because you can put them together without reading the instructions. It's not that they're not smart. They typically are. They studied women's history or geology in college. They get graduate degrees in social work. They do needlepoint or garden. They have a dog named after an obscure musician (Costello, or Niko, or even

Ramone). And they stand there looking up into the eyes of one Jimmy Voltage, giggling and talking about last weekend's "show," and they don't show an ounce of the insecurity that lies beneath all of our surfaces.

Because the schmoo is lacking in the one thing that makes dating so incredibly painful and awkward for women like Siren and me— they don't have ego. I mean, sure, they have enough to survive. They're actually incredibly confident and cool and uncomplicated, but that's the thing, ego isn't confidence. It's the part of you that tells you that you are so much better than the schmoo, that she is the Ikea girlfriend and you are *Architectural Digest.* Then you tell yourself, perhaps with some honesty, perhaps with self-sabotage, that you will never win. And so, we anti-schmoos give awkward hugs and sleep with guys on the first date. At times, we act like we are the greatest things on the earth; other times we are on our knees, begging for them to stay.

Three days later, I find myself sitting across the table at Canter's, a local Jewish deli, with my date Rob. Rob is the organic nutritionist with the PhD. And unfortunately for him, I find myself trying to forget yet another man on one of our dates. But this time, it's not Oliver; it's that damn schmoo lover I have been doing so good not thinking about. But perhaps even more disappointing is that between the last date and this one, Rob has shown some disturbing personality trends.

I was supposed to go out with Rob the night before but had gone to the dentist after work and found myself with three fillings and a mind-numbing amount of pain afterwards. I called Rob to reschedule. He had just left work and as I told him about the pain I was in, I could hear him scoff.

"What's wrong, Rob?" I asked.

"Nothing. It's just, it's Friday night, you know. You really shouldn't be canceling a date last minute on a Friday night."

"I'm in bed, Rob. I'm in pain."

"I know, I hear ya. Still, it's Friday night. It's a little rude."

Something in my gut says I should hang up on the guy, that I should cancel the date, but whether it's my good manners, or the place in me that still wants to beg people to stay, I don't. I apologized again, I hung up the phone, and I put in the movie *Rear Window.*

Oliver once said that I resembled Grace Kelly, not so much in my looks, but in my demeanor. When watching her last night, I understand why. Because though she looks fairly cool and collected, she is actually a fast-talking spaz under the surface, and when her mouth gets going, all she can hear is herself. And in *Rear Window* she is the perfect woman; so perfect that Jimmy Stewart is afraid to marry her because he thinks he would prefer someone more bland, someone more schmoo. Grace gets him in the end. But then again, she's Grace Kelly. She married a prince. And of course Jimmy Stewart is so much like my Jimmy here that I cannot help but feel that this is how the universe laughs at us.

"It's been three years for me," I say as I tell Rob how single I am over dinner. I know I sound a little morose. I sound like all my dates who just shrug once they realize they're not interested. I don't even hide the fact that I am depressed.

"Wow, three years, what's wrong with you?" He laughs and then bites into the pastrami and rye that has just arrived. Apparently Rob might teach others about organic diets, but he himself can dig a meat sandwich from time to time.

"I'm not sure. I've been trying to figure that out." I shovel a large spoonful of potato salad into my mouth. I talk with my mouth full. "And you? Ever been married?"

"No, I was close once, but it didn't happen."

I tell him how Siren and I are bored by the male sex. "I guess we're just beginning to feel like you're all so predictable. And we adore you, we do. It's just, well, we have your number. And that's dangerous. It's dangerous to not be surprised."

Rob laughs. "What are we, recipes or something?"

"Kind of."

"I think," he jokes, "I would be a cranberry pomegranate reduction —pretends he has read more books than he actually has and masturbates twice a week."

"Mmm, yeah, except for you're lying." I take down another flight of potatoes as I mumble through them, "You masturbate more than that."

"And lies about how much he masturbates," Rob quips.

I have to laugh at that. And then I decide to just drop one.

"I quit masturbating," I say.

Rob shakes himself. "What?"

"Yeah. My libido is just gone." Rob might be shocked but not as much as I am.

"I have an idea," Rob says. I brace myself. He suggests that we go to a sex shop around the corner.

"We won't buy anything; we'll just see if we can reprogram you," he suggests.

"I don't know."

"I promise we'll keep it innocent. No matter what, we will end our night with a kiss on the cheek."

And that's a plan I can agree to. We spend the next hour jousting with dildos and making dirty sounds between the shelves and trying to figure out how someone could look themselves in the mirror after fucking a foam pussy. I actually begin to forget about Jimmy and about Rob's previous behavior because this is fun. We leave the sex shop, laughing and bumping into each other in the parking lot. I drive him back to his car, and I pull over. It's a busy street, and I am in the red. There are people walking by, so I don't take my foot off the brake. I don't put the car in park. I don't even undo my seatbelt because I am hoping that Rob and I will keep our pact to go to the sex shop and end the night with a kiss on the cheek. Rob undoes his seat belt and turns toward me.

"All right," Rob announces. "I am going to try to kiss you again, even while you attempt to fend me off."

"Rob, I'm sorry, but that's exactly what I am going to do. Can't we just do what we said? Can't we just end it with a kiss on the cheek?"

"Whatever." He leans in, and I think he is smart and is going for the peck, but suddenly I feel his tongue pushing into my mouth, and it's wrong. I keep my mouth closed, and Rob pulls away.

"You're really not going to kiss me?" he hisses.

"No, I told you that. I want to take this slow, please."

"It's our second date. That is slow!"

"So? Is there some rule in place?" I'm a little taken aback.

But Rob gets pissed. "That's bullshit."

This guy really is an asshole. "I'm sorry, Rob. But if I don't feel like kissing you, then why should I?"

"Because we're not ten. I bought you dinner; we had a fun night. You normally end a date like that with a kiss."

"Well, I don't."

"Well, you're a freak," he says, and quite frankly I think we're both surprised by his behavior. Silence. I let that one sit there.

"Look, Rob, that is just how I feel, and if you're not interested in going along with that, I won't take any offense. Really."

"I'm sorry. It's just weird to me, that's all." Rob tries to back down. But the card has been played, and from here on out whatever Rob might say or do has been destroyed by the word still bouncing around my car. We just went to a sex shop together. We talked about masturbation and terminal singlehood. We had fun. And he ruined it. Rob gets out of my car, and though I know he feels bad, it doesn't change anything. I can't help but wonder if my instincts actually worked this time.

And so I hope that I can apply those same instincts to Jimmy. After the meeting is over on Tuesday, he saunters over and asks me how I am. Except he pulls me back up into that same hug, and though I am so confused, I try to focus. I try not to act all crazy Grace Kelly, but I can't.

"Guess what?" I nearly yell in his face. "I got a promotion at work!"

Jimmy still has his arms around my waist, and mine are around his shoulders.

"Really, that's awesome! What will you be doing?"

We slip apart as I tell him, "I'm gonna be asking rich people for money."

His face falls, and he looks a little sad as he says, "You'll be good at that."

It's a strange response, and I can't help but feel that he thinks I'm some fast-talking grifter, just a sassy and sophisticated con whom he couldn't figure out so he turned to the nearest schmoo. He asks me if I'm hungry, and if I want to join him and John for dinner. Before I can confirm, I am in a conversation with someone else, and I see him and John walking off.

I know it's for the best because just those few seconds in his arms scrambles me up again. The next morning, I am sitting in another meeting, and I begin to fantasize that Jimmy and I never ended in the first place. That we have been dating now for three months and that we're hitting that place in a relationship where new challenges might be showing up, but the excitement that this is really happening makes the little bickers and nags fairly invisible. I imagine that he had come to my work's holiday party and that we had spent New Year's together and that when my mother visits in two weeks, we would have been in the place where he would have spent some quality time with her. I imagine as I am sitting in the meeting that he would have come in a little late and put his hand on my neck as he sat down behind me. I would have turned around and shot a sleepy glance in his direction. People would at this point know us as a couple and comment on what a great pair we were. And I would have gotten the boyfriend who, for a moment, looked like mine.

Date Twenty-Three: That Old Dylan Song

I meet Marcus at Philippe's French Dip in Chinatown. Marcus is an art designer for movies and TV. He is tall and skinny and looks his forty-four years of age. He's also dressed incredibly cute and has an easy laugh and asks an enormous amount of questions. Though I wasn't entirely smitten from our e-mails, he resembled a boy I once loved in high school and that was enough for us to set a date over roast beef sandwiches on a Tuesday night.

I've got half a French dip in my mouth when Marcus asks me how my parents met. I talk through my sandwich. "That's a good question."

And the reason why my existence was decided by a single nanosecond of fate. I would have said that latter part too, except this is why dating is hard. So much eating and talking at once.

"My mom was actually vacationing by herself in Florida. The weird thing is she can't quite remember why she was there. It was to visit a friend or something. She had just graduated high school, and I guess was killing time while she tried to figure out what to do with her life."

"Where did she go to high school?" Marcus should be a reporter.

"Dallas. That's why we ended up moving back there when my parents divorced. Anyway, she was there in Ft. Lauderdale and was standing at a stoplight when a man walked up next to her with this big Irish setter. Red Dog."

To this day my family cannot mention Red's name without saying, "What a good dog." Because Red was special and was, until me, probably the love of my father's life. I tell Marcus how my mom commented, "What a beautiful dog." Even today the story confuses me. Because my mom doesn't talk to strangers on street corners. And she certainly doesn't talk to random men. But I guess that's just the simple twist of fate. Seconds and words and street corners lining up just right so that our windows of opportunity become clear. Clear enough for my dad to look over and see my mom and know that he had to meet this naive, little redhead complimenting his Irish setter. "So are you," my dad replied. And though my Mom might have been nervous that he had just called her a dog, she couldn't help but feel the excitement that flows when you stand on the edge of your life and slip right over.

Marcus listens intently as I continue, "My dad followed my mom into the juice bar where she was headed, insisted on buying her a juice, and well, here we are."

A little over a year later they were married. Another year later I was born, and in 1981 my father was sentenced and went away for the next twenty-five years. They got divorced when I was six, and at the age of eight my mother took me to my favorite park and sat me down to have what would be a very serious conversation. I knew something was up. I knew my parents were divorced, so it wasn't that. Our white poodle Gigi had already died the year before, leaving us with no surviving pets, so I checked that one off the list too. Maybe she found out I had stolen the colored chalk from my second-grade teacher. I prepared myself for the stern lecture and shaking head and narrowed eyes that would come to haunt my ill-behaved life. But it had been over a year since the theft, and by the swell of tears in her eyes, the way her mouth fell soft and open, she looked far too sad to be on the verge of punishing me. She slowly explained, "Daddy is in what they call a correctional facility." Not jail, not prison—a correctional facility. And so we began a lifetime of glossing over the truth of who my father is.

I don't tell Marcus all of this, of course, because I don't air my dirty laundry as easily as I used to. Marcus is put in the awkward position of airing his, however, when I ask, "So how long have you lived in Chinatown?"

He looks down, "Well, I guess now I get to tell you the long, sordid story." My interest is piqued but Marcus's telling of it is neither long nor sordid. In fact, I can tell I am getting the much-shortened, guarded version of the tale. He is divorced and has a four-year-old son, and it seems they all once had a house together up the street. When it came to a tragic end, however, Marcus was forced to move into an apartment in the area, and has been there since. I can tell some serious shit went down when he says that he and his ex are finally on friendly terms and that she now has a boyfriend.

"I've pretty much been out of work since, which sucks, for obvious reasons, but I do get to help out a lot with my son, so it has its perks. I just wish I lived in Germany or Italy where the birthrates are low, so they actually pay you to take care of your children."

"Really? They pay you for having kids in Italy?" I ask.

"They do."

"Shit, that's perfect." I tell him how my friends and I have made a pact that should we not get married and pregnant by a certain age, we plan to move in together, have children, and raise them in a multi-parent household. I nearly gush, "But if we do it in Italy, we can also make some cash. And we'll be close to the Prada outlet."

"Sure," I can sense Marcus is not as enthusiastic about my revelation.

"Marcus. I think I might have found the great solution," I say, and I am not kidding. Because when he tells me his ex isn't angry anymore, I know the divorce was Marcus's fault. And I wonder whether it's worth it. Whether you finally meet the guy, have the kid, and he ends up fucking it up anyway. And sure he might be good for child care but that's only when he's unemployed and living tenuously off the profits of the dream house you bought and renovated together before having to sell it amidst pain and tears and betrayal. I want to ask Marcus if he cheated on his ex, but I don't. Instead, I tell him the world turns on the backs of women. He laughs, but only a little, and I know he can't help but admit that it's true.

I think about John's fear that I will hate men by the end of this. And once again, I decide that I won't. Because whatever mistakes Marcus has made, I have made them too, and I sit there across the table just as single and confused and slightly jaded as he is. We get up to go, and Marcus stops.

"So should we go out again?"

I have begun to realize that my easy banter and tendency to laugh is often mistaken by men as romantic interest. And I am not interested in Marcus. I am too young and vibrant yet to end up in someone's Chinatown apartment, taking care of their four-year-old son, pretending I am happy when I never even felt a spark in the first place.

But what else can you say when you're standing in a historical restaurant filled with roast beef and slaw, and you've already shared quite a bit of your own histories, and you feel bad for how much this guy standing there, looking at you, has gone through, and you know he would take it all back if he could.

"Sure."

I get in my car and call my father. Two weeks ago, he sent me roses and chocolates and a little teddy bear that has managed to go to bed with me every night since. He has called me numerous times over the last two days, begging me to return his call, telling me that he decided not to pursue his old career. He says he is living with a friend and is writing the book about his life instead. I talk to Nana earlier in the day, and we agree that I should return the call but only to ask him for some more time apart. That he needs to focus on what he is doing and show me that his change is in action and not just word.

I call him, and I think he might be drinking. His voice is heavy as he tells me that he is staying on a farm in Tennessee. "Look, K. I just want to say that the last conversation we had, it's dead, okay? It's dead and buried."

I would disagree as it is still very much alive for me, but I have begun a new template with my father where he talks and I remain quiet, and then I say what I have to say and try my best to prevent his frequent interruptions with the phrase, "Please, let me speak."

"Dad, believe me, I know that you love me, but sometimes we don't know how to love people the right way."

"Aw, Jeez, Kris, you sound like you're from L.A. Come on, we don't know how much time we have on this earth."

"I agree, and I respect that. It's because of that, because we only get one shot at this, that I want to do it right. That's why…"

"Kris…"

"Please, let me speak. That's why I need time to decide how I want to progress, to see whether I want to even participate in this relationship."

He falls silent and then says, "Oh, so, is that how it is?"

He sounds like so many of the men I have dated. I stay calm as he tells me that he needs my help getting his book published. "I'm not calling you just because you're my daughter, you know. I want you to be a part of this. We could make some good money here. With my stories and your connections."

I ignore this. Ignore the fact that my father is in essence telling me he is using me. I ask him to give me a month. He feels bad and says that he wants me to visit, that he will pay for it, that he wants to see me. But I remain strong. "Look, Dad, call me in a month. We can see where we're at then."

I hang up the phone and choke back the tears. I am trying to create boundaries, but I also can't help but wonder whether I am punishing the guy. I have it in my head that if only I could be healthy and strong in my relationship with my dad, then I could be healthy and strong in my relationships with men in general. Rob, my date from the sex shop, said he hates feeling like he is being punished for another guy's mistakes. And I wonder whether I am now punishing my father for all the mistakes the guys I have dated have made. Or if I have punished all the guys for the mistakes of my father.

On my last visit to the shaman, she told me that some people get to do all their work within the space of a relationship, but some of us must do the work before we can even get into one. I am beginning to think that all the work in the world will not bring me a mate any faster. In fact, maybe it does just come down to those seconds and words and street corners lining up just right so that our windows of opportunity become clear. Like the ones that brought me here, to this night, where I see the flaws of two fathers: the one that just bought me a roast beef sandwich, and the one that bought my mother a juice over thirty years before.

1 2 3 4 5 6 7 8 9 10 11 12 13 14 15 16 17 18 19 20 21 22
23 **24** 25 26 27 28 29 30 31 32 33 34 35 36 37
38 39 40 41 42 43 44 45 46 47 48 49 50 51

Date Twenty-Four: The Lies of Coco Van Dyne

I'm beginning to have trouble keeping track of all these dates. I am talking to Ivan, on my way to meet yet another man I met on *The Onion*, when I explain to him, "I feel like I need a cheat sheet to keep them straight. And I'm not sure who I've told what and whether I am repeating myself over and over."

"I put it all in my Outlook," Ivan tells me.

"Really?"

"Yeah, just some basic facts. Then I check my iPhone before going in, and I know who's who."

"Well, I don't have an iPhone."

"Sucks for you."

"Anyway, I don't think I want to know Alan," I explain to him. "I don't think I want Alan to know me."

"Then don't tell him anything about you," Ivan suggests.

"That's a great idea."

"Of course it is."

"I will lie," I tell him.

I have trouble finding Alan at first, which is the worst. Because there's nothing like poking around a coffee shop, trying to figure out which man sitting alone is the one you're supposed to join. I have seen too many headshots by now to remember what Alan's looks like. Thankfully, Alan approaches me. Alan is a nice, short Jewish man, who I probably wouldn't have recognized even if I did remember his picture.

At this point I can't even remember why I said yes to the date in the first place, but I also know that I am trying to be open to possibility here, even if I am not quite sure what will come of it.

"I am going to lie to you for the entire portion of our date," I tell him off the bat.

"Okay." Though a little confused, he accepts my proposition. Basketball plays on the TV. I start to watch, but only because I'm not in the mood to talk with the man sitting eagerly on the other side of the table. I can tell he wants to talk, and I understand now how Micah must have felt with me poised with all my interview questions, chomping at the bit.

Alan notices the game and asks, "You like basketball?"

And my own game begins. "Love it. Lakers rule, baby." I couldn't even tell you who plays for them outside of Kobe. "I'm pretty much an avid sports enthusiast."

"Really?" he asks.

"Yeah. I've got about fifty-six sports channels through Direct TV and spend the better part of my time watching football. All kinds of football, even high school, and rugby."

I pause. I am breathing a little heavy while I talk. Kind of like Tony Soprano. I wonder if my false sports persona is increasing testosterone levels as I speak.

"I dig extreme sports too. Motocross, BMX racing. Even rock-rappelling. Aquatic dancing, spelunking, you name it."

Alan knows that I am making shit up, and so he plays along. But I try not to let him. I just keep listing random sports.

"Lacrosse, tennis, shot put, track and field, of course, archery, gymnastics, hockey." I finally run out of Olympic events.

Alan asks, "What about cross-country shooting?"

There is a photo of me on *The Onion* at the gun range where I am holding the electrician's shotgun.

"I am actually training to become the world's greatest cross-country shooter." I lean across the table and whisper, "I am also a hired assassin, but not for pay."

Alan should be more concerned by that admission, but he isn't because, as I quickly guess, he is a writer. Another, fucking, writer. Just a dude like me with the big dream and the day job and the little apartment that holds it all until we make it big and grab that house in the hills.

I go back to lying, but I try to intersperse some truth because those are the most believable ones. I tell him I worked in film development and for the crazy book publisher. "But my real job. The rest was just a front. My real job was as a high-end call girl in Paris, but then I got tired of walking the streets."

"Aha," Alan calls out. "There's a hole in your story. High-end call girls don't walk the streets."

I don't even blink. "They were fancy streets."

I try to make it as funny as possible so I don't come off as mean. I am supposed to leave the date by 5:30 p.m. to go try on a bridesmaid's dress for Nat's wedding in October. And I am less excited about that than I am about this date.

Nat and I met after I relapsed and got sober in L.A. Like Siren, she was one of the first women to reach out to me. Though she was six years younger, she had more sober time, and we quickly became friends. Soon after we met, however, Nat met Reggie, and she pretty much disappeared from my life. Sure, we would run into each other at meetings. Every once in a while we would plan to meet for coffee, but Nat was the type of woman, who once she had a man, didn't seem to have much room for friends. For all intents and purposes, Nat is a schmoo. Though she is funny and smart and absolutely self-conscious, she is incredible at blending that into the perfect male-focused confidence that the opposite sex finds so intriguing. I have watched as men fall at her feet in easy succession. She is attractive, but I know that's not necessarily what it's about. It is about her ability to make them feel safe, feel loved, feel a devotion that I, for whatever reason, can only muster in a creepy, begging way. And I resent her for this. Wholly.

However, when she came to me a few months ago and told me that she was looking for a new job, the words, "We have something at my organization" flew out of my mouth before I could even think about it. And so, not long after, Nat joined my nonprofit as another assistant, and our subtle competition found a whole new stage. Not long after

Nat and Reggie got engaged, she asked me to be her bridesmaid. I wasn't surprised because for all our jealousies and resentments and competition, Nat and I kind of love each other. We are like sisters, bound to one another whether we like it or not. Still, being her bridesmaid hasn't been easy.

As I explain to Alan: "I guess I can just see me standing at the altar, single, as my much younger friend marries her soul mate, and they run off to their newly purchased home in Echo Park together. And I kinda want that too."

Alan looks a little excited. And I realize that after lying the better part of the date, this is probably the one subject on which I shouldn't be telling the truth. Because I do have recurrent dreams about living in my own house in Echo Park. I know the floor plan in every detail; I know what the kitchen table looks like and where I keep the spices, and though there is never a man in the dream, there is always a sense that there is a man present, somewhere.

I told my uncle Vic recently that I had horses to ride and lives to live, and I wanted a man that had as much zest for the journey as I do. He sighed, "You sound just like Coco Van Dyne."

Ah, Coco Van Dyne. My uncle's high school girlfriend. Back when he still dated girls. I remember growing up hearing stories about her, and she seemed like exactly the kind of gal I wanted to be. All wild and unfettered and feisty. She was gorgeous and owned horses and seemed like she would jump off a fence and start a fight for no reason at all. She is now fifty-two, single, and walking dogs for a living. She keeps trying to get sober, but it won't stick, and she keeps telling my uncle that they should get back together because they are both single and depressed. Somehow she is willing to ignore the fact that my uncle has been gay for the last thirty years, but that's Coco Van Dyne for you. She never gives up the fight.

And when I hear that, I wonder whether I will be able to either. And then I know why I am upset about being the bridesmaid and not the bride: I do want to feel settled down. It's just that I want to feel a little shaken up too.

Alan is not going to be my settler. That much I am sure. Sometimes when I go on a date, and I am really not excited, I hope that it means I will be meeting the perfect guy, and then years later we can tell our kids how we were not looking forward to our first date, and isn't that ironic. But there's no irony here. So I bullshit instead. Alan seems to think that I am interested because I am being so insane and laconic. Maybe he's the crazy one. But not in the right way.

I thank Alan for the coffee and the lies, and I go to try on the dress. And it's really, really pretty. For the first time, I get excited about this wedding. As I spin around in the swaths of satin, I forget that I am resentful of Nat's easy engagement and marriage. I forget how tiresome these dates are beginning to feel. I forget about Coco Van Dyne and what it means to settle down. I remember that anything is possible.

1 2 3 4 5 6 7 8 9 10 11 12 13 14 15 16 17 18 19 20 21 22 23 24 **25** 26 27 28 29 30 31 32 33 34 35 36 37 38 39 40 41 42 43 44 45 46 47 48 49 50 51

Date Twenty-Five: Otorongo

"So you don't smoke pot anymore?"

I sigh. My father asks me this far more frequently than I care to admit. I try again to explain. "No, Dad, I'm sober." I stretch the word as though that will make him understand better. "I don't drink alcohol. I'm even thinking about quitting cigarettes. And no, I don't smoke pot."

"Huh..." My dad thinks for a second. "Well, that's a shame, K. My real hope for you is that one day you'll be able to enjoy a blessing again."

I am driving on the 10 Freeway and use the excuse of having to change lanes for my lack of response to both the comment itself and the fact that he just referred to pot as "a blessing." I have been speaking to my father again recently, which is not an easy task. I know that my request for space has been hard on him. I know that he remembers a time when I loved his wild stories, when I agreed that pot was a blessing, when I thought he was the sun and the moon and all the stars in between. But then I got sober.

And his tall tales didn't seem as interesting. Whereas we used to talk about legalization and outlaws and the evil American government, whereas we used to talk about cheating the system and living on the lam and breaking the rules, whereas we used to talk about bullshit and pipe dreams and plans that never materialized, I don't really believe in any of that anymore. And I don't really believe in him.

He is still at the farm but has recently made an agreement with the FBI to work as a consultant. He wants to have an easy and light chat with me: the type that fathers and daughters do every day because he feels like a normal guy who should be able to call his daughter in California at the end of his work day on the farm.

The tough part is there is nothing about our relationship that is normal. And try as I might to be friendly and easygoing, I find myself being awkwardly silent and responding to everything he says with, "Uh huh" or "Great!" because I can muster no more words than that.

He finally says, "Well, I can hear you are rushing off to somewhere. It sounds like you need to get off the phone."

"Dad, I'm sorry. I don't know what to tell you." I sigh. Again. "I don't know why it's awkward to speak to you. I know that we had no problems talking for years, but I do now. It's just how it is."

"I know why, K. It's because you're not too sure." I assume he means about him, and if that is the case, then he's right. He decides to take a different tack. "Hey, have I ever told you about the day you were born?" My dad thinks that by going down memory lane we might find some common ground, and he's right again.

"No, you haven't," I say. At first I warm to the story because he is telling me about my mom and Lamaze class, and I can just see that tiny little lady with that huge beach-ball stomach, and it warms me to tears.

And then my dad tells me where he was when my mom was going into labor. "God, what a day, Kris. I had wrecked a Mercedes the night before. Did you know that? It must have been around four in the morning. It was crazy. We went straight off the Merritt Parkway and flipped the car right over into the goddamn pines. It was the pines that broke our fall. We all walked away without a scratch. Shit, do you know that was the second Mercedes I rolled that week?"

He laughs. I fall silent. What the fuck kind of story is that to tell about a person's birth?

The apex of my father's career came during his marriage to my mother. For those brief five years, he found himself as the main smuggler of marijuana out of Jamaica, and according to him, Panama and Columbia. We had houses, and cars, and helicopters. And then he was arrested, and all my mom had left was me, a Buick Regal, a handful of Louis Vuittons, and one Rolex watch that my family still won't let me wear.

My mom has insinuated that my father was not sober the day I was born. When I hear that he was out partying until four in the morning the night before—partying to the point where he flipped a 1970s-metal Mercedes off of a highway—then came directly to the hospital, I know he must have been coked up out of his mind to stay awake until my arrival at 2:45 in the afternoon. I almost want to say something to this effect. But I can't. My voice gets trapped again.

That's where Lidia and I begin today. So much has happened since I last saw her. I am starting my new position at work. I just moved into my new office and put in the order for business cards and went to my first conference to meet and greet and start asking those rich people for money. I love my work so much—the children, the people, my boss.

The last time I was with Lidia, she had me create an altar at home. On that altar I am supposed to keep photos of me as a child, a candle, any sacred rocks, flowers, or memorabilia that mean something to me. I did what I was told and have been spending time each day at my altar, trying to communicate with that scared little girl inside who clams up when she most needs to speak and who knows the great truths of this existence, but only shares them when no one is around.

My father escaped from prison when I was five. My father is well known for his escapes. Connecticut, Mexico, Connecticut, Florida, Connecticut, Nevada, Connecticut. On the Florida break, the prison officials had made a mistake by letting him get his teeth fixed at a civilian dentist's office. He was left alone for two minutes. By the end of the first minute he had found a door with the word "Exit" above it and was gone. He was out for a year and a half before they caught him again. During his break, however, he came through Dallas where we were living at that point. He stayed for a few days in various hotels with various lackeys around him, but one night it was just him, and me, and my mom, and the Galleria Mall.

The biggest mall in Dallas, and I think at one point in Texas, the Galleria has a glass sunroof and five levels and a large ice-skating rink where I still dream that one day some man will propose to me. I spent my childhood shopping there with my grandmother, my teen years loitering there with friends, and now as an adult, we still go for last minute holiday gifts and lunch at the Corner Bakery. But for some reason, we went there one night—my mom, my dad, and me. It was the last time I would ever be with my father outside of prison walls and certainly the last time that I would be with both parents together.

I can still see the lush brown carpet, the stores beginning to the close, the Chinese restaurant I thought was really fancy at the time. I remember walking up ahead a bit and turning around to see my parents holding hands. The three of us went to a record store. My dad had bought me a Polaroid that day, and so one of them snatched a picture of me in front of the kids' records. And my look is priceless. I am standing there in my little red sweater with a heart patch sewn on the front. My blonde hair dangles around my face. My eyes are stretched wide in fear or shock or paralysis, or perhaps all three. I am adorable, but as Lidia says when I show her the picture, "Wow. Are you caught up in your head or what?"

Because though this night is supposed to be the best night of my life, though I have been waiting and praying for this night for nearly two years, though I am finally getting everything I want—this night with my mom and dad—I am caught entirely off guard. If a five-year-old is capable of an anxiety attack, it appears I am in the midst of one. It is the same look I have on my face when I begin to like someone, and I fear that they are pulling away. And it is the same feeling I go through while talking with my father that day, driving on the 10, listening to his bullshit stories about the day I was born.

I found out recently that Lidia is a form of shaman called a curandera. She has been trained by the native peoples of Peru and Mexico to bring the special brand of healing that happens in the little room where we now sit. She is curled up in her chair, still in her loose white linens, and smiles, saying "Sweetheart, we can only love as much as we are willing to be hurt. And I can't imagine that after years of loving your dad, and only being hurt in response, that you wouldn't be, that you could be anything but terrified to do that in a genuine, real way with a man."

And so I clam up, and that look comes across my face, the one from the record store twenty-five years ago, when my dashing, romantic father finally came home, and all it did was make me panic. I think I knew then what I am finally seeing now—that my father was never made to be a father.

My mom's youngest brother, my uncle Tom, is one the greatest men I know. He is also, along with my uncle Vic, the great male role model in my life. But being that Tom is a responsible, mortgage-paying, conservative-voting business owner, and Vic is a gay man with a penchant for suicidal depression, Tom assumes the father role a bit more naturally. Has he been perfect? No. Did he play a typical father role? Hardly. But when I was hitting my alcoholic bottom in L.A., and I had no money, and I was falling apart, it was my uncle Tom who asked me to come home to Dallas, to live in his house, and to get clean. And during that year, my uncle took care of me. He loved me. And when he calls me on the phone, he always refers to me as "Puppy" or "Little Moose" or some other endearing nickname that makes me want to call him Dad. And that is what my father has lost in me. Because someone else rose to the challenge and took his place.

Lidia tells me about the great jaguar of the jungle, a spirit named Otorongo. And I can picture him immediately. In my studio at home, I have a large watercolor painting of a cheetah. She is the first thing I see every morning, and so when Lidia tells me that "the Peruvians believe that if asked, Otorongo can hunt for those truths, for those fears, deep in your heart, and catch them like any prey and bring them to your door," I understand because my cheetah greets me each day with that same sense of honesty. And I can feel that amazing beast circling around my legs, ready to lead me deeper into this forest of who I am, who I was, and who I wish to be. Lidia has me lie down on the floor and search for why I can't speak the truths that ring so loudly in my head. Why I get caught in that head and can't get out when I need to the most. It takes a few minutes of her shaking her magic rattles and helping me to get the energy moving, when it hits me, "If I tell the truth, he will leave." And that is the big fear. Whether it's my dad, or some other man I love, I fear telling the truth because the truth is heavy and big and means something, and by saying it I might weed them out of my life. And because I often decide I want someone before I figure out whether I should want them, I prefer to hold back on the truth rather than risk losing them by it. And instead, I lose them because of it.

Date Twenty-Six: My Momma's Still My Biggest Fan

I once asked my former sponsor Louise how I can be in a healthy relationship when I've never seen one up close. She reminded me that I have my mom and her boyfriend Raymond as an example, and she is right. My mom was single my whole life. She never dated. There were never any strange men coming in and out of the house. She had her work to which she was a slave, and she had me. Nana, on the other hand, retired from men at the age of fifty. Of course, by that point, she had been married four times. The last of which was a sham marriage in the late seventies to my uncle Vic's boyfriend. They exchanged vows, rings, and she took his last name, but it was only so he could get a tax break, and she could fly for free on Delta because he was a pilot with the airline. He later died of AIDS in the eighties, but my grandmother still has his surname. I find it incredibly funny that it will be his name that goes on her tombstone—a con even in the afterlife. But my mother is a different story.

When my father was arrested and sent away, my mom didn't go on a drinking binge, she didn't have a nervous breakdown, she didn't throw dramatic tantrums, as I know I would have done. She got a job, she went back to school, and she started working at the company where she still works twenty-five years later. And dating, well, there was no room for that. So I got used to it being just my mom and me, with my grandmother as the third member of the triumvirate. When I was in college, my mom was transferred to her company's New York office just so she could be closer to me while I went to school. We left Nana behind, and the two of us learned to love New York City together. My mom went back for her bachelor's degree at NYU when I was in college myself. And though I might be the more philosophical, my mom was the one to graduate with honors. Because she does things the right way.

And then in 2002, I decided to leave New York. I think sometimes people can't be open to love until it doesn't look like there are any other options left. Until there is space in the heart, and time in the schedule, to make room for another.

With school out of the way, her job not taking up all of her time anymore, and her daughter and only friend preparing to move to the other side of the country, my mother, on my uncle Vic's urging, asked out the guy in her building's gym she had been eyeing for quite some time. And that guy was Raymond. Raymond is my mom's first boyfriend. They make dinner together and go to the movies. They go on vacations and play golf every time the weather's good. They are in love, and they are one another's best friends. And though I could throw out the codependency word, I also realize that sometimes a little codependence is the glue that keeps things together.

"So I was thinking you should come out for Presidents' Day weekend," I tell my mom as I sit in my car at the stables. I stare out my windshield at the jump arena, watching as horses and their riders go over a series of fences.

"Presidents' Day? That sounds like a good idea."

"Really?" I ask, a little surprised by her quick acceptance of the plan. My mom doesn't visit me as much as I would like.

"Sure. I think I can do that."

I start counting down the days for her arrival. Because my mom has seen how much I have changed. She has seen me become more able to pay the bills and show up for my family and be a woman, even though she has not had the chance to see how I live. I pick her up in my clean car at LAX with a dozen roses and decent clothes and trimmed fingernails and clipped-back hair. I pick her up, and we begin a regular weekend in Kristen's life. I show her the work that my nonprofit does. I make her dinner. I take her to one of my meetings.

The next day, we start one of the best dates of my life. We go to the Observatory, and my mom loves the Sparkling Ribbon of Time. And she looks at all the brooches and pendants and points out the ones she likes. And she joins me in being at once awed and humbled by the size of this world. We go outside and stand by the café, looking at the big, beautiful view. I tell my mom how I've recently been thinking again about Jimmy Voltage.

"I just wish he would stop coming to my Tuesday night meeting," I tell her.

"I don't know why you don't talk to him about it," she suggests. "Ask him what happened."

I look down into the drop of the landscape below; the dry harsh ground of Griffith Park surrounds us. Right in the middle of the valley, there sits a small desolate hill, as though rising up against the paved road and wealthy homes and the stark Observatory that hovers over it. It is green and beautiful and I am sure the envy of every developer tearing up the land around it. But that's the thing about L.A.; there are some parts about us that no one can change. And maybe the same goes for Jimmy.

"I wouldn't know what I'd say." I shrug in response to my mom's question. "I don't think we're that comfortable with each other to have that talk. Besides, I already know what he wouldn't be able to say."

"And what's that?"

"That he thought he was dating a woman and ended up getting a scared little girl."

But I'm not sure if it's that simple, that I somehow fucked it up. I know Jimmy has his own issues too. RAD was around long before I was.

My mom squeezes my hand. "Don't worry, K. It'll happen."

We go to the stables, and my mom watches me ride Arrow. Afterward, we hang out with this horse who means so much to me and as he nuzzles into my arm, my mom laughs. "I don't know why you're bothering with all these dates. You two look pretty in love."

And we are. As I show my mom my life, I get a birds-eye view of it myself. Of the hiking trails and the road trips and the healthy meals and horses and sunny days and fresh flowers that fill my world. That night we lie in my bed and talk about what my mom was like before she had me.

"It's funny because I can't even remember really being a person then," she tells me. "I was just so shy and confused."

"Like a ghost person?"

"What's that?"

"Oh, you know, they're the type of personality that never quite touches down to the ground. Like Keanu Reeves or George Bush. They're here in the physical, but you can't really feel that they're truly part of this world."

My mom thinks about it; she is playing with my hand. "Yeah, in a way, I was."

Just as my mother gave me life, so I brought her the gift in turn. Because my mom is a whole, true person today. She is funny and kind and not afraid to share her opinion. Like most parents, she lived in a certain state of denial when I was drinking and using, and I know, though I am healthy now, she wishes desperately that I had never been sick in the first place. And therein lies the great difference between my mom and me. Because I don't regret my dark places. I feel so fortunate to have seen the sad and the sick parts of life and to have emerged from them.

But even more than that, she doesn't want that kind of pain for me. Ever since I was a kid in elementary school, my mom and Nana have done everything they could to protect me from the harsh realities of life. They worked overtime to make sure I was never left alone in stores, never walked home from school by myself, was never put in a position where I could wind up on the side of a milk carton. While other kids went out and participated in a myriad of adventures, they said no to summer camp, to Indian Princesses, to sleepovers, and as I moved into adolescence, to any number of opportunities for me to get wild, get in trouble, get hurt. I have diary upon diary filled with the entries, "They won't let me…" And it ranges from getting sugar-filled cereal, to going to all-ages nightclubs, to being able to wear Daisy Duke shorts, and finally, when I hit fifteen and found myself a boyfriend, to having sex.

And it's probably no surprise to anyone but them that I would grow up to become a woman hell-bent on adventure and sexual freedom.

But I also know that no one could have loved me the way that they did. That overprotecting someone is sometimes the great price of unconditional love. Because how can you care so deeply for another, love them with every ounce of your being, be born by them and give them your life all at once, and not wake up every day, petrified that something bad could happen to them?

The next day we drive up North to an outlet mall, and we go shopping. For years my mom took me shopping. She threw clothes and money and privilege at me to make up for the hours she was at work, for the fact that my father was missing, or because Nana could be mean. But since I got sober, we refrain from such guilt-ridden enabling. But this weekend is different. I am saving money on my own now, and I have just gotten a promotion that demands I get my first business suit. As we drive up, Dixie Chicks begin to sing "Landslide" on the radio, and I turn up the volume.

"I love this song too," my mom says as she turns it up more.

It still fills my car, this memory of driving with my mother through the green hills and misty mountains of California. Me singing, and my mother stealing glances in my direction as we both know that I am growing up, that I have changed, and the one thing that never will is our huge, magnificent love for one another.

149

1 2 3 4 5 6 7 8 9 10 11 12 13 14 15 16 17 18 19 20 21 22
23 24 25 26 **27** 28 29 30 31 32 33 34 35 36 37
38 39 40 41 42 43 44 45 46 47 48 49 50 51

Date Twenty-Seven: Revelations

On Saturday night I go to a party at Mimi's house and begin to question her mental state. She called me Thursday morning at 7:15 a.m., nearly out of breath. Since we've recently started taking morning hikes together, I think she might be on her way to my apartment. But she's not, she's just excited.

"I have the perfect man for you," she squeals.

If it weren't seven in the morning, I might be more enthusiastic.

"No, really, Kristen. He could be, like, the one."

I don't mean to be callous, but Mimi's Jewish matchmaker can get the better part of her. I have seen her do this with other female friends, and it's scary. Even scarier, I have become her latest target.

"Imagine Jimmy Voltage but with advanced degrees and a trust fund," she knows she has me on this one. I haven't heard her speak the words "Jimmy Voltage" in a long while, so it must be time for the big guns.

I'm not necessarily on the hunt for a rich man, so the latter part, though nice, isn't the clincher. But all in all, Mimi's description sounds like exactly what I am looking for. Maybe Mimi got this one right. Maybe this guy Joel will be my second coming.

Mimi and her boyfriend Carty have just moved in together, so there could no better place for me to meet my future partner than in the glow of their own partnership. When Mimi and Carty met, she didn't declare off the bat, "He's the one!" as I have a tendency to do. And though they had slept together by their third date, there was something rather relaxed about the way it started, about the way it has progressed.

I walk into Mimi and Carty's new house and know immediately that Joel is not my future partner. Because Joel is an alcoholic. I shoot Mimi a look, but she is trying to get Joel's attention. Joel is busy dancing by himself in the corner. And though I like people who dance by themselves in the corner, I can tell by the large pint glass of whiskey and coke in Joel's hand that he is not looking for a sober woman with an active spiritual program. He is most likely just looking for another drink.

Mimi has been sober for almost seven years. I consider her one of my elders in that sense, and as I have struggled with the ups and downs that come with living sober, it is Mimi to whom I traditionally go first. So why she thought this clearly active drunk, albeit a hot one, and I would make the couple of the century is beyond me. Five years ago, sure, we probably could have started some tragi-comic romance that involved a lot of fighting and devastating benders. But now?

We start talking because so far it is a small gathering, and we both know why we are here. I crack a Red Bull, and Joel doesn't even seem to notice that I am not joining him in the Whiskey and Cokes. Joel seems to be pretty oblivious to everything as he talks about the limo he is renting for his birthday and the tattoos he has been trying to get lasered off his arm and how L.A. has begun to bore him. He is thinking he will move back to San Francisco.

Though he's drunk, there's an ease between us, and it's no surprise. Because, though I'm sober, I'm still an alcoholic, and we get each other. We're the same type.

"Why would you want to move back to San Francisco?" I joke, playing off the long-standing L.A./S.F. rivalry. "The women are so ugly there."

He laughs. "I know. That's why they'll let you do the naughtiest things to them."

I agree because I understand the misogynist mentality. I can certainly be one myself. Mimi is inside, watching us, and when I come in to get another Red Bull, she takes me into the bedroom under the pretense that she wants to show me their new game for Wii.

I see through her ruse because Mimi hates video games. Me, on the other hand, well, I can definitely state that Nintendo was my first addiction. I am already swinging aimlessly with the Wii controller when she asks, "So what do you think?"

I throw a right jab in an attempt to knock out my enemy on the screen. "About what?"

"About Joel, asshole."

I grunt as I dodge my opponent. "I think he'd be an incredible hook up."

"Come on, don't waste one on him. I think this could be more than that."

I barely hear her because I am in video-game land, and to be honest it feels more realistic than what Mimi is proposing. But she presses on: "You guys should get to know each other. I really feel this could be exactly what you both have been searching for."

I am getting a little out of breath—Wii is hard. "Mi?"

"Yeah."

"I don't know if you noticed this...Bullshit motherfucker!" I have a bit of Tourettes while playing video games. "But your friend is an alcoholic."

"Yeah, I know, but I thought you could help him."

I'm really into the game now. "You want me to convert him?"

Mimi is watching the screen, which is a good thing because I might have had to take aim at her too. "No, I thought you could be his angel."

"Bitch! Bitch! Bitch!" I yell at the TV.

And this is how I've grown. I have absolutely no desire to save Joel's lost soul. No human power can. I know because even the ones who tried to save mine failed. And I loved them. Dearly. No, soul saving is for higher powers only.

Thankfully, Joel is not trying to get sober that night. I come out to find Joel sitting on the couch, taking pictures of himself with his iPhone. He doesn't seem all that interested in talking to anyone at the party. He just keeps hitting the "capture" button while he stares into his cup. And I get that too. I used to look into my cup all the time.

Fearing that it would end soon, wishing it would end soon, hoping somehow that there was an answer down there, and I just needed to get to the bottom of it.

Joel sees me and lights up. He doesn't seem to care that I am not drinking; I think he just likes that I am willing to have fun at this relatively boring, grown-up affair. He asks me to pose for his pictures, and we end up doing our own photo shoot. Not sexual ones. Goofy photos. One where I am curled up on the floor like a cat. Another, we're both throwing gang signs. One where we are head banging. Regular all-American fun. One o'clock hits, and I am about to leave. I plan to leave. And then everybody else starts leaving, and I realize that Joel is spending the night there. I sit down on the couch, and he comes and sits down next to me. We are getting tired, and he lies down against me. And then I feel it. The stir that had gone missing these last few months. The pulse I had once known with both frequency and intimacy—my raging fourteen-year old hormones. My libido's back, and I'm gonna get in trouble. Mimi and her boyfriend, Carty, sit on the opposite couch, and it's as though Mimi knows this when she suggests, "Kristen, why don't you stay the night?"

Yes, why don't I? Surely, I shouldn't be driving home the four short blocks between our houses. I am sober, and it is before 2:00 a.m. "Okay," I agree as Joel begins to quietly rub my leg. Mimi and Carty go to bed. Joel and I make room for the both of us on their couch. I am having trouble sorting out all the pillows, and I don't like being in control in these situations and am playing the dumb blonde to get out of it.

Joel laughs. "And you're the sober one."

"But I'm still the girl," I whine. Even pouting my lips for good measure.

And that's all I need to say. Because instantly Joel goes into action. He sobers up. He sorts out the pillows, takes off his shirt, positions me on the inside of the couch, curls in behind me, pulls me in close, and it is on.

It has been years since I had sex like that. Hair-pulling, hickey-leaving, love-making sex. The type you see in the movies when it looks like the actors are about to devour each other and names get uttered over and over. And then it feels like the back of your brain just got blasted out, and your bodies go slack, and your mind goes dull, and it isn't love. And it doesn't matter. Because I never do this. And I get to enjoy it with the same amount of satisfaction as if it were the real thing.

Joel knows this is just play acting. We're both pros. We know how to pretend we're in love for one night. And it's fun to do it with such intensity: We don't ask too many questions; we don't pretend this is the beginning of anything; we just kiss and snuggle and find something quite nice for a night. Something that both of us have been missing in our very different lives. Me with my rigorous sobriety and my clean and healthy choices. And Joel? Joel is still living the life I used to live. And it shows. It shows in the dark circles around his eyes. In the clench of his jaw. In the graying hair around his temples.

I fall asleep praying for him. I pray that his higher power saves him as mine did me. I pray that he gets the chance to live a responsible and healthy life. I pray that he grows up.

Date Twenty-Eight: California Country

I've been listening to a lot of country lately. And not even good country—cheap, modern, pop country. Shit like Taylor Swift and Shania Twain and Billy Ray Cyrus. When I was a kid growing up in Dallas, country made me nauseous. It was everywhere, like football, and created an immediate, visceral reaction. The first twang of Travis Tritt or the roar of the stadium crowd created an anxious churn in me, which I can only guess is what one feels during a heart attack.

To this day the mere sight of a football green will make me light-headed, but my opinion on country has changed. Now it seems to be the only type of music that truly relaxes me. Which as I am singing "Red Neck Girls" on my way home tonight, makes me wonder whether I am becoming more Texan. Because I never felt at home in Dallas. I still don't. I read too much, thought too much, and definitely talked too much to ever be accepted there. And though I have friends and family in that town who love me, and whom I love, I know that I do not belong there, anymore than I belong on a football field. But Texas… well, Texas is all about horses and guns and independent women. And those things I am.

Which is why when Frank invites me to go shooting for our first date, I can't help but be excited. Frank is a lighting consultant on blockbuster films. He is from a suburb outside of Chicago. He reads authors like Thomas Pynchon and Jonathan Kozol. He is extremely funny on the phone, and from what I can tell by his pictures, really cute. And I am actually pretty excited about this date. I even shave my legs because I want to feel pretty. And I worry about what I am going to wear and end up putting on a sexy top, paired with my trusty decade-old cowboy boots.

On Thursday, I went for my first trail ride in Griffith Park. As much as I have loved learning how to walk, trot, and canter in the dust-streaked arenas of the equestrian center, the hills that surround it had begun to beckon me. My friend Jen introduced me to a British horsewoman named Jane, who teaches neophytes like me how to race a horse up a mountain without falling off. With the same thick, woolly hair that all of us horsewomen seem to have and the perfect London accent, Jane quickly became my hero. I borrowed one of her horses, and we went through a tunnel that runs under the 134 Freeway, and she took me up and deep into the Griffith Park hills.

Growing up, all of my report cards were littered with the same comments, "Refuses to listen," "Won't follow directions," "Doesn't pay attention." I hated them like I hated country music, but they weren't altogether wrong. Later, I would take that inability to listen and bring it into workplaces, relationships, and my conscience. But as I rode with Jane, I paid close attention to her British accent and her wise words about how to stay on a horse while riding on the side of a cliff.

She explained to me how to give and take with the reins so that my horse didn't rear on the narrow paths. She taught me how to lean forward while the horse cantered up the mountain so I didn't bounce off. And as we hit the top of the old landfill that stands above Mount Hollywood she showed me a view like I have never seen. To my right were the Griffith Park Observatory and the smoggy haze of Hollywood. To my left were the high and folding peaks of the mountains of San Gabriel Valley. And in between was us, caught between these incredible worlds of city, country, and ever-winding freeway. It was sunset on a Thursday night. Most people get off work and then go home and watch TV. And normally that's what I would do too. But that night, I sat on a horse, and I caught my breath because that is the kind of country I pay attention to.

The following Saturday night, I walk into the Japanese restaurant where Frank, my Pynchon-reading, lighting-consultant date, and I are rendezvousing.

"Frank?" I hesitantly ask the lone man waiting by the hostess stand.

Frank greets me in turn, and I fear he can see the look of disappointment cross my face. Frank looks nothing like his pictures. I am not sure whether it's because I don't have the fancy, $25-a-month version of *The Onion* personals, and so all the pics are thumbnails, or if it's because Frank has posted photos of himself that are as old as my boots. Because Frank is old.

He's got longish, graying blond hair. His eyes are too light and his body not right, and as we sit down to dinner I look at his soft, pale, ill-defined hands, and I know this isn't going to work.

"Yeah, this whole online dating thing kind of throws me," Frank tells me as we sit down at the Sushi bar.

Whenever you go out on an online date with someone, they always have to mention how weird online dating is. I don't get it. We live online, we shop online, we chat online, we look at porn online. Why would meeting someone on the Internet be such a source of anxiety?

I shrug. "I guess."

"Or maybe it's just dating in general."

That I get. "Yeah. I've been doing a lot of it recently, but I didn't go on my first date until I was like twenty-five or twenty-six. It's still pretty new to me," I tell him.

"Me too. Although mine is because I've been with someone for a long time."

"How long?" I ask.

"Thirteen years."

"Wow." I can't help but say it, "That sucks."

I feel for him. At least I have been on the dating scene for some time, even if most of my dates, hell, roughly all of them, have taken place in the last six months. After we eat, we go to the gun range as Frank had promised. I blast away at an easy target with my 9 mm, but when I attempt a real one, with a bull's-eye and not just photos of fake terrorists, I realize that I am a terrible shot. Frank comes over and shows me how. He explains it in depth and gives me my first real lesson in target practice.

"You should get a .22 next time. You can't focus your aim with something like a 9 mm. Even my dad, who competed, practiced with a smaller gun."

Frank and I finish shooting, and though it doesn't feel as though the date should end on such an adrenaline-rushed high, I have to get to Hollywood for a birthday party. Nat's fiancé Reggie is celebrating his two-year sober anniversary at midnight, and I need to be there. I want to be there. So we take our paper targets, and Frank drives me to my car. We hug, and though I am not sure, I think Frank might realize I am more into shooting than I am into him.

I drive to Canter's, where my friends and I are meeting. I walk in and go toward the back of the room where I see a large table with warm faces. I give Reggie my target with the terrorists on it, with a Happy Birthday note, and I hug my lovely friends. I sit down and laugh and listen to the lives of those I love. Because I do listen now. I listen all the time.

Date Twenty-Nine: Cinderella
Does Not Smoke Marlboros

"I just quit smoking." These words do not surprise my date Tim as much as they do me. I decided two weeks ago to not have one, and I haven't since. And it's spooky. I have been smoking Marlboro Mediums since I was eighteen and have a love for them that surpasses most of my human relationships. So why and how I am on the verge of making it to twenty-one days without my oldest friends is beyond me. And the sad thing is I really don't miss them.

"That's good," Tim replies.

We are sitting at a bar on Franklin. Franklin Avenue is the quainter option if one is driving from Hollywood to Silver Lake. I used to take it all the time because it is also the street on which Oliver lives. We used to drink at this bar. But now I sit watching my date drink, and I wonder whether he is legal to have one. Whereas Frank from the shooting range looked a good ten years older than his posted age, Tim looks ten years younger than his listed "28."

"I've been smoking since I was twelve," I tell him.

Now, Tim is surprised. "How do you start smoking at twelve?"

"I was stressed out," I shrug. When I was eight years old, my mom, Nana, and I moved into the condominium complex that became the setting for my childhood. Situated between a nice neighborhood and a railroad track, it was the perfect analogy for the awkward class position in which we found ourselves. And also the awkward age I found myself at when I turned twelve. Gone were the days when I was the cute little blonde in the class picture. As my boobs failed to develop, and my permanent teeth twisted into an awkward snarl, and the confidence I once had turned into a fear of boys and girls and Nana, the one place I felt safe was that condominium complex situated between a nice neighborhood and a railroad track.

Nana couldn't keep me inside after school, and I learned that I lived in a fairy-tale place of adventure. Whereas I spent much of my childhood playing teacher by myself in our one-car garage, I was now given unlimited license to roam. I would do a serviceable amount of homework before slumping down on the couch next to Nana. This was the beginning of CNN in our household, and my grandmother was glued to Wolf Blitzer and the First Gulf War.

"Nana?"

"Huh," she would grunt, watching the SCUD missiles fly high above Israel.

"Can I go for a walk?"

She would look at me suspiciously as she had begun to always look at me at that age. As though she too was confused as to what had happened to the adorable little Barbie I had been just two years before. She sniffed the air. "Your breath smells. Go brush your teeth."

"Okay, but then can I go for a walk?"

"Fine. Just be home in an hour. I'm putting the chicken on."

An hour would barely give me enough time to smoke my rationed-out two cigarettes and make sure I didn't smell, but I would take it and rush out the door.

"You didn't brush your teeth," she would call out after me. But I would, just after I got home. After I walked up to the Food Lion and stole my pack of Turkish Camel Unfettereds. After I put on my Walkman and turned on the *Pump Up the Volume* soundtrack. After I pretended I was someone else.

Some days I would walk along the tracks, and I would be tough and cool and dangerous. I would listen to The Velvet Underground and pretend I was a junkie dropout like the real tough and cool and dangerous girls in my middle school. Other days, I would play in the gazebo that sat at the entrance of our condominium complex, and I would marry a prince, or accept an Oscar, or act out any number of strange scenes that I am sure made the commuting crowd driving by look twice. Once it started to get dark, I would amble back intentionally late to our condo and prepare myself for Nana's, "Where have you been?"

"Walking," I would mumble, lying down on the couch.

"You're late. Finish your homework," she would yell at me as she breaded the chicken tenders.

"I don't have any homework."

"Yes you do."

"No I don't. And what do you know anyway?"

She would come in from the kitchen, towel in hand. "I know you have homework to do and that you are thirty minutes late, now move it."

She would swat at my feet hanging off the couch, and I would scream as though she had just taken a belt to me, "You hit me!"

"No, I didn't. Besides, I'm the boss here," she would say as she walked into the kitchen.

"No, you're not. Mom is. And you're not my mom!" This had become my rallying cry during these years, before it got so bad that Nana had to move out.

But my mom would be safe at work. And she would come home hours later, after we had eaten our chicken tenders in silence, and I had gone to bed. And I would lie there waiting for her car to pull into the garage, and I would imagine what my life would be like if I had just jumped on one of the trains that regularly ran past our condo. Because I figured if I couldn't get rich and become a princess, I should probably just hop a boxcar and become a hobo. Either way, I knew I needed a cigarette. And I was eternally grateful during those years that the Food Lion made it so easy to steal the small delightful packs of Turkish Camels.

Tim is looking at me like I am telling him about how I had to walk forty miles in the snow to get to school, and I know I have probably just told him too much. But I also know that I can say anything here because I am not interested in Tim. Whether eighteen or twenty-eight, I am not into younger men. First of all, I like my guys a little more road-weary than that. I like some chest hair, and wrinkles around the eyes, and the certain roughness of skin that age creates. Tim is incredibly smooth, so much so I wonder whether he can even grow a beard. People are always shocked when I tell them I'm thirty. Apparently, I look fourteen, but next to Tim I just look old. And I feel even older, referencing Wolf Blitzer and the Pixies and Christian Slater in *Pump Up the Volume*.

I learn that both of Tim's parents are deaf, and I ask him if he signs.

"No, I never learned," he says, shrugging.

"Really? They never tried to teach you?"

"Oh no," he tells me. "They tried for years, but I wasn't really interested."

I am floored. As much as Tim might think it's strange that I once stole cigarettes from the local grocery store, or that I would perform small plays by myself in a gazebo overlooking rush-hour traffic in Plano, Texas, or that I feel the need to divulge stories of my adolescence on a first date, I find it all the more weird that he can't sign with his parents.

Because as much as my grandmother and I screamed a lot during 1990, we still spoke each other's language. And though I might have started smoking at a precociously young age, I cannot imagine refusing the adventures it brought me on, real or imagined.

Earlier in the day I had been at one of my organization's preschools. I was coordinating a donation of toys when one of the little girls came up and asked me in her quiet, three-year-old voice, "Are you a Princess?" I said that I'm not, but that I would like to be. Before I knew it, I had a small gathering of three-year-olds around me. They explained that they were Jasmine, Snow White, and Belle, respectively. The little one who first came up to me took hold of my hand and told me, "You can be Cinderella."

Years after walking along the tracks, I actually got on the train. I smoked my Marlboro Mediums, I did my cocaine, and I flipped the ultimate bird at my mom and grandmother for trying to raise me to be a princess. But then I found out where the boxcar takes you, and it wasn't as exciting as it had seemed. It was a lonely, dead-end place. As I stand in the circle of chanting three-year-olds I know I don't have to be the sulking, smoking girl anymore with bad breath and a thieving habit to still live the adventure.

Tim has two drinks. He sips them very, very slowly. I think in the time it takes him to drink two beers, I have had somewhere around seventeen seltzers. I always used to say that I wasn't an alcoholic so much as I just drank fast. I wonder whether I wish those club sodas were Beam and Cokes, but I would have had almost as many and probably would have slept with Tim. I look at Tim as he talks and think about what it would be like to have sex with him. My stomach turns.

I leave the bar and walk to my car, and though I want a cigarette, as is tradition at the end of all of my dates, I don't. Because I'm Cinderella, and no matter how poorly she's treated at home, no matter that she misses her real mother, no matter that she is caught between the better neighborhood and the railroad tracks, Cinderella doesn't smoke Marlboro Mediums. And for today, neither do I.

Date Thirty: The Perfect Date

It's been a long time since I've had a straight, male friend. In college, I had roughly forty of them. I was in a fraternity filled with funny, smart guys with whom I drank, got stoned, and for a good handful, screwed throughout the four years I was a part of higher learning. I recently found my old camcorder that has more hours of college footage on it than I would ever want to watch. But I threw in a tape anyway.

The image is grainy, and it takes me a moment to identify the friends in the shot. And then it focuses a bit. My friend Flannery is lying on the kitchen floor of our frat house amidst beer cans and other litter.

I can hear my voice: "Come on, Flannery, when do you not have anything to say?"

Flannery explains to the viewer: "This is typically the part of Morning Tails where I lie on the kitchen floor of whatever fine establishment we have crashed and give my yearly summation."

He takes a sip of his drink as he says, "But this is our last Morning Tails."

Morning Tails is the final party of the semester. It starts at 6:00 a.m. in the morning on the last day of classes. It is and will always be remembered by me as one of the best times of my life. Flannery is a gregarious Classics student who later goes on to become a lawyer in the D.C. area. He is never lacking words, in English, Latin, or Greek. Until that moment.

And then in the video, a figure emerges from the dark, and it is my closest male friend, my heart of hearts: Reeves. He is so young, and sweet, and not yet damaged from his own alcoholism. He is wearing Flannery's straw hat and takes it off. Reeves is the quiet one of the bunch, and so it goes to him to give the annual summation. With the hat over his heart, Reeves says, "I guess we say goodbye today. Though we'll never really say goodbye. We are in our house this morning."

Flannery and I both howl. Reeves just smiles. "And I couldn't think of two better people to be here with. I love you guys."

He places the hat on Flannery's head and lifts his Beam and Coke. "Here's to an awesome four fucking years."

The tape goes dead because even in my college bravado there are some moments too special to catch on film. I cry when I watch this. Because it is all so innocent and fun and loving.

They are my boys, and I am their girl. And we still talk but no longer in the same cities and not with the same intimate passion that we did when we were stoned and hopeful at Hamilton College. Since that time, I have discovered that is hard to make straight, male friends after college. Because everyone's looking to mate. They're not looking for new buddies. And either you become more than friends, or you simply don't have time to keep up any sort of active friendship. This is why outside of Ivan, and a couple of sober men, the only other male friend I have in this town is a guy named Adam. Adam and I met three years ago right before I moved from L.A. He was working as an independent producer, and their offices were housed in the same building as my own. I was dating Sabbath at the time, but Adam and I hit it off from the get-go. He was from Houston, and we became natural friends.

We stayed in touch when I moved to Dallas, and about three months in I got a call. Adam was in town and needed somewhere to crash for the night. He came over to my uncle's house where I was living, and I couldn't help but wonder if something might happen between us. I was newly sober and spent the better part of the evening getting Adam drunk on White Russians.

Adam and I sat outside talking for hours—him getting loose-tongued and misty and me realizing that I could not sleep with this man. Perhaps because I only had three months of sobriety, and my nerves were too raw. Perhaps because I was watching someone get smashed, and it's not that attractive. Perhaps because I found out that Adam is three years younger than I am, and I don't do younger men. In the end, I put Adam up in my room and left his disappointed face to sleep in another bedroom.

A few months later, Adam came back to Dallas, but I was working and was unable to meet up with him. In return, he left me a voice mail telling me he was in love with me. I could tell he was drunk in the message, and so I never brought it up and neither did he. Instead, we stayed friends.

Adam's follow through on our friendship is remarkable. Most guys would have forgotten I existed by now. But not Adam. I know I've got some good qualities, but I can't help but be surprised that he still wants to hang out with me. We hadn't seen each other in months when Adam e-mails me recently asking when we are going to catch up. I suggest we go shooting because he too is a fan of the gun club. He calls me up, enthusiastic, and offers that we go to Little Tokyo for dinner. I tell him I am dying for some good sushi, and he says he knows a great place.

"You ever go to Sushi Gen?" he asks me.

"I love you, Adam! Sushi Gen is my favorite."

And I wonder whether maybe now I really could love Adam. We do complement each other nicely. Adam picks me up, and we drive to the restaurant, and I wonder if this is a date. Because Adam is cute, and he dresses well, and he's funny and articulate and spontaneous—everything I say I am looking for in a man—and maybe I have grown up enough to get over the fact that he is younger. Maybe I have a little cougar in me after all.

"So, how's the house?" I ask. Adam lives in a big house in Nichols Canyon with a revolving door of occupants. It's sort of like the *Real World* but without cameras.

"Good," he tells me. "We just got a new roommate."

"When don't you get a new roommate?" I laugh.

"Yeah, that's true. Except, well, she's a girl. One I've been dating for a while now, so it's a little different."

And I realize—this is not a date.

My dad calls me the other day. His transfer to Houston was recently complete, and so he is living there in various motel rooms as a consultant for the FBI.

"I'm not a rat, K," he tells me again. "But they said that they can clear my record, give the old man his name back. I haven't been Dan McGuiness in years."

And I can't help but wonder if the old dog might just be willing to learn some new tricks. Adam already knows this story of my dad, so when I tell him the latest update, he has the same reaction as most straight males.

"Who is he going to be informing on?" he asks.

I tell him that I don't know. I try not to ask too many questions. I prefer not to know.

Adam and I go to the gun range and afterwards, Adam asks, "You wanna get gelato?"

And off we go to Pazzo. I explain the gelato criteria, and after Adam orders, he asks if he passed. And he has. He asks me how our own non-date is going.

"Pretty good," I tell him while spooning the world's greatest gelato into my mouth.

"Come on, it's probably one of the best."

Adam is flirting with me but only innocently. Because I can tell he is madly in love with his girlfriend, and I know that he is not the type to cheat. Adam and I have a perfect itinerary tonight with all the things I love. And he loves them too. And I ultimately confess that this is one of my best dates yet, and I mean it. But as much as I wish I could feel I missed the boat, or that someday Adam will be mine, I know that's not true. Instead, I am genuinely happy for him. I am happy for my friend.

169

1 2 3 4 5 6 7 8 9 10 11 12 13 14 15 16 17 18 19 20 21 22
23 24 25 26 27 28 29 30 **31** 32 33 34 35 36 37
38 39 40 41 42 43 44 45 46 47 48 49 50 51

Date Thirty-One: The Council
of Butterfly Ancestors

The minute I walk into Lidia's house, I feel better. It is one of the few things I can count on these days. My mom senses the depression in my voice, and without asking about it or intimating as much, she says, "It's a good thing you're seeing Lidia this week." And it is a good thing I'm seeing Lidia this week. I have a lot to tell her.

Last night, I was talking with my best friend from college, Liz, which normally doesn't trigger a depression, but then she said, "I talked to Jake the other night."

I was sitting in Echo Park. My Tuesday night meeting was about to begin. I normally could not care less that she talked to Jake One the other night. Jake as in my evil ex-boyfriend. Jake as in the guy who tried to strangle me to death. Jake as in the convict who just got out of San Quentin. Even on his MySpace page, it says for occupation, "Parolee," and I wonder whether Jake is more institutionalized after two years in prison than my father is in over twenty. But either way, what I do care about is what Liz said next: "Yeah, he's living with Maria in Echo Park."

I gulped. "Liz, I am in Echo Park right now. I am in Echo Park all the time. It's right next to Silver Lake."

I couldn't help but look around. I was half expecting a rap at the window and for Jake One to be standing there. But more than that, I am really pissed that he has a girlfriend. And I am pissed that they are living together in Echo Park because that's the neighborhood in which I fantasize about living with my future partner. And right now, I feel like I couldn't be farther away from seeing that fantasy come true. Though I love my new job and my hikes with Mimi in the morning and my recent visit from my mother, I am getting that feeling again that I want something more. I want things to change.

As I sit across from Lidia I tell her about my recent run-ins with Jimmy Voltage. "I feel so stupid, Lidia. It's like what happened with Oliver. I know that Jimmy doesn't want anything with me. I can see that, but yet I still can't stop thinking about him." I laugh. "My God, it's been four years, and I'm still thinking about Oliver."

"Let me ask you something." Lidia smiles at me, and I get a bit of relief that I might not be as stupid as I feel. "What attracted you to both of them? When you think about still wanting them, what is it you want?"

I think about it, and I know. I know so well. "Magic. I think everyone I dated has had that. Oliver, Jimmy, Sabbath, even Jake One. They were just magical to me."

"Sabbath?" Lidia asks. And I realize that I have never mentioned him here before. I explain how he was the last man to play the role of boyfriend. That he just wanted to be there for me, but that I couldn't see him for what he was worth.

"And where is he now?" Lidia asks.

"New York. I tried to call him a couple of years ago; tried to get together for coffee, but he never called me back." I shrug. "That's the thing, Lidia. I look at Jake being able to have a girlfriend, and I wonder what is wrong with me that I have to keep going for these guys who want nothing to do with me, guys like Jimmy, and I just can't like the ones that like me back."

Lidia stops me. "Did you not like Sabbath?"

I think about it. "No, I liked him, but I was so fucked up. I was so hurt from Oliver. I knew I couldn't be there for him, and then I got embarrassed, and I got angry, and I just feel like, whenever somebody does want to love me, I decide they're not good enough. And so I end up with guys like Jimmy. And I lose the ones who want to stay."

I start to cry. "It's not fair. Why can't I make this singlehood business end?"

In that moment, I don't care about this stupid book. Or about meeting the right one. Or about my inner growth. The tears are coming down, and Lidia hands me a tissue.

I want to be in love like Mimi. I want to get married like Nat. I want to be attracted to someone who won't disappear. But more than anything, I want to come home from work on a Monday night, put the laundry in, make dinner, and curl up in bed with someone who loves me. And instead, I find myself, night after night, sitting on my bed, watching TV by myself. If you surveyed people who killed themselves, probably 98% of them were doing just that the hour before they died. Because it's depressing. Really depressing.

I tell Lidia all of this, and she smiles sweetly at me. "Kristen, there are caterpillars and butterflies in this world, and you are a butterfly. You're smart, you're self-aware, you're evolving and changing, and you're interested in that growth. And that's no judgment call against the caterpillar. The caterpillar is beautiful too. But they're a lot more caterpillars than butterflies. The butterflies are rare, the male butterflies even more so. And it will take a special man for you to fall in love."

"I'm not even attracted to the caterpillars," I sniff.

Lidia smiles at me. "And they are not attracted to you."

I get it. Though there is nothing wrong with being a caterpillar, I'm not in the space yet where I want that, where I am ready to stay close to the ground, foraging for food, and hoping that I won't get squashed. I still want to fly. I want to be taken away into some dream world with Jimmy and Oliver and not into the reality that someone like Sabbath demands.

As I walked into Lidia's house I saw a "For Sale" sign in her yard. I comment on the fact that I am going to miss her house, and she says so will she. She tells me that she and her husband are splitting up. And I am thrown. I have always wondered how such a strong, magical, sarcastic creature could have achieved the American Dream. The husband, the child. She seemed like so many women I know in her age group: divorced, maternal, and wiser for both. The fact that she was married almost didn't fit. The fact that I can see the pain of the split on her face when she mentions it makes me realize that even the most magical of the butterflies still have to face the pain of living.

Lidia and I get down on the floor for the energy work. She has me choose a stone, and once again, says it's perfect. I lie down, and she places it right on my pubic area. I trust her enough to do that, and she is so respectful of space, it doesn't feel weird or awkward. Before I begin wondering why the stone is perfect, she tells me that its purpose is to help us focus on the first chakra, which is the baby-making, lovemaking section of the body. It is the place where we as women find our center.

Before we begin, she asks me to picture my ancestors. "Kristen, they are your ultimate spirit guides. I want you to think about the ones that came before you. The women that brought you here. The woman that you are to become."

And I see them. I see me. This long line of women who thought too much, and felt too much, and just wanted to soar because they couldn't stay on the ground long enough to be hurt. And then I see me. I see me as the woman who finally finds a way to do both. Who lives the adventurous life but is still able to create relationships which stay.

"Okay, let's picture that woman. Picture the grown, strong woman you can be. Bring her into focus," Lidia tells me. And I can see her. She is taller than me, and she is a healer, and she helps others and is strong and of faith. I am supposed to picture her in an environment, and I see her in a desert. She climbs on top of a boulder. The boulder has soft edges and is large but surmountable. She watches as a storm clears, and then we begin channeling spirit. Trying to use the magic I easily contain in my palms, we start moving the trapped energy between my first chakra and my mind. Moving it up through my gut, my heart, up my spine, and out of the top of my head. It's funny, but I have become sensitive enough to know when the energy is pulsing and when it's not, and it's not at first. I kind of have to pee, but I don't want to interrupt, and I think it's more than that. I think it is where the real problem lies. Learning to unite my heart, and my mind, and my spirit, and my loins, in an honest, mature and loving way.

Lidia tells me to continue the work every night at home. She asks me if I pray, and I tell her yes. "Then try praying to your ancestors this month. Ask them to guide you wherever you are supposed to go and ask them for the strength to get you there." If ever anyone has suggested a god in which I can believe, it is this. When I was twenty years old, I studied abroad in South Africa, and maybe that's the soil, the dark rich ground in which I can believe. Because I learned about this notion of ancestors from my friends there, and though I might not believe in the traditional Creator spirit so many people call God, I can believe that the spirits which shared my blood might get a say in my destiny. We Italians trust family above all else. So whereas a god who tells me what to do and what not to do is kind of terrifying, those crazy Italian, Hungarian, and Irish brethren who left this world before me feel like much better advocates for my life.

I get up, and suddenly the energy is pulsing within me. I feel better. But I also feel scared. Because though I know faith is as much about accepting one's circumstances as it is about changing them, though I believe that I am being guided to where I am supposed to go, I can't help but hope it's where I want to be.

Date Thirty-Two: Nana

It has been my lifelong campaign to convince Nana that we are Jewish. I have been pushing this for years, but she still won't give in and confess. The Nazis themselves wouldn't have been able to break her. Nana arrived yesterday for one of the two-week trips that have become a tradition since I moved back to L.A. and got sober. The day after she comes to town, we lie on my bed talking and as she tells me about her childhood I become all the more convinced of our Hebrew heritage.

"We're not Jewish," she says, trying to ignore me.

"And your father's depression started right around the time that people would have been finding out about the Holocaust," I continue.

She sighs. "It was the Depression, Kris. Everyone was depressed."

"But your chutzpah…," I begin.

"I'm Hungarian, okay? All Hungarians have chutzpah."

Nana's obsession with blond-haired, blue-eyed children borders on Aryanism, so it's no surprise that she bristles at my claims that she is a Jew. But I have always wanted to be Jewish. Growing up, there was only one Jewish girl in my elementary school, and with her menorah and her mezuzah, she was the most exotic person I had ever met. And I wanted to be just like her. I wanted to be Jewish. Once I started finding out more about Nana's upbringing, I began to sense that we might still have a chance.

Which is why Nana's refusal to admit the truth of which I am so convinced, only makes me surer she is. She is clearly a self-hating Jew. This is why her whole life she wanted a golden, Gerber baby—the ultimate evidence of her goyishness. But after three kids that look more

Sicilian than Scandinavian, she only had one final shot at a golden child. And that child was me. And though I was technically my mother's, with my blond hair, green eyes, and fair skin, I quickly became Nana's too.

When I was in elementary school, Nana dressed me every day and curled my hair and told me regularly how beautiful I was. I never went to school without looking like I was in a fashion show, and maybe that's because I was in fashion shows. Nana signed me up to model at Bloomingdale's and Neiman's. I would strut the little catwalk set up at Prestonwood or Valley View mall, and we would get some free clothes to take home to add to my already fashion-savvy wardrobe. No matter how little money we had, or that I shared a bedroom with my mom, or that we couldn't afford many things that my wealthier friends could, Nana was determined to make sure that we dressed well.

But then I started growing up. I started choosing what shoes I wanted to wear and how I wished to style my hair, and the fight began that rages to this day. The wrong shirt was enough for Nana to hurtle insults at me that lasted well into the week. And so I was caught between desperately trying to please her and, at the same time, trying to assert my own style. Whether that meant wearing fake Doc Martens, or socks over my tights, or the year I started sporting a bow tie, Nana would have none of it. And it only takes a week into her trip for a new battle to erupt. Like the debate over our Judaism, but far, far worse.

We are getting ready to go to Nordstrom's because Nana only likes to go to three places: Nordstrom's, Neiman's Last Call, and Walmart. Since the only Walmart in L.A. is in the hood, and the Last Call is about an hour and a half away, this will be our third trip to Nordstrom's this week.

I put on a dress that Nana had bought me so I know that I will be safe with my choice, but then I decide I want to add a bright, summer scarf. I know it's hot out; I know that most people don't wear scarves on eighty-degree days, but I am part of a culture that does. We wear our scarves all the time. Nana does not agree.

"I'm not going with you if you wear that," she tells me.

"What?"

"That stupid scarf. I'm not going out with you in it." She sits down.

"Too bad for you then," I tell her. "Because I'm wearing it, so you'll be sitting here alone."

I go about getting ready as she watches me, smoldering. "You look ridiculous, Kristen." She never calls me Kristen, always K or Kris, or more often, Krii-iis, but I know she's mad. There is nothing like an ill-placed accessory to piss my grandmother off. I know it's dumb; I could remove it, but this is what family is for. We are there to argue about the principle of things. About what is right and what is important and how we all should have the freedom to live how we wish. Even if that means wearing a scarf when it's hot outside. She finally relents, getting back up to finish putting on her makeup.

She gets in her final comment as we walk out the door. "You look stupid, just stupid."

Later that night we go to a big meeting for sober people held in my neighborhood. Nana was originally against my admission of alcoholism because if wearing a bow tie was bad, being a coked-out drunk was far, far worse. But then she came to a meeting with me, and she began to see how much hope was in it. And then she saw me change. And now she frequently tells me how proud she is of me for being sober. As we sit there waiting for the meeting to begin, my scarf conspicuously absent from around my neck, she takes hold of my hand and says, "You're the prettiest girl here."

I smile at her and squeeze her hand, and then I see him. Ben. Toxic, sober alcoholic Ben. We haven't seen each other since that night at the bowling alley, but then the speaker gets up, and all I can do is motion for Nana to check him out.

I go up to him after the meeting as Nana watches from a short distance.

"Hey, do you remember me?" I ask.

He smiles. "Of course, the 51-dates girl. Kristen, right?"

"Yeah." I smile. "Ben, right?"

As though I am not sure of his name. As though I didn't know it before the night of the bowling alley. As though I haven't recorded and even repeated it here. And as though there haven't been a few lonely nights in bed when I may have uttered it in my fantasies.

"So, you still down to be my last date?" I attempt to flirt.

"Of course."

"Okay, get ready then." I toss my head and giggle. And somehow I think I say this twice because he looks at me like I am a little crazy and says, "I'll be sure to wax."

I'm not sure what I think of that. I don't know how I feel about the guy who always has to make the lewd comment. I used to be really perverted in my humor, but I also feel like I am kind of over using sex as an easy joke. But I decide not to hold it against Ben. As my 51st date, he might just be my last chance for recorded love. And though I am still not sure whether I am the prettiest girl in the room or stupid, just stupid, I think there's something about Ben that would get all that too. He is Jewish after all. Surely his mother is not so different from the woman lurking behind me while I talk.

I take Nana to the Observatory on her last day in town. As we walk up to the building I take pictures of her with my phone. And she looks so young and sweet and pretty that I forget all about the unkind words that have been uttered between us. Because there will be no greater pain for me on this earth than when my grandmother dies. As much as my relationship with my mom is perfect, and as much as my father is significant, it is Nana who completes me. As we walk around the Observatory holding hands, we are mesmerized by the same words, the same images, the same pretty, pretty things. She stops with me to read about the Sparkling Ribbon of Time and look at the large pieces of meteor that might one day send us into our brilliant, obliterated end. And I know as she slowly shakes her head at this one overwhelming image of our universe that she too recognizes what an impossibly small role we play.

On this trip Nana told me that more than any man, more than any of her children, that I alone am her soul mate. And I know I am. I understand her when no one else can, and likewise, every time I have found myself lost, not knowing where to turn, it is Nana who has guided me. And though there are certainly differences in who we are and how we dress, she and I, we are cut from the same cloth.

181

1 2 3 4 5 6 7 8 9 10 11 12 13 14 15 16 17 18 19 20 21 22
23 24 25 26 27 28 29 30 31 32 **33** 34 35 36 37
38 39 40 41 42 43 44 45 46 47 48 49 50 51

Date Thirty-Three:
The Chores of Romance

Nat comes into my office today and asks how the dates are going. I generally get riled by this because I can sense an air of engaged superiority in her sing-song questioning. And it's not that she doesn't genuinely want me to find someone, it's just that I can sense her disapproval on how I am going about it. She feels I demand too much and that I appear to prefer to be single, both to her and to my respective mates. The worst part is, I don't think she's wrong. I just don't want to be forced to admit that. But on the other side of her charges is the fact that in my heart I know what I want, and I know that I just haven't found him yet. And I don't want to waste my time on a futile and false relationship.

"So…," Nat leans in my office. "Who's the lucky guy tonight?"

I tell Nat about Jeff, my date for the evening. Harvard-educated, business attorney for an entertainment law firm, kind of nerdy, Radiohead fan. I can almost see the flash of jealousy in her eyes, but then she morphs it into enthusiasm. "He sounds perfect!"

"I guess. I don't know, Nat. I have been on so many dates that by now they're feeling more like trips to the post office than any real chance at me meeting someone." Because though Jeff sounds perfect, I am not excited. I feel no fervor.

Nat scowls at me. "Well, you're not going to meet anyone with that attitude."

I shrug. "You try going on a date a week and then tell me what sort of attitude you have."

But Nat isn't going on a date a week because she is sitting at home watching *Idol* with her fiancé. Oh, how green that grass always looks on the other side.

I get home and have time to kill before Jeff and I meet at 8:30 p.m. for dinner. Rather than wash my greasy hair, or even shower, I decide to go for a hike through my neighborhood. I have recently discovered a great walk that takes me up through the hills of Silver Lake and down one of my favorite streets, where all the houses are so individually charming, all Craftsman and Spanish tiled and mid-century modern, it makes my heart break. I love this street. And as I walk, I imagine living on it with my husband, and our kids, and our wonderfully eclectic, slightly eccentric, always exciting life. I even see a guy who could have gotten the part had he not ended up in some other woman's movie. He is taking out the trash, and in the driveway sits their Audi and their Volkswagen, with their matching Obama bumper stickers. He looks at me but not in any way that is flirtatious or wrong, just with the neutral gaze of a good man well married.

And I wonder if that's what I want. Do I want the man who is able to do that? Not even a spark of appreciation for the woman walking by. Because in my book, I'm not sure if that's devotion or death. I get home and only have ten minutes to get ready so I rush over to the restaurant, greasy hair and all. I stand outside of the cute French bistro Jeff has chosen for dinner and text Ivan because Jeff is a few minutes late, and I am trying to look busy. Jeff shows up and recognizes me right away, which is a good thing because much like my first date Richard, Jeff is much better looking than his photos. He's tall with a great build and nice shoulders and long legs and a thick head of brown hair.

He is also nervous. And suddenly I am nervous too. Jeff and I sit down, and the configuration of the table is a little awkward, and the waitress won't leave us alone, and the restaurant is strangely empty, and we're so busy laughing and talking and watching the pixie dust flit around us, we forget to order. After the waitress's fifth trip to our table,

I finally try to concentrate on what I am going to have and mutter, "All right, it's time to get serious."

I begin to look down at my menu as Jeff laughs. "You're really entertaining to me." I look up, and we catch each other's eyes, and I feel that long absent thump in the left side of my chest. I breathe in and smile and am so happy that at the last minute I threw on makeup.

Jeff is from a good home outside of Pittsburgh. His parents are still together; he's close with his younger sister, who used to be a bit of a wild child but has now settled down and is married with a new baby. Jeff is an uncle, and I can tell he wants to be a dad.

"So, I saw on your profile you like Salman Rushdie?" I ask this hesitantly because more often than not I am disappointed by people's literary tastes.

"Yeah, *Midnight's Children* is my all-time favorite book," he tells me.

I stop. My breath gets caught. It's not like it's an entirely obscure work, but still. I nearly whisper, "Mine too."

And the flutter across Jeff's eyes speaks for both of us.

We don't go into anything too heavy: presidential elections, old-school Nintendo, college life, past jobs. I've had this conversation with many of my dates. Some were far more in-depth, some more serious, some more comedic, but none with as much chemistry as Jeff and I have. The food is excellent, and the place well lit. Jeff is wearing a button-down and blazer from work, and I have on a cashmere turtleneck with some of my good jewelry. We both look very adult. We both are very adult. And I feel normal.

The fact that my father was in prison my whole life, the fact that I used to be addicted to cocaine and go to meetings to keep me sober, the fact that I have herpes, and a dirty mouth, and a sexual past that could rival a few NBA stars—all of those facts seem very far away. And instead I feel like the well-bred, well-educated, well-mannered lady that I can be. All soft edges and dry humor and small bites that I am as much as I am wild and brazen and libidinous. We shut the restaurant down, and we get up to leave. He walks me to my car, and we laugh. I like walking next to him, and I can feel his body even though he's still a few inches away. I look down to see he is wearing Chucks with his work clothes, and though at this point, it might not put him in the great shoes club, it doesn't oust him to the bad one. And in a way, they fit him. Boyish with his maturity and fancy degree and funny ways and handsome face.

"I'd like to see you again," Jeff says. A simple statement, but one I can respect.

"I think we can do that."

"This weekend?" he asks.

"Sure. Although, I have something on Friday."

"Saturday then. There is a party I need to go to, but we can just lie about how we met each other—we don't need to mention *The Onion*."

I laugh. "Aw shit, it's 2008. I think we can tell them."

I go in for what I think will be a hug and kiss on the cheek, and before I know it, he's swept me up and is kissing me. Really kissing me. And his body is pressed against me, and I can feel him against my leg, and though I might have been worried that Jeff is too nice, he is apparently still naughty enough to pull a fast one. I am so caught off guard that I kiss back, and I am not sure if I am melting or popping or fizzing, but when someone walks past us and comments on the kiss, I am disappointed that we pull away. It doesn't take long before we try again, but another couple walks past us, sing-songing "K-I-S-S-I-N-G." I don't know why a young couple making out on a quiet street is causing such a stir. Jeff says, "You would never get that kind of attention in New York."

And it makes me love L.A. all the more. Because we take notice here. And I take notice too. I take notice of how I have been on the best date yet and will be going out again on Saturday with Jeff. I get in my car and call a friend and wonder if an alcoholic like me can be the type of woman a normie like Jeff could actually date. But more importantly, I wonder whether I will be able to date him. I have described to my sponsor before that as an alcoholic I sometimes feel like the aliens in *3rd Rock from the Sun*. If I emulate the humans well enough and for long enough, they might not notice that I'm different. But ultimately, I fear they will. Or worse, I will fault them for being human. I will expect magic and miracles and mysticism from people who, though smart, handsome, and mature, are simply not made up of such powers.

187

1 2 3 4 5 6 7 8 9 10 11 12 13 14 15 16 17 18 19 20 21 22
23 24 25 26 27 28 29 30 31 32 33 **34** 35 36 37
38 39 40 41 42 43 44 45 46 47 48 49 50 51

Date Thirty-Four: Being
Reese Witherspoon

The hostess leads us through the all-white decor of the Mondrian Hotel, through Asia de Cuba, and outside onto the back patio, which nestles into Skybar. My old coke dealer used to be stationed here, and I cannot help but scan the scene to see if he is there. Jason one ups the hostess and pulls out the chair for me. He seats me with my back to the crowd, which gives me a wonderful view of the lighted grid that is Los Angeles but which feels somewhat strategic on his part. Like he doesn't want me looking around, or he doesn't want people looking at me.

Jason is not from my side of town. He lives in Beverly Hills. And here is where the problem begins.

A couple of weeks ago, I stumbled across a list of numbers from when I worked for the notorious publisher. One of her authors was famous for writing a book on how to be a male player. We'll call him Neil Strauss. I've never met Neil, and I doubted he would remember me, but I called him anyway. When I recently told Siren this, she immediately responded, "Wow, that Shaman is really doing something, huh?" And I laughed and said yes. Because I have been doing my energy work every day at home as requested—the work that tells me not to be afraid to ask questions, to ask why, to ask for help, to ask for what I want. So I called Neil Strauss, and I told him about my 51 dates, and then I asked, "Are you single?"

"Oh, for one of your dates?"

I felt like such a schmuck. Like the star of a bad reality show trying to find candidates for my affection. I found out Neil is already seeing someone, but I pressed on. "Well, if you know of anyone, even one of your nerdy, player dudes," I offered. Because Neil is actually the man who spawned one of those bad reality shows. His was the one with the Tommy Lee look-alike in the Jamiroquai hat.

"You want a nerdy, player dude?" he asked.

"No," I laughed. "Not really. I just figured you might have one. I'm just trying to figure out how to get dates. It's a lot harder than it seems, even when you ask your friends. And I am so tired of online dating. If I go out with one more Prius-driving liberal who reads *The New Yorker*..."

Neil cut me off because I was nervous and rambling. He told me, "I think I have someone for you."

And that is how Neil Strauss set me up with Jason. Jason and I started e-mailing and it's actually pretty exciting. He is smart and disturbingly funny, and I was beginning to think that Neil had done pretty well for not knowing me. And then I told Jason I lived in Silver Lake. He sent me back a botched version of the Red Hot Chili Peppers lyric, "You can only find East Side loving on the Westside."

First of all, he quoted Anthony Kiedis. Albeit incorrectly. Anthony Kiedis is one of those sober douchebags who demands a certain kind of hot tea during interviews and makes people meditate with him. And the quote itself? I don't even get it. What does "East Side loving" mean, and how does it only take place on the Westside? I know Jason is trying to get in a dig, but the insult isn't really clear, which is why he follows up with another e-mail. In that one he tells me the only good things about Silver Lake are that it is near the Department of Immigration and that our homeless have good tans.

Often when I speak at my meetings I open with a reference to *Brave New World*. In the classic book mankind is divided into two groups: the Alphas and the Betas. The Alphas are good-looking, strong, popular, the dominant species. And the Betas, well, the Betas are like Danny DeVito in that movie with Arnold Schwarzenegger—they're "the shit left over." And I have spent my whole life with the Betas assuming I was an Alpha. All the while, having the Alphas take one look at me and know that I am a Beta.

And it is no different now. The Westside is filled with the beautiful, the tanned, the dominant, and also the incredibly, painfully unaware. The East Side might be the shit left over, but it's good shit. I feel comfortable amongst the houses, the hills, the untamed gardens, the Latinos, the hipsters, the small, winding streets, and the sense of wonder that my neighborhood inspires when I go on my morning hikes. So many nights I park my car and walk down my street, and the streetlamps hit the palm trees just right, spotlighting them against the darkened, starry sky. The air smells cool and clean, and I forget we are a city made of smog. I walk past the rose garden that sits on the corner of my block; I stop and close my eyes and hear the barking of dogs and sirens in the distance. I feel the warm spring breeze of an April night against my face, and I fall in love all over again. Because I love this city, but I am in love with Silver Lake.

I am not in love with Jason. He is good-looking, strong, and popular. And just the right type of smart for his side of town—witty, charming, and cruel. He loves his friends. And he talks a surprising amount about his dad, Fred. "Ah, Fred. What a guy."

"You're close with your dad?" I ask.

Jason thinks about it. "Close? I guess. We work together so I see him every day. Fred's a total character. I like to describe him as a cross between Hannibal Lecter and Archie Bunker. Although, he's a bit more vicious."

"Wow."

"And fucking hysterical."

"I have a grandma like that."

"Really?" But Jason doesn't care. He goes back to Fred. In fact, he won't shut up about the guy. I am a little thrown by why he keeps doing this until I realize that even Alphas need a security blanket. The easy topic they can grasp onto when they're not sure what else to say.

I can see through the gap of Jason's button-down shirt that he has a nice tanned chest with short brown hair with a small smattering of grey from his thirty-nine years of bachelorhood. When a piece of food falls off my plate, Jason picks it up with the calm briskness of a man who cannot have anything out of place but realizes that calling too much attention to that fact might get him labeled as OCD. And Jason is not down with being diagnosed. I am sure his home is immaculate.

"I'm up in the Hills," he tells me.

"Oh, Hollywood?" I ask.

"No, Beverly. Right behind the hotel." Jason sort of looks over my shoulder, and I am sure he is checking out some anorexic model with big tits, but he's respectful enough to bring his attention back to the woman with whom he is sharing a table.

"I love that neighborhood. I go hiking up there."

He lights up a bit. "I'm right there. I've got that Art Deco number as you're walking to the trail."

I know which one is his, and I'm impressed. "God, that's a great house."

"Yeah. The neighborhood signed a petition trying to make it a historical property so I couldn't tear it down." He shrugs, and the light goes out of him. "I still plan to... I mean, give me a fucking break. We all know that modern homes have the best value."

He says this with a bit of a sad laugh, and when I say that I love dark Craftsman homes, he says that so does he. And it's odd that we share the aesthetic. For a minute, we actually look like we might be natural and honest here. It is a beautiful evening with Los Angeles sparkling before us. Jason points out that Catalina is out there, and we can almost see the light of the ocean. And for a second, we get a little soft and sappy over the city we both love so much. And then Jason's friend Martin and Martin's girlfriend sit down and join us at the table.

I should say I was thirty minutes late for the date. I was at a meeting in the Valley, and well, there's this little thing called L.A. traffic I hadn't accounted for. And by that time, Jason had run into Martin and his new girlfriend. The girlfriend has lumpy implants, a fourteen-year-old son, and seemed to apply an incredible amount of lip gloss as an alternative to speaking. I walk up apologizing, and Martin ribs me for my tardiness. He asks how I know Neil, and I explain I used to work for Neil's former publisher.

Martin immediately quips, "You look like you're from New York. Is your last name like Witherspoon or something?"

I don't know why Martin is on the offense with me. Maybe it's because I was so late; maybe it's because it's how I'm dressed; i.e., not wearing a bikini top and Juicy Couture sweat pants like his girlfriend. Either way, he seems to think I am some sort of Tracy Flick character. Or maybe he just thinks I'm Reese Witherspoon.

When Jason and I move to our table at Asia de Cuba, I think we have shaken Martin for good, but then just as my date and I begin to move past our stereotypes and actually enjoy each other, Martin and his lip-glossed lady sit down.

"Dude, did you see those waves up past Zuma last week?" Martin says, interrupting any conversation that may have been in the works. I hear the word waves, and I'm out. I don't mind watching surfers take off their wetsuits, but outside of that it might as well be football.

"That was fucking sick." Jason becomes the dude I figured he would be. "I just booked my flight to Belize last week."

"I was just there!" Martin nearly squeals.

"No way. Did you get some pussy?" Jason asks and then apologizes to Martin's girlfriend. "I'm just fucking with him."

But she's tuned out as well, although I get the feeling hers is a more permanent condition. Martin needs an out because by the shifting that's going on in his seat, he probably did.

"Aw, poor Kristen. She can't join us in this conversation." Martin gives me a nasty look, and I just laugh at him.

"No, really, it's okay," I shoot back. "Tell us about the pussy, Martin." Jason likes that one, and we share a laugh at Martin's expense.

Finally everyone is done with their appetizers because this date is not making it to the entrée. Jason and I walk out together, the other couple disappearing behind us.

I am parked up Sunset, and Jason walks me to my car. I turn down toward the garage, and it is a steep hill. I am wearing heels, but before I can even worry about negotiating the terrain, Jason grabs my arm and holds me up, and then it hits me: I don't want Jason, but man, I do love a guy who can do that. Who knows how to manipulate the conversation, who is strong enough to walk me to my car even though it's out of the way, and then bold enough to grab me and lead me when I am walking downhill. We go into the underground garage, and the warm night air is whipping at our backs, and suddenly, I get playful. Under Jason's sturdy grip, I feel free. I take the lead. I can see that he didn't realize that underneath the witty banter and the sarcastic remarks of my Beta self, was a seismically Alpha girl.

But there's no time to get to know her. I drop him off at his car. We talk, we laugh, we kiss on the cheek. And that is that. Because I have fucked Jason before. Many times. Back when I partied, he was just the type of rich, hot asshole with whom I would do a lot of blow, talk some serious and honest bullshit, and ultimately bang when the sun came up. And then, like now, we would never speak again. This time I go home. And I don't end it like some scared little Beta girl who's playing with the wrong team. I end it like a classy Alpha from the East Side. Because I've got enough assholes on my side of town, I certainly don't need to fight traffic to date one from Beverly Hills.

Date Thirty-Five: Fake Cannoli and Pixie Dust

The South Beach Diet is interesting for a myriad of reasons. One, I am losing weight. I wasn't fat; I wasn't even Bridget Jones heavy, but the extra ten pounds I can carry makes me go from svelte to frumpy pretty quickly. I think it's because I already have a round face, either that or a demanding self-image. Anyway, the one thing you cannot eat on South Beach is sugar. And that is hard. Because it's like Mimi once said, "When you're single, sugar is how you find that sweetness that you're missing from lack of romance. That little mmm, mmm, good."

However, South Beach does give you recipes for substitute mmm, mmm, goods. Like mixing ricotta with Splenda and a little bit of cinnamon. Basically, it's the low-carb version of a cannoli, and being half Italian, I love cannoli. Last week, I bought some genuine curdled ricotta. It even had a basket in it, so you could remove the cheese from the watery liquid in which it stews. The ricotta fell apart, and when I mixed in the sugar substitute and the cinnamon, I closed my eyes, bit in, and felt like I was being kissed. This is what happens when you remove sugar from me.

On Friday I go to the grocery store, and I try to repeat the experience. I buy a cheaper brand of ricotta, though, because I'm feeling pretty confident in the South Beach trick. Today, I open it up, all excited for my Sunday treat. I mix it up. I bite in, and ick. The ricotta is not strong enough, authentic enough, curdled enough to create the same reaction. It tastes like paste.

And I am afraid the same goes for Jeff. I am disappointed but only as much as I am about the bowl of bland cannoli sitting next to me as I type. This has happened before. Many times. Richard. Peter. The first date they're funny, they're smart, they come from loving families, and drive decent cars. They seem cool, or cool enough, and I know that my mom would like them. And then they pick me up for date number two. They do not park and get out of the car. And I know parking spaces are tough in my neighborhood, but there is illegal parking right in front, and if you put on your flashers, and just got out to greet me, it would make a world of difference. Jeff doesn't park; he doesn't even double park. He is in a driveway down the street, and then when I come up to the car, he nervously reverses out, so that I am negotiating between his moving vehicle and the oncoming traffic. He isn't rude, he's just nervous, and he doesn't know the best way to handle the 2,000 pounds of metal that is his BMW.

I get in. A little ruffled, but with the weight loss, looking like I have always wanted to look when getting into a date's BMW. Mimi loaned me a very grown-up dress from her line, and my hair is a little wild, and I am wearing heels and holding a clutch, and my lipstick (I am wearing lipstick) is on perfect. I sit down and cross my well-lotioned legs and say, "Hi." Jeff looks at me, glances down at my legs, smiles nervously, and says, "Hi" in return. And though I can see he thinks I look pretty, he doesn't say it. And not because he's an asshole, but because he's too scared.

Jeff is a grown professional with a nice car, a good job, a well-gym-ed body, and a Harvard degree. He should have the self-confidence to be able to say to the gussied-up dame sitting next to him, "Wow, you look great." But he doesn't, and so we move into the humorous banter that served us so well on Wednesday. We go to one of my favorite restaurants. It's situated in the heart of Laurel Canyon, next to a country store that has been there for decades and surrounded by amazing houses that, if I did not love Silver Lake so much, I would dream of living in one day. Jeff pulls into the restaurant's drive, and I can tell he is still nervous. He gets confused with which entrance to use, and then when we get out of the car, he has difficulty communicating with the valet. I stand there and look over at the far end of the parking lot, and while he gets his ticket and hands over the keys, I fade away to a memory that happened in that same lot so many years ago.

Oliver and I had been on the verge of starting a relationship for months when it happened. He was deciding between staying with his girlfriend and leaving her for me. At first, when it all began, he had told me they were almost broken-up, that it had been agreed upon that he would be moving out at the end of the month. But as the end of the month drew near, as he took her to New York for a film premiere, as he continued to have his trysts with me and return to her at the end of the night, I saw where it was going. I might have been a cheat myself once, and at the time I was nowhere near sober, but I was aware enough to know that I didn't want to become any more of the other woman than I already was.

"Oliver, this isn't fair to me," I said. He was in New York with his girlfriend and had called me while walking home alone late one night.

"I know."

"And it's certainly not fair to her."

"Kristen, I want you to know that I see this ending only one way. I am just trying my best to negotiate through it all."

"You're in New York with her Oliver. That's not negotiating. That's taking a vacation. I'm sorry. I don't want to be a home wrecker," I explained.

"It's a little late for that."

"Fuck you."

"Look, I just need some more time," he told me.

"Fine. I'll give you two weeks. Don't call me. Don't e-mail me. If you haven't decided by then, your decision will be made."

Days went by without him calling, and though I was hurt, though I felt there was something there worth investigating, I had begun to move on from the idea that I had met my match.

Until one night. I went with a friend to the MTV Movie Awards, I wore the shortest dress in history, and I drank an obnoxious amount of champagne. I ended up at a party on Laurel Canyon and was flirting with an old friend. The friend in question later went on to have a brief but public affair with Britney Spears, because that's just how things go on that side of town. I remember going outside to have a cigarette when I got the text message, "What if two weeks happened early?"

It was Oliver, and he had broken up with his girlfriend. He had been at a party at the Chateau Marmont and asked where I was. In minutes, I was on the street outside of the party, and he was walking with a friend, who had driven him over to me. We were still on the phone, because the excitement was too great to hang up. He saw me from a distance and I could hear him inhale as he asked, "Is that you?" And it was as though in the drunken universe of time, he launched across that distance in a moment's wisp and was in front of me, and I was in his arms and in the air as he repeated over and over in my ear, "You're so beautiful. You're so beautiful." And we kissed and laughed and spun around in the parking lot of this restaurant I go to with Jeff.

At dinner, Jeff tells me about how when he was a kid, he had a lazy eye, "It was horrible. I had to wear this ridiculous patch for two years, until they moved me into bi-focals."

"Bi-focals?" I cover my mouth, trying not to laugh.

"It's okay. You can laugh. Let's hope I'm over it by now."

"Did you have friends?" I ask.

"Not really. I mean, having weird eyes doesn't win you too many points with the other kids. I couldn't play sports so that was out..."

And I now understand his drive to achieve. His determination to fit in when during his developing years, he didn't at all. I feel for him, and I can still see the experience's effects in his current behavior. He tells me about how he had a little bit of a nervous breakdown when he worked for Teach for America, and I know that he doesn't like admitting it because in his world, pain and weakness should not be. There is no beauty to them, only the lesson to do better next time. And I also know that I could no longer share any of these observations with him without feeling mean or strange. He would not understand.

We go to a party at a friend of Jeff's. It is the girl's birthday, and she has an amazing two-bedroom townhouse with sweeping views of L.A. The minute we walk in I realize that this girl is in love with Jeff.

"Hi Jeff," Sarah croons as she hugs him. And then she sees me. "Wait, I thought you were coming with Lily?" Lily is obviously some platonic co-worker they both know. Sarah is cool with Lily. Sarah is not so cool with me.

"No, she's at a show. This is Kristen," Jeff says, introducing me.

"Happy Birthday!" I enthusiastically hold out my hand. Sarah shakes it but only because she has to. She turns back to Jeff. "Did you get the Radiohead tickets?"

"No, but I'm still working on it."

"I talked to my dad, and he said he might be able to help," she offers.

"Is this for the show in August?" I ask.

Jeff grabs hold of my hand. "Yeah."

Sarah turns her back, and I can feel her disappointment. For the rest of the night she keeps popping up to stare longingly at my date, and I can tell this has been going on for a while. I can also tell that Jeff is oblivious. We walk around and admire Sarah's Hollywood Hills home. As we stand outside looking out at the skyline, I notice all the other people smoking.

"I haven't had a cigarette in sixty days," I tell Jeff.

"Really? Do you want to go inside?"

I shake my head. "No. That's the weird part. It doesn't bother me. In a way, it feels like I never smoked."

"Oh," Jeff says. "I've never actually had a cigarette, so I don't know."

I try to ignore the Normie gap I sense widening. But as I watch Jeff try to joke with other people at the party, and get ignored, I wonder whether this is the kind of man I want. And I know that I share many of these weaknesses that I am now judging in Jeff—the fear, the insecurity, the humor, and warmth that we all trap inside when we want something so bad and just aren't sure how to get it. But I also know that at the end of the day, it all comes down to that magical pixie dust that made our date Wednesday seem so exciting, that made my love affair with Oliver so powerful, that makes romance worth the pain we know it so frequently demands.

Jeff and I go inside, and we drool over the Warhol original of Mick Jagger (signed by both Andy and Mick) that this girl's father has just given her as a birthday present. We try to ignore the fact that there is no way this girl is paying for her multimillion dollar life with a job as an associate A&R rep in the music industry. And as we sit down on the couch, I lean over to Jeff and whisper, "God, this girl's dad gives her everything."

But much like my own loving parents, he cannot give her what she wants more than anything else, which, oddly enough, is my date. But that's the thing about pixie dust: no amount of money, or fancy dinners, or Harvard degrees, can make it appear if it just ain't there.

It's nearly one in the morning, and I have been at the stables all day. Before I left my ponies, I went into Arrow's stall and reminded myself again that even if I am struggling with romance, my life is incredibly full. I rested my head on his shoulder and heard his beating heart, and I remembered that love comes in many forms. I used to feel the same way about Oliver—about his silhouette. The way love puts you at peace.

That first night I spent with Oliver, we left the party on Laurel Canyon and went back to my apartment. We might have already had sex but it was the first time we had gotten the chance to spend the night together. I lay there in his arms, his soft, tanned chest beneath my head, and I was home. His eyelashes flitted against my cheek, my body fit like the perfect puzzle piece against his own. His hand slid along the side of my face, and in his kiss I found everything that I had been searching for in the empty lines and the short skirts and the obnoxious amounts of champagne that I thought I needed to be happy. And I didn't ever want to leave.

Jeff drives me home later, but I don't get the same sense of peace and belonging. We kiss but only because we did the first night, and I am too tired to have that conversation.

Today, I wake up feeling great. Later as I drive past Oliver's house, I almost want to stop in and tell him that. I want to show him how I have become the woman he always wanted. I imagine ringing his buzzer, and something in the pit of his stomach knowing who it is even before

I utter, "It's Kristen." I imagine entering the courtyard of his building as he walks out to meet me, and space and time shrinking as it did when we were together. And I know that's how it would happen, but the thing is, the woman that Oliver always wanted me to be doesn't do that sort of thing. She thinks about it, and she keeps on driving.

201

1 2 3 4 5 6 7 8 9 10 11 12 13 14 15 16 17 18 19 20 21 22
23 24 25 26 27 28 29 30 31 32 33 34 35 **36** 37
38 39 40 41 42 43 44 45 46 47 48 49 50 51

Date Thirty-Six: This Brother of My Mother

My uncle Tom and I have always been close. Ever since he moved to Dallas when I was six, he has done his best to fill in the gap left by my father. He came to Dad's Day at my schools, he taught me how to ride a bike, and he took me horseback riding when no one else would. He would always tell me that my dad loved me very much and that he wasn't there to replace him but rather to fill in for him while he was gone. My uncle had once been good friends with my dad, and that is another thing we share—this belief that somehow my father could be a better man.

So when Tom called me and asked if I wanted to drive down the coast of California with him for his birthday weekend because his girlfriend was traveling and he didn't want to spend it alone, I jumped at the chance to be there for this man who has always been there for me. And then he asked me if I wanted to stay in Big Sur, and this is why I love my uncle. I have been dreaming of going to Big Sur forever. I have planned more solo trips up there than I could count. Siren once told me, "You'll get there however you're supposed to get there." And I do.

My uncle pays for me to fly up to join him in San Francisco. He takes the train to the airport from his hotel so he can meet me there, and we rent the car together. Tom loves nothing more than a good deal so he makes two reservations at Thrifty, one using his slightly bogus travel agent membership, and the other under my name, using what they call a "Wild Card." The Wild Card wins, and we get a convertible at an incredibly reduced rate. My uncle and I jump and cheer. Our sales agent Shirley laughs at our antics, and my uncle and I like nothing better than playing the hams.

It can be awkward traveling with a fifty-year-old man who looks so young for his age, and if not for the very different styles in dress, could be mistaken for my boyfriend. I know most people don't have this type of relationship with their uncles. I can tell them anything, and I have been the bearer of many of their secrets as well. On the outside, Tom and I couldn't be more different. He is a conservative insurance agent with suburban homes in Dallas and Atlanta (talk about Red States) who likes Classic Rock and water skiing and pleated khakis. I am L.A. and New York as much as I am Texas. And if you saw us together, you wouldn't think we would have much to say to each other, but I think that on its best terms, this is what family is because the love between us is real.

We drive down the Coast, listening to the E Street Radio on XM. Once we get to Monterey, we take the top down, and it feels like we could do this forever. My hair blows in the wind, and Tom drives. We pull over frequently to drink in the view. We get to Big Sur and check into our cabin with our twin beds and a wood-burning fireplace. We go for a ten-mile hike, and I tell him about this book and my romantic troubles and the shaman and my very single life.

"I don't get it, Bo. What's wrong with these guys?" My uncle frequently calls me that—Bo and Puppy and Little Moose.

"Neither do I, Uncle T. You'd think I'd be able to find someone who would want to stay."

"You're just..." He looks at me and cups my head with his hand. "You're such a terrific girl."

My uncle was married before. He had been with Tonya for almost eight years when they finally got married. Tonya was as much a sister to me as an aunt, and when two years into their marriage, she was diagnosed with breast cancer, we all felt the fear that only cancer can instill. One year later, at the age of twenty-nine, Tonya died. And my uncle gave up on the idea that he would ever be a father, and for a while, he gave up on love. But then he met Cindy—his new girlfriend. Cindy is his age and has grown children of her own already.

As we walk I tell him, "For whatever reason, God didn't give you children, just as he didn't give me an active dad, but I'm glad he gave us each other." I know my uncle does not want to take the place of my real dad, but for all intents and purposes, he has. I want to be his daughter because he would have made the best father, and I am so sad that he never got the chance.

We stare out at Big Sur, the wall of ocean pulling down on itself, and the wide great sky hovering bright blue above us. We seem so small here in this landscape, just two little ants, worried about the crumbs that might not fall from the table. I tell my uncle about the guys that will get out of the car to greet me, and those who park down the street.

"See, I get out of the car." Tom walks next to me, and I smile because of course he does. "How else can you properly greet your date?"

"I need to find someone like you, Uncle T." My uncle just shakes his head as though he is at once mystified and disappointed in his fellow man.

We get home that night, and Uncle Tom gets the fire going. He sits in a reclining chair and pulls up a blanket. I pull down the comforter from my bed and lie in front of the fire, and I read to him the first seventy pages of my father's memoir, the one my dad has been writing while I have been writing this. And in a way, my father is there with us. As I read to my uncle about my father's early years of smuggling pot through California, the same great state we have been driving through, as I tell him about the Mexican prison and the early days in Haight Asbury, as I listen to myself tell these outlaw tales of the man who is my father, I feel him there. I feel protected by both of them. The man who I have been learning to slowly love again, and the one lying in that chair falling asleep.

205

1 2 3 4 5 6 7 8 9 10 11 12 13 14 15 16 17 18 19 20 21 22
23 24 25 26 27 28 29 30 31 32 33 34 35 36 **37**
38 39 40 41 42 43 44 45 46 47 48 49 50 51

Date Thirty-Seven: High Fidelity

I feel a moment of intense honesty tonight when I say to Jeff, "I promise you, you will find a lovely, beautiful, amazing girl someday, and it won't be long because I can feel it. She's coming soon." I don't normally make romantic predictions for my dates, but I can tell Jeff is bummed out, and I can also feel that he will meet an amazing girl someday. Just not the one in question.

I went out with Jeff again on Saturday but only because I promised myself I would. And my mom pretty much made me. It's amazing how a Harvard degree has the power to hypnotize people, particularly parents hoping to see their daughters marry well.

A few days before the date, I was telling Jeff about my weekend in Big Sur, about the incredible views, and the power of a convertible along the coast.

"I've never done that," he said.

"Done what?"

"Driven down the coast... driven anywhere really. I hate road trips. I get nauseous."

I didn't know how to respond. If I could, I would move into my Honda Civic and drive around the world for the rest of my life. But they still haven't built a bridge between here and the rest of the world, so California will have to suffice.

"Oh, wow. Yeah, I'm pretty much a trucker," I replied. And the silence that sat there said it all.

I speak to my father again, and for the first time he grasps that this book I am writing is memoir and not fiction. That these dates are all real. Immediately, he puts up some awkward pretense of fatherly concern. "Oh, K, don't tell your old man that."

"It's all pretty innocent stuff," I explain.

"Yeah, but you don't need to be dating."

"Dad, I'm thirty years old. I better be dating."

I think my father forgets or fails to understand how old I am. Because he hasn't been an active father since I was four, I am some median age between now and then to him.

"I want to have kids someday," I tell him. "I should probably start by going out to dinner with a few potential mates."

"I guess." Then he thinks about it. "I would like grandkids."

I take the conversation further, explaining that I am the last of a very interesting genetic line, and that I don't want it to die with me. And I am. Besides a missing half-brother in Mexico, I am the last of my father's DNA and the last of my mother's.

"It's a pretty wacky bloodline, Dad. I'd hate to see it go to waste."

"Wacky? It's not wacky."

I sometimes forget that my father is sixty-two and that he has been in prison since he was thirty-five, and that we do not share a vocabulary. When I was in college, I remember once telling him that I was shanking on some work. To me shanking meant procrastinating; to my father, it meant getting knifed during lunchtime in the mess hall. Needless to say, wacky to me means fun, wild, crazy, loving. To my dad, wacky means weird, bad, dorky. I explain what I mean, and I tell him that's why I believe in finding the right mate.

I think he should understand this. Last month my father moved to South Texas to live on a citrus farm. From what I can tell, he spends his days smoking pot, fishing for clams, and helping a local breeder raise Blue Tick hounds. He crosses the border to Mexico for cheap beer and women, and I think that if anyone would get why I am looking for a more interesting partner than one who hates road trips, it would be him.

I come from a family who regularly dances to Madonna after Christmas dinner. We go clubbing together. And when I drank, we were basically a frat party without the Greek letters. But even now that I'm sober, there is nothing formal about the way we treat other. And all of us, including my mom simply by choosing my dad, have been incredibly wild in our time. I think that's why Jeff's response to my road trip bothered me because whomever I bring into that fold needs to be able to keep up. I will not let our concentrated eccentricities be dulled by a man who couldn't fit in as one of our own. But perhaps even more importantly, I don't want our children tempered by some safe and boring bloodline. My father is a little thrown that I have put so much thought into this. And I realize that this is the great fear of all men. That they are somehow always being interviewed for their semen.

This makes for an even more awkward conversation with Jeff. Jeff and I decide to go to a movie on Saturday, which is pretty couply for a third date, but I also welcome it. I haven't been to a movie with a man I was dating in years. Jeff picks me up, and we get burgers on Sunset. We have time to kill, and so we decide to go to Amoeba Records. We get out of the car in the ArcLight parking lot, and Jeff corners me. Not in a threatening way, just in the way that Jeff wants some kind of reassurance of my interest, and I have been a little vague in terms of hand-holding and hug-returning. So he comes up and tries to kiss me, and I back off.

Before I went on the date, I did some energy work, asking my ancestors for the strength to be honest. And it works because I stand there in the harsh glare of the movie theater parking lot, and I ask Jeff not to engage in the physical until I have a better idea about whether there is something between us.

I don't say it like that of course because I am new to this honesty, so it comes out like a language that is foreign to my tongue. "I can't. Please. I need... I'm not good at this. I want to see what's here. What I want. What... oh, shit. Can we stay, the physical, stay away, the physical. I'm not good at this. Do you understand?"

Though disappointed, he understands. We continue to walk to the record store.

"I'm writing a book," I tell him point-blank because we have gone too far now for me not to. "I'm going on 51 dates this year, but that's not why I didn't kiss you."

He laughs. "Oh, I hear you. I've been on so many dates recently, I should write a book."

We walk into the record store and are going through the racks of Used Rock. I pretend I care about the music as I say, "I guess in the end, it just all comes down to chemistry."

"Well, if you think that, and you're not sure about us, that doesn't sound good."

"Jeff." I look down. I cannot hold his gaze. I cannot hide the truth.

We keep moving through the store, up the stairs to Hip Hop because I want the Kanye West CD. I keep thinking that if I buy a CD, it will make Jeff feel better. He has explained to me how the record industry is on its last leg, and how he represents many clients from it. I figure if I can't like him romantically, the least I can do is support him professionally.

We hit Hip Hop as I explain to him, "I'm just trying to decide, okay? All I am asking for is the physical space for me to do that. Oh, God. I guess what I am trying to say is that it's not necessarily a no yet."

Jeff stops with his hand on a Rihanna CD.

"Yet?" he asks.

"Uh..." maybe that was the wrong answer.

"That's like in *High Fidelity* when the girlfriend tells John Cusack that she hasn't slept with the new guy. Yet. We all know what yet means."

I cringe. Jeff is quoting Nick Hornby at me in the middle of a record store, in the middle of the crowded hip hop aisle nonetheless, and it's a little embarrassing for us both. He realizes this and asks, "Can we get out this section? Let's go to foreign film or something."

We end up in the used VHS area as I try to weave some sort of web of compassion and honesty. I decide not to buy Kanye because I can tell by the look in Jeff's eyes that it won't make any difference to him whether I purchase a studio album or not. We go to the movie instead.

Jeff drives me home, and we agree to speak in a few days, which is when I tell him, "I promise you, Jeff, you will find a lovely, beautiful, amazing girl someday, and it won't be long because I can feel it. She's coming soon. But I just see us as friends."

He tells me he doesn't see that happening, and I understand. I know I am breaking his heart a little bit, and since I have had the same done to me recently, I am pretty cognizant of how it feels. And I know it sucks. But I also know that Jeff will find a lovely, beautiful, amazing girl someday. It's just not me.

Date Thirty-Eight: Sober and the City

My mother moved to New York City my freshman year of college. But that was not my first experience with the town I once loved so much. When I was fourteen years old, I went up to Connecticut to visit family friends. We took one afternoon to go into the City, and that was when it happened. When I fell dramatically in love with the place. I remember going to Saks, and the Plaza, and seeing Tony Bennett eating next to us at Planet Hollywood, and getting to do all the things that people do when they are tourists in New York and don't know better. I also remember getting on the train back to Connecticut and crying for the better part of the trip because I didn't want to leave.

On Thursday, I fly into New York City on the red-eye, and the next morning I get on the subway from JFK and begin to make my way to my mom's apartment. I love riding into Manhattan on the subway. There is no better way to feel immediately a part of the city, not as the tourist I was when I was fourteen, but as the resident I still like to consider myself as being. As I ride in, I remember the day that was the catalyst for why I left six years ago.

September has always been my favorite month: it's the one in which I was born; it has the most beautiful weather; and Neil Diamond sang a song about it. It has a lot of great qualities. And that morning when I woke up, got ready for a my job in book publishing, and headed out the door at twenty-two, thinking I had it all together, despite the terrible hangover I was rocking, I had no clue that it was about to end. For all of us.

I was getting ready to go into the first big meeting of my career when the news came in. Planes, falling buildings, we know the drill. I waited for my best friend Liz to arrive; our friend Courtney joined us. We picked up a couple cases of beer, some wine and whiskey, went over to my friend Ally's and began to drink. Sure, we watched the news, sure, the bars were filled all over, but when four o'clock hit, and we were out of weed and couldn't get any blow, Ally and I decided we would go downtown for some nitrous.

I lived in the East Village, so we were able to get past the blockade to make it to the bodega on St. Mark's that sold cartridges. We picked up a few boxes and were so desperate to get home and get high, we decided to take the bus. And that's when it hit me. I was an atrocious human being. I remember swaying on the bus, giggling with Ally about our nitrous score, while people stood around us, some covered in dust, all in a state of shock and terror. We were obviously drunk, people were giving us dirty looks, and I remember thinking, "This is not how I should be." Nine months later I moved to Los Angeles, and I was never able to love that city the same way again. And I think, in many ways, it couldn't love me.

But as I get on the 6 train and make my final leg up to Mom's apartment on the Upper East Side, I feel that New York state of mind that I haven't felt in a long time. The advertisements for dermatologists, the poetry sponsored by Barnes & Noble, the warnings about walking between the cars, this is my New York City. This will always be my New York City. Because there is something about the place—the honking horns, the shining steel, the lurch of my subway car—that makes me feel like anything is possible. I get to Mom's house except for it's not my mom's house anymore because, as of the month prior, my mom is now living in Raymond's apartment, even though it is in the same building. But despite the fact that I might miss the comfortable couches I have known from her place, and the floral calendar in her kitchen, and the picture of sailboats I would wake up to every morning in her bedroom, I am happy for her. And for them.

Because my mom has just moved, she still has a bunch of photo albums that I haven't seen in years. Siren is coming from Philadelphia to meet me in New York, and my mom needs to go to work, so I lie down on her couch and fall asleep looking at these photos of my childhood—of me with my mom and dad—memories that have been lost, like my love for New York City for so, so long.

Siren gets into town, and I go and meet her at the Chelsea Hotel, where I have reserved a room for her birthday. I had always wanted to stay at the Chelsea, and just like in Big Sur, my time had finally come. We luck out when we get there because Stanley, the famed manager of the Chelsea, is the one who checks us in. I decide to go bold.

"So when I called before, I requested a special room," I tell him.

Stanley looks at my reservation, "Well, then, why aren't you paying a special price?" I am in an economy room, the least expensive possible.

"Because I'm cheap," I offer.

Stanley likes that, and so he gives us Janis's old apartment. As in Joplin. The room where she famously gave Leonard Cohen head. Siren and I go up and channel all the crazy energy in the room because we can feel it. That shit is heavy, man.

That night I take Siren to my mom and Raymond's apartment, and I show her the pictures I found earlier in the day.

"You have got to be kidding me," Siren says, laughing at a picture of me she is holding in her hand. I am wearing my grandmother's panty hose and nothing else. It is the time in my life when my dad is still a kingpin, and we have cars and houses and cash. And it shows. Because that little girl is not wondering if she is the prettiest in the room—she knows she is. That little girl is not afraid to ask because she demands. Because that little girl has yet to lose her daddy, she channels him and that shit is heavy, man. I am posing and posturing and pimping in front of the camera. And already at the age of three, you can tell, this kid's gonna be an asshole.

Later, Siren tells me how her own father has been trying to get back in touch with her. She tells me how he has been living with his mother in Bucks County, drinking all day while his mother slowly dies in the back room.

"Have you talked to him?" I ask.

She shakes her head. "He just leaves messages. Sometimes I can tell he's really drunk. Sometimes he cries."

My dad doesn't leave those kinds of messages because he too is posing and posturing and pimping in front of the camera, trying to project who he thinks he is supposed to be. But I know he feels just like Siren's dad. He is old and tired and drunk, and he just wants love from that little girl he left behind so many years before. And I understand why Siren can't call her dad back, but in that moment, I see in her father what I often refuse to see in mine. That they are now broken men, and though we might hate them for who they have been, it wouldn't hurt us to try to love them now. Because they need us.

My father has been asking me to visit him down on that South Texas farm. And I keep telling him to get settled there, and I will come. But as I listen to Siren tell me about how she cannot call her father back, that she just isn't ready, it hits me that we might never be ready. And if I want a chance to love my dad, this might be the only chance I've got. I know I will call him when I get back. I will make the reservation.

I take Siren to an old jazz club, and as we settle into our seats I realize what a perfect night this is. Siren and I walk through the West Village afterward. Down the empty, cobblestoned streets, laughing and holding hands. There is so much magic in the air that I love the city as though for the first time.

We go back to our historical apartment and wander the halls of the Chelsea Hotel. Some say we're born alcoholics. Others think we become them. I think it all comes down to *The Shining*. When Stephen King wrote his famous book, he was in the grips of addiction. And in the story, the Jack Nicholson character decides to take the job at the hotel because he is running from his own drinking problem. And I think that in a way, the Shining is alcoholism. It can kill us. It can brutalize the people who love us. It can turn otherwise lovely, charming people into monsters bent on destruction.

And so as we sneak around the hallways that comprise the Chelsea Hotel, I am not surprised when we stumble upon a photo of Jack Nicholson on the shoot of *The Shining*. It is the scene where he sits at the bar talking to the phantom bartender. And in that instance, my own chimeras call out to me. The ones that tell me that I too can have a drink.

But I don't. Because that night in New York, I get to cross the cobblestoned streets with my friend. I get to have dinner with my mom. And I get to appreciate every moment of this city I left after that fateful September day years ago.

Date Thirty-Nine: The Condors of La Cañada

Last Thursday my wheels fell off again.

It all started when I went to a new meeting in Pasadena. Noelle had asked me if I would house sit, and since I have adopted her golden retriever Rocky, I quickly agreed. Plus, Noelle's house is exactly the house I want to have one day when I grow up. Noelle lives in the now-suburban enclave called La Cañada. Back in the day, La Cañada was known for its sprawling farms and rather staunch conservative ranch folk. It was a bit like Texas, but to the west of Pasadena. Since that time, new money with newer Priuses have moved in, but there is still an independent air to the town and horse crossing signs at nearly every intersection.

Noelle's house is nestled into one of the foothills of La Cañada. It is an old Spanish-style hacienda with brightly painted walls, a large backyard with a swimming pool, and books upon books about mysticism.

I figure that my extended stay in La Cañada also gives me a great opportunity to try some new meetings, and maybe even meet some new men. And that's when the shit hits the proverbial fan. Because as I am sitting in one of those new meetings, the secretary gets up to make announcements and I feel like I have been hit by a lightning bolt. I have been waiting years to feel that full body tingle again, that time-space continuum of *Who is that?*, that great, big, powerful glimpse of love at first sight. I see this man whom I do not know and because I am so mesmerized I do not even hear his name.

There is a smoke break and since I don't smoke anymore, I could easily go up and talk to him. I could ask him any number of questions. I could ask his name. I could at least act as though I notice him when he is standing five feet away from me talking to someone else from the meeting, but I don't. I am terrified. And even though he is by no means the hottest guy in the room, all I can think is that he will not be attracted to me, and so I freeze. I freeze. And I hate myself all the more for it.

That weekend Mimi comes out to La Cañada for a hike, and while we are walking through the neighborhood, I tell her about my issues with talking to Mr. Pasadena.

Later that night, Mimi and I go out again because she is determined that I practice my flirting skills. She tells me that once I see someone I like, I just need "to keep my eye on the prize." We go to a bar up the street from my apartment in Silver Lake, the one with the sober bartender I think is hot. Braden is still there, but he's not sober anymore. I explain to him my flirting problems.

"You know," he says as he leans across the bar, looking pretty darn sexy, even for a relapsed alcoholic, "it's as much what's behind the eyes, as how you look at people."

I look up, and Braden is staring at me, and we lock gazes. We're incredibly close, and I try desperately to bring it forth. To show him what's in there, but I can't, because for all the fire and feeling and passion I have in me, I cannot expose it in this moment with him. So I drop my eyes, and for the rest of our time there, he flirts with Mimi. And I know why. Because Braden is wrong—it's as much how you look at people. What good is it if I got all this behind my eyes, and I won't share it?

I wake up the next morning more depressed than ever. Because I am thirty and single and now, apparently, don't even know how to flirt. Not good. Not good at all. I feel like getting some rope and finding a sturdy limb. Depression takes over with a heavy hand, and all I can see or feel is my loneliness and rejection and the fear that there is something very wrong with me. I get into a huge fight with both my mom (who tells me, "Well, sometimes you do talk too much, and when you start telling a joke, you just can't stop. It's like, K, enough!") and my grandmother (who tells me, "Well, you *can* be gorgeous."), and herein lies the problem. Because as much as I can intellectually state that I am smart and kind and funny and attractive, when you put me in front of someone I like, I think I am having one of those days where I am not gorgeous and that if I open my mouth, I will talk too much and go on for too long. So I shudder a smile and shuffle away. Like some strange combination of Pat from *Saturday Night Live* and *Shrek*—one part androgynous misfit, one part ogre.

I explain this to Lidia when I see her the following week. The night before had been my second chance to talk to the Pasadena man. At the break I saw him go outside, and I sensed my opportunity, but I got nervous and decided to go to the bathroom to look at myself in the mirror instead. I left the bathroom and confidently walked down the stairs. So confidently, I even smacked the ceiling in the place where it was low enough for me to reach it. That's right, I got it. I hit the landing, looked up, and Mr. Pasadena was right there. He was staring at me. He was also in the middle of talking to an attractive girl who was around my age. I could have smiled. I could have stood up tall and said hello. I could have kept my eye on that prize as Mimi had tried to train me to do, but I didn't. I think there might have been a small spasm around my mouth, but before it could resemble anything like a smile, I put my head down and hurried past.

"What are you thinking in that moment?" Lidia asks. God love her for recognizing these experiences as real challenges to wholeness, and not just some dumb girl complaining about some dumb dude. And I remember the moment clearly, remember my thought in it, "She is skinnier than me." That girl to whom Mr. Pasadena is talking, and she is skinnier than me.

Lidia and I go through what age this all comes from, and it's pretty clear to both of us that this sounds like preadolescent anxiety. The middle school years, where I was undeveloped and unpopular. Also, the years where my grandmother and I really went at it. Where whatever chance I had to feel good about myself was always undercut with the sense that I could be "better," "cooler," "more gorgeous," but that I just couldn't make the cut.

These wounds are old. I wish I was done with them, but when I can't even lift my head and smile at someone I like, they're obviously still getting to me. I go to choose a stone before lying down, when Lidia begins telling me a story. Years before, she had been in Peru, hiking as part of her training with the Shamans. She was on a three-day vision quest and between the small amount of food she had, the torturous climb she was doing, and the altitude, she had begun to feel that she couldn't make it back to the camp.

"I was petrified, Kristen. I couldn't move. I just stood there, clutching the wall of the cliff I was climbing down. Terrified that I didn't have it in me to take the next step. And then a miracle happened. A condor came flying out from the side of the cliff. And he flew around me three times. Back and forth in front of me. So close that had I reached out, I would have been able to touch him. Do you know what we pray to the condor for?"

And I do know because I have been doing this for long enough with Lidia to have begun adopting her prayers as my own. "The big picture," I answer.

"Exactly," she says, smiling at me. "In that moment, it was as though I could see the world through a bird's-eye view. Our struggles, our fears, they're only as big as we make them. And we can let these little things stop us from reaching our potential, or we can see them for what they are and keep walking."

"I want to keep walking, Lidia. I am trying to do the things to just keep walking."

And then I tell her how on my way to her house, I called my dad, and I told him I would find a flight to visit him.

"Really, K?" he barely whispered.

"Really, Daddy." Because I know that I can blame Nana or my dad or that little girl inside for all these fears and failings, but the truth is until I make them right, I can only blame me. I look down at the stones Lidia has laid out for me, and I choose a small crystal in the shape of a snake. Lidia tells me it's perfect.

"Why?" Finally, after months, I get up the courage to ask.

"Because it is the stone that allows you to find the truths that you keep hidden inside."

Before I lie down, I tell her, "Lidia, I feel it. I feel that my preteen self knows so much about this. That she holds the answers."

And so we go in to find her. Lidia begins by holding a crystal pendulum above me to gauge where the energy is flowing. And though neither of us can explain why or how, the pendulum begins moving with a momentum that would be scary if I didn't feel like I was the one causing it. And then I am in a full vision: I am in a maze, holding my middle school self, and she is vomiting it all out. All the nasty words and insecure thoughts and unnecessary fears. She falls back on me, and I continue to hold her. My real body is practically levitating with energy while I do this, and I can tell that something in me is fully turned over to this work. I don't know if it's real or not, but I don't care. I need it to be in that moment. I need to heal these wounds. And so far, this work with Lidia seems to be doing the trick. It seems to be showing me things I haven't been able to see before. It seems to be giving me a hint of the big picture.

"She wants chocolate." I come out of it and can feel my teen self desiring something sweet.

"Chocolate is often the reward for magic, like in Harry Potter," Lidia informs me.

"She also wants to go to the arboretum."

"Then, take her."

Later, I get a chocolate milkshake from McDonald's, and I look to see if there is an arboretum with a maze anywhere in Southern California. There is only one, and it is in La Cañada, home of Noelle and my future life. On Sunday I go to the arboretum, and when I ask the sweet Eastern European lady working there where the maze is, and she takes me by the hand and leads me to it, I know that this day is charged with magic. Even though I can see above the hedges, I still let myself get a little lost. I get to the middle and follow Lidia's direction, "Sit in the middle of the maze and imagine there is a spike of energy going from the top of your head through your first chakra." I get to the middle where there is a donor memorial—stone tablets on the ground with the names of people who have passed away. Smack dab in the middle is a stone that says, "In memory of Nana," and a shiver so strong bolts through my body.

I sit on that stone, and I channel that energy. And then I open my eyes and look around, and I know that someday I will not do this alone.

223

1 2 3 4 5 6 7 8 9 10 11 12 13 14 15 16 17 18 19 20 21 22
23 24 25 26 27 28 29 30 31 32 33 34 35 36 37
38 39 **40** 41 42 43 44 45 46 47 48 49 50 51

Date Forty: Archetypes Away

"We are not on a date, Henry Monk!" I shout. But we are standing in line at the silent movie theater, and he is buying my ticket. As I hit the relatively nice button-down he has dressed himself up in, I know, that whether I want it to be or not, I am definitely on a date with Henry Monk.

And it's really no surprise. Henry and I have known each other for well over a year, and started a 7:00 a.m. Friday meeting together last spring. He is a poet, a father of two, and an incredibly cerebral man. He is also in construction, is as big as a bull, and looks a lot like Bruce Willis. It's not that I don't find Henry attractive because in certain instances, I do.

When I saw Henry at a meeting over the weekend, I found myself in an easy conversation with him about lying in bed all alone on Sunday mornings and our current states of mind on the subject. I told Henry that I spent my day watching *America's Next Top Model*. I explained that I view the bed as my personal cell phone charger. It restores me to full strength.

Henry laughed. "You really have this thing wired, don't you?"

"What thing?"

"Life. You've got it down. You should go around and teach seminars or something."

I laughed, but my current grasp on life is temporary, and I know that. Just last week I was waking up caught between the loneliness and thoughts of suicide that Henry had just told me he had been fighting. So my techniques are by no means a perfect science.

"Well, I figured I'll at least try to stay alive until tomorrow because they're playing *Satyricon* at the Silent Movie Theater," Henry joked.

Henry looked around the room, and though I didn't know if that was an invitation, I couldn't help but ask, "Fellini's *Satyricon*?"

And that's how I end up not on a date with Henry Monk. Because I really do want to see *Satyricon*, and I kind of want to go on a date with Henry Monk. But it's much easier to admit the former than the latter. Because I'm not sure what my motive is.

Henry Monk was at one point an up-and-coming musician on the mean streets of punk rock Hollywood. He hit his bottom like many do, with a speedball in his arm, dying in a motel bathroom stained with his own shit and vomit. Most actually do die there. But not Henry. At that time Henry had a four-year-old daughter and a five-year-old son, and their mother could no more take care of them then Henry could. So he went from Mr. Motel to Mr. Mom. He got sober, raised two kids on his own, continued to write poetry and be an inspiration, and still managed to find himself broke, single, and suicidal at the age of forty-eight.

His kids are now grown, and last year, when I first met him, he seemed to have everything I wanted. He wrote and performed poetry. He had a dog named Tennessee. And a gorgeous girlfriend named Camille. And he seemed to be a sage to those who knew him. Then as I got to know him, I realized he was a nerd like me. And not long after, the gorgeous girlfriend and he broke up. And more often than not, I see him riding his bicycle, not because he wants to but because he doesn't have the money for gas.

I do have the money for gas, so I drive us to the theater. We get there early and go to a great little arty bookstore up the street. They have The Criterion Collection DVDs, and stellar production value, and annoying clientele, and incredible bookbinding. I love books. The way they feel and smell. Their texture and color and design. They were one of my first addictions. Henry walks past me and makes an aside, "Stick with me kid. I can show you around."

I want to say okay. Do that. I have been dying for someone to show me around. To lead me to the hidden bookstore on Fairfax, to the silent movie theater, to the underground Vietnamese restaurants, and the best trails in the hills. I have been waiting for the person that knows and loves this town like I do, that can unlock the door and lead me even further into her wonderland.

And I get the feeling that Henry could be that kind of guy. But I know that he also never could. That I would learn what I wanted from him and be gone. That in the end, we would both be left embarrassed.

We walk back to the movie theater, but we still have some time to kill. We sit down at an outdoor chess table across from the movie theater, and I don't hold back. The sun is setting right across the street from us, and it could feel romantic until I ask, "So what happened between you and Camille?"

"Oh, God." Henry rubs the top of his balding, closely shaven head.

"What? I've always wondered. You two seemed so much in love."

"We were. We probably still are." He looks back over at the movie theater, into the setting sun, because these are always tough topics. "But we were also incredibly toxic for each other."

"I hate that," I tell him.

"Yeah, I think we'll always love one another. I do. But we've gotten together and broken up too many times to ever try it again. It wasn't even painful anymore. It just became frustrating."

I thought so. I knew that's how that one worked. You could see it in them when they were together, and I saw it in her eyes as much as his when they broke up. And I know what that's like because as I sit there and listen to Henry describe their relationship, I cannot help but think of Oliver.

My uncle Tom called me the other day to tell me that he and Cindy are breaking up. I would like to say I'm surprised, but I'm not. Because just like Henry and Camille, just like me and Oliver, they have tried too many times to get around the issues of fear, bad timing, and ultimately, the indifference that comes when you just can't put yourself on the line anymore.

Henry and I sit in a comfortable silence, and I look out as the sun begins its final sink over the setting. We both watch as it slips behind the hills and off into someone else's horizon. And I remember when I was seven years old and dreamt about Oliver. Of course, I didn't know it at the time. In the dream a boy came to me asking for help. He was around eleven, and I loved him immediately. I asked my mom and Nana if he could stay with us, and they said yes. But when I went back to tell him, he was gone. I went to school the next day, and I told everyone about that dream. And I wondered if I would ever find him again.

It was only about three weeks into my relationship with Oliver when I did. I was helping Oliver move into his new place, and I was unpacking a box of pictures when I found a school photo of that eleven-year-old boy. The sandy brown hair, the scared brown eyes—I even remembered the slight pout in his lower lip. I didn't need to ask it, but I did. "Is this you?"

Oliver was putting books away on the other side of the room. "Yeah." He came over and looked at the picture. "Yeah, that was right after my mom left. Ugh," he said as he practically shivered. "I remember I had to borrow a shirt from the neighbor because my dad didn't know how to do the wash. It was a bad year."

He handed the picture back to me and as had become a routine in our romance, he pressed his lips into my forehead, his face against my hair, and I could feel in his breath, in the long, soft inhale of my scent, that he had been waiting for me too. But I never told him. Because how do you say to someone you've only been dating three weeks that they came to you in a dream when you were seven? That they asked for your help. That you've been looking for them ever since. And that is the paradox of love. Whether it is some ancient business from our souls, an old relationship from another life that we just have to play out in a typically painful pattern, or whether it's a question of chemistry—that which attracts also repels. Or whether it simply goes back to what Lidia said, "We can only love as much as we are willing to be hurt." And when we allow ourselves to love someone like that, when we search our whole lives to find them, we are just primed for destruction when we finally do.

Cindy, Oliver, Camille—the great loves are like that sinking sun. We are blinded by them, and we keep seeing them in our vision long after they have gone. They are forever burned into who we are, whether we get to keep them or not.

227

1 2 3 4 5 6 7 8 9 10 11 12 13 14 15 16 17 18 19 20 21 22
23 24 25 26 27 28 29 30 31 32 33 34 35 36 37
38 39 40 **41** 42 43 44 45 46 47 48 49 50 51

Date Forty-One: All-American Dates

On Tuesday night I go out on a real date. It's been a while since I've met anyone in such a traditional American fashion. There was no Internet. No drunken/sober hookup. No anonymous meetings for sober people. Just me and some guy standing outside of a bar, talking. As American as apple pie.

On Wednesday I go back to the Pasadena meeting, but this time with my wingman in tow. Sometimes I wonder if Mimi's boyfriend wonders where his girlfriend is because it appears she is as determined to see me coupled as much as she is to stay that way. But I also know that one day, when I do have a Carty in my own life, I hope to be as available and as in touch with my friends as Mimi is because despite the fact that she has all the fears and concerns and "what ifs" that are inherent to a relationship, she somehow manages to walk through hers with amazing aplomb.

After my last shuffle in front of Mr. Pasadena, Mimi offered to help me out, and so we both go to the meeting, and at the break we wait. We are standing in the middle of an aisle, and Mr. Pasadena is walking toward us. Everything in me wants to run, and much like Lidia on her Peruvian mountain I freeze. I do not know what to do, what to say, but Mimi is my condor, and she comes flying out of the side of the mountain and moves toward Mr. Pasadena.

"Thanks for such a great speaker tonight," she says to stop him. And he does stop. And though he thanks Mimi, he looks directly at me.

"Yeah, good choice, Mr. Secretary," I reiterate.

Mr. Pasadena reaches out his hand to me. "I've noticed you recently. I'm Chris."

And I smile and say, "Hi, Chris. I'm Kristen." I can feel Mimi beaming beside me, and I am so proud of myself in this minute that I almost forget to introduce her, but I do and am feeling a little more normal in this easy social engagement in which I take part nearly every day. Chris stands there smiling at me. "Do you live in Pasadena?"

But before I can answer, an older woman swoops down out of the blue. Another condor, but this one is not on my side.

"Christopher! I was looking for you, honey," she shrieks. And in an instant, Chris is literally being dragged away, still smiling at me but clearly attached to another. I turn to Mimi, and though I am disappointed, more than anything, I am relieved. I did it, and in a way that's all that matters.

Mimi shrugs. "I guess Mr. Pasadena already has a Mrs. Pasadena."

"I guess so," I say, smiling.

Mimi takes hold of my hand. "That's okay. We'll try again this weekend."

And so the following Saturday, we return to the bar where Braden works, and we drink our Red Bulls, and we flirt with some men. Mimi is pretty clear from the start that she has a boyfriend, so the attentions are quickly redirected towards me, and I hold my own. Unfortunately, there is no one with whom I would want to trade numbers until we are walking across the street to leave. I notice him as we walk out, but it takes a second for it to register. I turn back around to look, and Mimi proves yet again that she is a condor because she is not missing a beat.

"Who are you looking at?" she asks.

"No one," I say with a shrug.

"The guy in the button-down?" Mimi is relentless.

"Yeah, but we're across the street now." I had walked too far before I had thrown the look behind me and missed my chance for an easy introduction.

"Let's go back," she demands.

"Mimi, that's silly. I didn't like him that much."

"You haven't met him yet. We're going back."

And so we pull a ballsy U-turn, wait for traffic to pass, and then cross back over to the bar, walk up to the guy and his friend, and thrust out our hands.

"Hi, nice to meet ya'll," I say.

It was a bold move to be sure. And one not quite worthy of the intended destination. Brad from Boston. Brad didn't even have to tell me his name—I could have guessed it. Good, middle class upbringing. Small Northeastern school. Moved out here to be an actor. Now works in some entertainment-adjacent industry. He is also younger than me, which again never scores points. But he's nice, and we have an easy flirtatious banter outside of the bar, and he asks to take me out. And I say yes.

A few evenings later, we meet at a relatively nice restaurant in Silver Lake. We dine outside, talk about politics, and toss around some easy jokes. It is 2008. We are in the middle of an election. And I have begun to realize that the minute I start hearing the words, "after eight years, I can finally care about politics again," come out of my mouth on a date, it might as well be over. And that's not to say that my rediscovered passion toward American politics isn't worth anything, but it is to say that it is a very easy comment. Some sassy little turn of phrase I can use to keep the conversation moving.

On Monday my 51st date, Ben, e-mails me on Facebook. I had found him online a few months back, but it wasn't until my recent depression that I finally requested that he be my friend. He accepted but wrote no more than that. And then last Friday, I ran into him at a meeting. I saw him giving his phone number to a girl but didn't let that stop me from going up and saying hi. I ended up getting into a conversation with the girl instead and lost Ben in the mix.

They next day he sends me a message, and we began e-mailing. Big, extended, funny e-mails. We speak the same language; we make the same jokes. Ben compliments my writing and sense of humor. We end up exchanging numbers, and when I tell him I am about to go on date #41, he tells me to report back. So after my boring date with Brad, I call him. I am not nervous about it. Ben feels like a friend to me, and we end up talking for over two hours. In fact, I can't remember when I have chatted so easily with a man on the phone.

I feel incredibly comfortable with him, perhaps too much so. By the end of the conversation I have audibly and admittedly peed while being on the phone, and then just to prove how inept I am at snake- charming a man, I tell him how many people I've slept with. I could write the book on what not to say to romantic prospects, which I guess I am.

"So are you going with *51/50* as a title because you've fucked 51 men?" Ben asks.

"No." I am irritated by Ben's tendency towards the sexual until I realize something: "Wait! I have."

"I guess you've been pretty busy."

"Well, not all of us got sober when we were ten, Ben."

"That's true," Ben agrees. If I were being strategic, which I am not in love, ever, I would have probably thought better than to tell the sex-obsessed, slightly misogynistic writer how many men with whom I have slept. I might have been wiser to hold on to that card for a bit. But I don't because for all my shaman and program and deep breaths, when I get going, my mouth just speaks for itself.

We continue talking about love and romance and recovery. Ben has been single even longer than I have (seven years) and admittedly hasn't introduced a girlfriend to his family in forever. Ben is very single, but won't really tell me why. Maybe he doesn't know, but I think he does. He just isn't into showing his cards as easily as I am. We hang up the phone, and I wonder what the rest of this game is going to look like.

Date Forty-Two: Beautiful People

I shock myself sometimes. Really, I do. Because I should know better by now. I know that to do the same thing over and over and expect different results is the definition of insanity. I know this like I know my own name, or the serenity prayer, or the many other things we say in the meetings I go to not just to stay sober, but to stay sane. And then I go and do something completely fucking crazy, and I shock myself. I do.

I met Eli over a year ago in those said meetings, and though he wore an eye patch and was covered in tattoos, I still found him incredibly, naughtily sexy. We became friends if only for the reason that we are both very affectionate people. And so we would hug and squeeze each other and confuse all the other hipster girls, who once again would cock their heads to the side and think, "The yuppie?"

But then Eli relapsed, and I stopped seeing him around, and I stopped fantasizing about him when I had no one else to think about.

And then Eli reappears. And here is the dangerous part: Eli might wear an eye patch, he might be covered in tattoos, his hair might hang in greasy strings around his face, but Eli is beautiful. As in supermodel beautiful, and it isn't hard to see that he knows that, and he does everything he can to hide it. Or at least to make women like me think he is hiding it. Because that is the danger of beautiful people. It's like the rich. It always seems like they have it all, like they shouldn't have problems, but there is a laundry list of issues inherent to having money. And the one thing it does is always make you question why people want to be with you, what you are getting used for, whether people really love you, or if they just love your cash. And beauty is no different.

Traditionally, the most beautiful people I know are the most fucked up. They grew up with adults always looking at them funny. Either cooing in their direction, or for those who weren't well enough protected, often far, far worse. And then they become adults, and it is the source of their power as much as it is the source of their insanity.

And I know better. I know that I will not be dating Eli. I know that the affections we share, though sweet, are not the beginnings of any sort of romance. But he is so pretty that when he comes back into the meetings and starts turning his attentions on me, I forget the dangers of the beautiful people. I forget that there are finely drawn lines between physical classes and that you will normally be disappointed if you cross them. And I forget that to do the same thing over and over again and expect different results is insanity.

I can't even say it starts innocently enough because it doesn't. By the end of the first night of texting, I am suggesting that I come over with my riding crop and half chaps. And just as I did for the better part of my drinking, I find myself pretending to be someone much tougher and rougher than I actually am. Because as the texting exchange gets dirtier, as the ante keeps going up, and my bravado with it, I have promised things I don't know even know how to do. By 4:00 p.m. the following day I realize that I am no longer a woman who can go over to a strange man's apartment and do things with a riding crop without paying a heavy price.

What I could once get away with while drunk doesn't work quite as well sober. There's no boozy brain to fall back into and that is why I call Eli and tell him that I cannot come over. I can already tell what I am going to feel like the day after—the guilt, the remorse, the shame.

And then I get the text message, "Why don't you come over and watch a movie with me. If I give you an Eskimo kiss, it will feel organic and not something weird and planned. No riding crops allowed." And I destroy the good decision in the space of one text. Because I don't read, "it (meaning sex) will feel organic." I read, "watch a movie with me... I give you an Eskimo kiss," and I get excited. I want so desperately to curl up on a couch with some lovely man and watch a movie and eat popcorn and be sweet and adoring to each other. And so, I respond, "Perfect."

I go over, and he gives me the tour of the ramshackle guest house where he lives. Eli builds bicycles when he isn't working at a psychiatric ward. He makes us popcorn in a frying pan. He shows me the plant that he has nearly killed a thousand times. And when I tell him about my obsession to learn how to build furniture, he pulls out books that he has on woodworking and joinery, and we look at pictures of different types of wood and benches and chairs.

We watch an old Czech film with no real plot or dialogue or even narrative for that matter. We eat our popcorn, and I think, as we watch the lead actress stare dolefully at the camera, that this is probably the type of woman who interests Eli. Quiet and mysterious and incredibly beautiful, but in a creepy way. Or maybe that's just what I think about Eli. Either way we are leaning against each other, and I like it. He makes fun of me for dropping popcorn on myself, and it's odd, but for someone who smells like he hasn't showered in a while, I can tell Eli likes things in an oddly ordered fashion.

We finish the popcorn, and before I can even say, "That was good," he puts the bowl down on the coffee table and is all over me. The kissing is pretty darn nice, but I don't want this to go further.

I pull away. "Eli, look, I want to keep this G-rated."

"What does that mean?" he asks.

And with all my little heart, I say, "Pants on."

"Okay." And then he is on top of me again.

Someone once told me that the minute you sit on a guy's bed, you might as well just take your clothes off right there. Because basically, you're screwed. Which is why when Eli stands up, takes my hand, and leads me into his bedroom, I know better. I know what the results are going to be here, and I don't want them. I don't want to have sex with this man. I don't want to add another number to my notch. I just want him to hold me and tell me that I am beautiful and fall asleep to him kissing my back.

"I have herpes," I blurt. I don't know why I think this will help, but it does. Because though Eli's bed is adorned with a set of five-point restraints, apparently herpes is far more terrifying.

"That's okay," he tells me. "We can do other things."

But I don't want to do other things. I want to go home. There is something in me that doesn't trust Eli anymore, and I get up to use the restroom and try to figure out what I am going to do. I stand in Eli's dirty bathroom. It reeks of cat piss and a dirty litter box that I am tempted to scoop. There are urine stains around the toilet and tooth paste is caked all over the mirror in which I am staring, trying to figure out what kind of woman I am. Because I want desperately to be able to go into Eli's bedroom, give him a kiss on the forehead, put my shoes on, and go home. I just wanted to watch a movie. I didn't want this.

I take a deep, slow breath. I walk out of the bathroom and into Eli's bedroom. The lights are now out, and Eli sits on the edge of the bed.

"Come here," he tells me. I want to leave, but my legs are walking toward him, and my lips are against his, and then as he softly pushes my shoulders down, I am on my knees, and all I can think is, "I want to go home now. I want to go home."

But I don't. In fact, I don't even remember the next few minutes. I feel nothing but darkness, and though I can hear him moaning in the distance, I know that what is happening in this moment is very, very wrong.

Eli falls back on the bed. And I slump down like a rag doll. It takes him a moment to realize that something might be wrong with me. I am not crying out loud, but somewhere deep inside I am sobbing.

"Come here," he says again. And I get on the bed. I hope that he will hold me, that he will pay me in compliments, but he doesn't. I lie down next to him, and instantly he is asleep. And I feel like I did so many years before, lying in that bed with Oliver. Lying there, wanting so much more than this and knowing that I have once again given away a part of me for very little in return.

Nearly four years before, I turned twenty-seven. I was in the midst of my affair with Oliver and had decided that I would turn over a new leaf. I would quit smoking. I would quit cocaine. I would quit drinking during the week. And I would become the woman that I thought Oliver wanted me to be, and maybe I would get to keep him. But then my birthday party arrived, as did the cocaine and the cigarettes and the booze, and my new leaf failed to turn.

The day after my party, I woke up with a stuffed nose and bloodshot eyes and a broken heart. I was in Oliver's bed; he was already awake, reading for work in his living room, and I knew he was slowly but surely backing out. Though he had joined my party for the last several months, he was merely on a vacation on the island that had become my life. And it was time for him to go back to work. That morning at breakfast as we sat across from each other at a crowded Hollywood restaurant like any other couple, he asked between a bite of my omelet and a request for salt, "You wanna go to a hotel tonight?"

And just as casually I said, "Sure, why not?"

But I knew then what I could not admit. Oliver wasn't looking for a romantic night for two. Sure, we might have had some in the beginning before my addictions became so apparent, and the nights became increasingly tawdry. Nights where we lay in bed, drinking wine and listening to Bob Dylan, where his lips slipped around mine, and I could always see his eyes in the dark. That was there too. Even as we sat at that restaurant on that crowded Saturday morning. But more often we got an eight ball of cocaine, we partied with friends, and we tried desperately to hold on to each other through it all.

We got to the Rock 'n' Roll Hyatt in the afternoon, and the coke dealer made his first drop off right before sundown. By the end of the night, I lay there in our bed, watching as the sun crept through our tightly drawn curtains. I looked down at Oliver as he slept, and I knew there was no going back. Here was the one thing that I wanted, that I loved more than anything else, and I kept behaving in ways that only pushed him away, that only made me dangerous in his eyes, and not the safe harbor I had wanted to be for him ever since I was seven, and he came asking for my help. I looked at him, and I saw the boy he once was, the man he had become, and ultimately the father he would one day be. And I knew I would lose him. I knew that he would be okay. That he would stop this endless party, and mine would just continue. I looked at him, and I knew I had to change.

Eli and I settle into sleeping position, and I try to ignore that I don't want to be here. Eli begins to rub my back and kisses my shoulder, and I get what I wanted. But it isn't worth the price. And it never has been. Because at a certain point, I stopped looking for sex in the arms of one-night stands; I was simply looking to be held. And even though Eli's embrace is comforting, it's also counterfeit.

The next morning, Eli gets in the shower. When I realize he is not getting out until after I leave, I say goodbye. He pops his head out and tells me, "Hey, take that woodworking book with you."

Somehow the book is supposed to balance things out. And if I were a hooker, which I pretty much feel like, I have just sold myself for *The Complete Illustrated Guide to Joinery*.

I get home, shower, and call Mimi. And she meets me at a local meeting because that's just the type of friend she is. We walk into my meeting, and immediately I see Jimmy Voltage. As the way things go, he is the speaker for that day, and I have never heard him share his story before. As he does, I realize how different and yet how alike we are. I listen to him tell his own tale of bad decisions and regrettable mistakes, and I remember that we are not perfect.

Afterward, I go and hug Jimmy, and he pulls me in for one of the biggest, tightest, safest hugs ever. And I smile up at my friend, and I say, "I loved your share."

And there is nothing counterfeit about it. Just as I did with Jimmy so many months before, I know I need to pick myself up and brush myself off. Jimmy invites me to see the new house he lives in, and though I can tell we will only be friends, I also know that this is how things change. We fuck up. We get hurt. We move on. And we try to do it better the next time around.

Date Forty-Three: Love Will Tear Us Apart

Fantasy has never done anything but disappoint me. In fact, I can almost guarantee something will not happen once I have a fantasy about it. But it never stops me. Oh no, the many magical moments, the great Oscar-winning scenes, the music videos of my life are some of my many great distractions, and quite possibly, fantasy is my most unconquered addiction. Lately, I have been driving around, listening to "Love Will Tear Us Apart," by Joy Division, and I have been envisioning the fabulous way in which this book will end. I was telling Siren recently that I do not know which man will ultimately get to star in the final scene, but I do like scripting it.

I almost want to ask Ben what he thinks will be my ending, but I don't. Though I feel unreasonably comfortable with him, I am not sure if that's in a romantic way or just in a jocular one. We have now been e-mailing for weeks—all of which have been long and funny and filled with literary jags and some serious details.

One thing becomes clear: we will not be able to continue communicating at this pace without getting a little worn out. I went to a wedding last Saturday, and I wondered as I watched the beautiful couple join a perfect union whether Ben will make the move and at least ask me to coffee. I sat at a table of mostly single girls, and I knew that we were all thinking about when it will be our turn. The night was thick, the weather warm, and the bride and groom happily, giddily in love. I watched them at their table for two, and I wondered if that's what I want.

"So, are you looking to get a husband out of the book?" Ben sits across the table from me, stirring his coffee. Two days after the wedding, Ben asks me out. Since Ben is also a writer, he does it under the pretense that we can, "ya know, talk about our books."

I shake my head. "I was actually just hoping for a three- to six-month relationship."

He laughs. "Isn't a year of dating an awful lot to go through just to get a three- to six-month relationship?"

I rethink my offer. "Okay, then, nine months."

Because the truth is I don't see myself with Ben for much longer than that. I could see us breaking down each other's walls a bit, letting one another in, teaching each other a thing or two about our diverse interests, and ultimately just not seeing eye to eye on enough things to go much further.

Ben takes me to the cake-filled café where I went for my first date in this little experiment, bringing me full circle. As we navigate the crowded restaurant and shift around the heavy wrought-iron chairs, and Ben gets back up because his coffee isn't warm enough, and I try to find honey, and my tea cup is shaking because I am nervous, and Ben forgets to get utensils, and I still haven't found the honey, I am just grateful that we have made it through all the pitfalls of social anxiety to actually make it to our table.

When we walked to the restaurant from our meeting, the sidewalk got a little narrow, and I found Ben walking at least three feet in front of me, and I couldn't help but feel strange. Why would he leave me behind? Even as the sidewalk widens, and there is room for the both of us, Ben moves at a pace that is too fast for me. And I am not about to break into a trot just to keep up.

"So, did you ever end up finding some honey?" he asks, referring to my tea.

"No. It was too hard. And I was already holding a cup of steaming water, and I don't know, I just get nervous," I admit.

"Do you want honey?"

I nod my head. "Yes, please."

Ben smiles and gets up to find me some, and for a moment I forget about the fast walking and his sarcasm. I wonder whether Ben's attitude of being jaded and aloof is really just a front for the kind person struggling to get out. He tells me off the bat, "I feel a little guarded around you."

"Why? Because I'm writing a book?" I ask.

"Yeah."

I think he means emotionally, and so I explain, "Really, Ben, it's not as much about the dates as it is about me, about my own lessons and observations and growth."

"Yeah, I get that," he says. "The thing is, I'm writing a book too. I don't want you using any of my stories." God love him for being honest, but really?

Ben tells me how when he was eighteen, he lived an entire year making decisions with a flip of a coin. He was already sober at the time, so he agrees he could probably chalk it up more to youthful folly than actually being fucked up. But almost every decision that year was made by the toss of one very fateful quarter.

"It was my higher power," he explains. And so he decided not to go to college right away (tails); he decided to break up with his girlfriend (also tails); he decided to move to Israel for six months (heads); and he decided to sleep with his best friend's girlfriend (heads, again). When I hear this I am in awe—what an incredibly ridiculous form of faith. To truly give up all power to some seemingly insignificant quarter and then to follow suit on it seems like exactly the type of ruthless bravery I have been searching for in another.

"I still kind of live that way," Ben says with a shrug. And I realize two things: one, I will use that story anyway; and two, it might not be the allegory I wished it would be. Because that's the thing. Ben is fine with going wherever the flow takes him. In fact, he seems so nonchalant about whether he finds love or passion or the house and kids, I wonder whether he will ever be able to stop flipping that coin, not caring about the outcome.

Ben and I walk back to our cars and hug. I can feel that something is there, some spark of intimacy and knowing. Much like the reflection I once so desperately sought, I see myself in Ben and him in me.

I get in my car and see that my dad has called. I call him back because, just that day, I bought my ticket to Texas. He answers the phone, but I can barely hear him.

"Dad?" I shout.

"Hold on." There are loud music and laughter and women's voices in the background. It sounds like a saloon. It takes a moment for the noise to die down, and then I can hear him.

"Hey, K." I can tell he got my message. I can tell he is excited. "I'm in Mexico tonight. And God it's beautiful here. The stars, the moon...we'll come down here for a night when you visit, okay?"

I smile because I am just as excited. "That sounds great, Daddy. And it's perfect. Because I've decided that you're gonna be my fiftieth date, so we'll have to have it in Mexico."

"Oh, I'm gonna be your best date."

"I know you will, Dad." And though I still feel a little awkward here, I know he will.

I tell him that I am flying into Dallas, but that I will be able to spend two to three days at the farm. Though he wants me to come for a whole week, I am learning not too rush so quickly into things. We hang up the phone as I arrive at my own house. I walk home, down my favorite street, and I look up at the stars and the moon my father and I share, and I flip my coin.

Date Forty-Four: The Magic of Growing Up

Three weeks after my night with Eli, Noelle calls me into her office. I have not spoken to Ben since our night out for tea, and I am beginning to feel that this adventure isn't getting easier. I am not sure if she can sense the crack in my spirit, but when she offers me her home for July Fourth weekend, I smile for the first time in a week. I tell my mom about Noelle's house, and it only takes a few minutes on the Internet for us to do something we have never done before. My mom and Nana will both be coming out that weekend to spend it with me, in Noelle's La Cañada and in my Los Angeles.

The next day, I go to my agency's staff retreat, feeling as though neither of these opportunities are going to save me from the disappointment I have been carrying around lately. But that's the funny thing about faith—it will always show up if you make room for it.

I am sitting in the retreat, bored. It is at the Los Angeles Cathedral. I look down at the agenda and am pleased to see that the next portion will be a client panel, meaning some of our clients will be coming to speak to us. They are parents of our children, teens from our youth center, young mothers and grateful fathers. As one of our clients speaks, telling us that our agency is the bright light in their dark world, that they would not be able to survive without the work we do, that they are so grateful to us for making their children's worlds a safer place, I see that bright light. And I know that I might make my mistakes, but I also make this. I am part of something wonderful. After the panel, a new presenter comes on to discuss child abuse. I walk outside and find three of our younger panelists sitting in the lobby. They cannot hear this part, these truths, these horrors of childhood that I fear some of them might have already endured.

Since they are bored, I offer to take them on a tour of the Cathedral. One of the younger boys, Michael, tells me he has never been, and we all walk over together. I have known Michael since he was eight, and as he approaches fifth grade, I am beginning to understand what it means to watch children grow up. That there is a magic to seeing these young lives mature. Michael takes my hand as we walk into the chapel.

I do not attend Church. I might have been born Roman Catholic, but outside of the traits of sexual shame and familial guilt inherent to its principles, I do not practice anything close to its demands. But as we kneel down on the padded bench, it doesn't matter what I believe. I sit next to these beautiful young children, who without the right education and the right direction will spend their lifetimes on their knees. They bow their heads, and there the four of us pray.

Two weeks later, I show up at Lidia's and immediately see that the "For Sale" sign is down. I am saddened by this. I love Lidia's house, with its Prius and work truck in the driveway, the aquarium in the foyer, and the large rambling front yard that I stare out at while talking with her. I ask if she is sad, and she says, "Oh no, not at all. I've found the perfect place." She tells me about her new home, set off a dirt road up in Box Canyon deep in the hills around Chatsworth. She says it's like entering a different world, and I can see in her eyes that this is all a good change. The divorce, the move, the next stage of her own journey.

I tell Lidia how I ended up at Eli's house, and I tell her what happened there.

"Why do you think you were so affected?" Lidia asks.

I look out the window, and then I smile at Lidia with tears in my eyes. "Oliver."

Oliver. The ghost of this story. The memory I have yet to expunge. Lidia asks if I still fantasize about having a future with this man I have not seen in two years. But I don't. I think Oliver wanted someone else. I imagine that the woman he marries cooks dinner every night using organic vegetables and amazing sauces. She plays the piano and works in an interior design firm. She probably has an absentee father or some troubled element in her childhood, but funnels it into being comfortable around a large, wood island in the middle of her Spanish-tiled kitchen. I imagine a lot of silk and linen.

Lidia has me get on the floor. And I cannot figure out which stone to choose so I choose two. Lidia places them on me, and I realize that this is no longer uncomfortable for me. In fact, I find myself channeling energy and spirit a lot more on my own these days. The energy has been giving me strength, and though sometimes that strength may be clumsy and a little messy, it's still there. As I lie down, I tell Lidia about one morning in La Cañada when I went hiking with my mother while we house sat. We had brought Rocky and were walking back to Noelle's when I told my mom about a vision I had while I was dating Oliver. He had asked me what I wanted from my life, and I told him that I saw myself standing at the edge of a yard, overlooking a cliff, staring out at the Mediterranean Sea, with two children standing on each side of me. They are my children, and we are vacationing at a home somewhere in Europe. In the vision, I hold their hands and stand in front of a white fence that lines the edge of the yard. I turn around and watch as my husband walks out of the house to meet us.

"Everyone has that dream, Kristen," Mom replied.

"Do you have that dream?" I asked. She said no.

"I doubt that everyone dreams as big as to think that they will vacation on the Mediterranean," I explained. "But it's really not about the location, Mom. It's more about what I'm looking for, about what I want. I want a life filled with magic."

And as if on cue, Rocky sat down and would not move. My mom turned around to look at him. We were worried he was tired or sick, and then we looked up, and our breath stopped short. A deer stood there, having emerged from the woods. A doe peeked out from behind him. They skipped across the road not ten feet from where we stood and leaped into the crags of the mountain on the other side. The doe disappeared, but the buck stopped. He turned around and looked back. He looked directly at me.

And I know that's what Lidia and I are working on: magic. Oliver believed in magic, and maybe that's why I still hold such a candle to him. But I also know that I cannot be true to the magic if I keep pulling disappearing acts. I need to stand strong like that deer. And despite the barking dog, despite the intimidating humans, despite all my fears, real and false, I need to stop, hold the gaze, and speak the truth.

I lie on the floor; Lidia sits over me. "Kristen, we are made of mother earth. And there is nothing that we can do with our flesh that she has not given us the right to. We can throw out those dogmas of our childhood. We can have faith that we are all cut from the same cloth. You can do whatever you want as long as you are okay with it. As long as it is part of your truth."

"I know." I am beginning to cry.

"Are you now ready to speak that truth?"

For a long time that's why I drank and used. So I could leave; so I could find the abyss. Lidia asks me when I first checked out, and I can't even tell her. I can see myself through the years doing it. At four, at five, at seven, at eight, eleven, twelve, sixteen, last week. I leave, but my choices and consequences are made in my absence.

It seems an awfully unfair way to live. And certainly not one that is going to help me find, channel, and create that energy I now see everywhere in my life. It just won't.

"Are you ready to be present now?" Lidia asks. "To join the council of your ancestors, to create your destiny, to be a real part of this world, even when you are scared, when you are hurt, when you most want to run away?"

I tell her yes, and she asks me to make the request myself. And I do. "Great Spirit, council of my ancestors, I ask for the strength, for the courage, to live my life here, now. To be present, to fulfill my destiny, to experience every lesson along this great journey."

The energy is thick in the room and tears stream down my face. I can hear Lidia getting emotional, and I realize that just as she is healing others, so she is being healed. And it makes what we do such a beautiful process. Because our energy goes both ways, it goes all around, and it fills the room.

And then I let it go. I let it all go. Fear. Pain. Oliver. Magic. Doubt. My future. I let the energy flow out, and I feel more real than I ever have before. Lidia and I close the session, and I get up. We turn on the lights and open up the blinds, and I don't even know what world I am in.

She stands in front of me and says, "You are the last energy session I have scheduled to take place here before I move."

I could be bashful and pretend like it isn't perfect, but it is, and so I speak my truth: "What a beautiful conclusion." And she agrees.

247

1 2 3 4 5 6 7 8 9 10 11 12 13 14 15 16 17 18 19 20 21 22
23 24 25 26 27 28 29 30 31 32 33 34 35 36 37
38 39 40 41 42 43 44 **45** 46 47 48 49 50 51

Date Forty-Five: The Sparkling Ribbon of Time, Act II

I am sitting in the button-down shirt I wore today and my underwear. A crumpled tissue sits by me. My eyes are swollen. My heart hurts. And I feel like I might have had one of the best dates of my life.

As I tell Oliver as we walk past the Sparkling Ribbon of Time at the Observatory, "Some dates are romantic. And some are truth-seeking."

"So this is a date?" he asks.

I shoot him a glance and smile. "Yes, but this is a truth-seeking one."

I called him yesterday morning after my 7:00 a.m. meeting. I leave a strong, professional, very dignified message, and he calls me back almost immediately. We talk for half an hour, and he is the same man I knew so many years ago. The same poetic rat-a-tat, the passion, the intimate knowing that always made me feel like he was on the inside of my brain. We hang up with plans to meet up, and my eyes swell with tears. Because I know instantly that I am still in love with him. And that no matter what, our date will end as the truth-seeking variety and not the romantic. At first, I say that it cannot end any other way. That I cannot go down that road again. But then I am talking to my sponsor, and she asks me why not.

Lidia also asked me that, and I begin to ask the same. Why not? Why can't this story end the way most people like them to—happily? The long lost romance reignites. The flame turns back on. Prince

Charming returns home. But that was always the problem—I was never Oliver's home.

We meet the following afternoon at the Observatory. I set it up that way because I have so far taken everyone I love there, and Oliver is no different. I also love a good setting. I get there ten minutes late because I have been at the stables, and I need to spend some time with Arrow before I can spend this time with Oliver. I text him as much. I get there, and I don't see him anywhere. I go inside and pull out my phone and see a message from him: "I'm jumpin." I think he must not have gotten my text. I think he is leaving. I go outside to call him, realizing how cruel it would be if I finally show up, present, whole and ready to go, and because I am ten minutes late, I will have missed him.

Thankfully, he is there. And after a couple of minutes, we find each other and go inside. I show him the ribbon of time. I want to stop and talk with him about the vastness of the universe and all the things that fuel my flame. But we are there for one reason—to talk about a little romance that happened between two people four years ago. Nothing more. And though we might lean slightly into each other, though we might still walk in perfect step, I can feel him holding back, and I know that there is someone in his life. But I don't ask. Not yet.

Because I don't want to know yet. I want to pretend for a moment that there might just be a happy ending here. We get water. I chat with the cashier and offer to pay, and I watch as Oliver bends down nervously to pick up a quarter he has dropped. And I realize that I am calm and cool and strong in this, and that my dear friend is not. I am in this moment, standing in my riding boots and my tight jeans, standing with this man who is real and next to me and everything I have ever wanted. I know that he can tell that I have changed, that he can see it in the way I smile, the way I speak, the way I lead us outside and take control when before I had none. And maybe that's what is making him nervous.

We try to find a quiet spot, and we end up on the observation deck, overlooking the entire span of this great city where we met. I pull out the last chapter I wrote from when I was at Lidia's, and I read it to him. Because in it, it says everything I could say, or want to say. It also opens us up to saying everything that needs to be said.

And we do.

Oliver tells me about me, about what I was like when we were together. He leans up against a pillar, and I can feel his energy. Not in an explosive way, though, just in the solid way that he is telling me things that have been sitting around for years waiting to be said. I listen to him as though he is describing what someone was like as a child. Because I don't really remember what I was like before I got sober. I know some things, but I forget sometimes that I wasn't all bad. That people loved me.

I ask, "Did you love me?"

He doesn't hesitate as he holds my gaze. "Yes. Absolutely."

Oh, God. Oh, God.

For years I never knew, and yet I always knew. I press forth. "Then, what happened two years ago? When we went out to dinner, and I stayed at your house?"

He is prepared for me to ask this question. "I don't know, sweetheart. I just got scared. I can't tell you why. I just did." He pauses, "And I think I might have just begun dating someone at the time. I think that's when it started."

And I already know as I ask, "Are you in a relationship?" He nods his head. I try not to let it hit me. I had prepared myself for this. And then for some reason, I had unprepared myself for it. So it hits me. As I look into his eyes, as I talk honestly with him, I feel her presence in our conversation. Oliver tells me about her. How he knew her for years, how she has brought a quiet wholeness to his life. How she helps him to focus and listen and do the right thing.

And I know right then what I have known all along: that Oliver found himself a schmoo. He tells me the woman I painted for him wasn't quite right, and I agree. Because I thought he would have ended up going a little exotic. But that was silly of me, because that's not what he would have wanted at all. He would have wanted to go home.

Oliver and I revisit memory lane for a bit. A few great kisses, a few hungry moments. He tells me how he has been reading about St. Francis of Assisi. Oliver always loved telling me stories. We had both hidden in books when we were kids. Once we met, we found ourselves again under the sheets, making a tent, whispering late at night when the rest of the world was asleep. We made up stories about our future; we peeked out as dawn began to rise; and we pretended the night would never end. And then we left each other, before we ever got a chance to see what happened next. But Oliver's stories, the poets he introduced to me—they were the keys that unlocked my sobriety and saved my life.

Oliver tells me about the small village in which St. Francis once lived. At one point the villagers found themselves attacked by a local wolf, and so they went to St. Francis and asked the great man for help. Apparently, this wolf had been eating their children. St. Francis went to the wolf and gave him a mound of bread, and the wolf ate it. He gave the wolf a mound of meat, and the wolf ate that too. The next day, St. Francis walked into town with the wolf at his side. He took a piece of bread out of his satchel and handed it to the wolf as they walked. The villagers all asked, "How did you stop this wolf from eating our children?" And St. Francis told them, quite plainly, "I fed him."

Just as he did so many times before, Oliver holds up the looking glass for me and shows me my metaphor. Because I am the hungry wolf. Walking along, starving for love like I once had, with Oliver and with others. And all I want is a piece of bread. But for some reason, they always fear that I am looking to eat their children. Oliver jokes that his current relationship isn't like the torrid tryst we had. I can't help but laugh even though it hurts. "That's a good thing, Oliver."

I look down and out across Los Angeles.

Our time is up and as much as I want to tell Oliver about my life, I think we've said enough. As we turn to go, he asks, "How do you know if you have a drinking problem?"

He had mentioned earlier that he was currently not drinking, and I knew something was up. I don't know what to say. I don't know that I can be responsible for opening that door. Or maybe it's the only thing I can do. So I tell him, "You know when it no longer works for you, and yet you still can't stop doing it."

But it sounds so cliché and easy that it gets tossed off in our conversation.

What I want to say is that seeing the ravages of alcoholism does not prevent you from having it. That is one of the first delusions that must be smashed. And then you go to a meeting, and you listen, and you get the book, and if you got *The Shining*, you don't kid yourself that there is any other way to do it and still live a happy, healthy, and spiritually productive life. And if anything else, by doing that sort of legwork, you will know whether you have a drinking problem or not.

That's it. That's all. The rest is up to you, my lovely friend.

Oliver walks me to my car. He reaches out and holds my hand, but in a good, kind way. We stop and hug, and there is no major chemical reaction or explosion, just two people who know each other enormously well. He tells me that we don't need to be strangers, but out of respect to him, his relationship, me, we do. I tell him I will e-mail him this chapter as he has asked, but otherwise, I will see him again in two years to catch up. I hold on to his hand as I open up my car door. I cannot look at him as I say, "I will always love you, Oliver." My voice cracks, and I hold on tight as he replies, "I will always love you too."

I get in the car. He stands there watching me go. I walk home tonight with excruciating pain and love for this world. I notice every leaf, every limb, every splash of light, and in a way, I trip the light fantastic. I feel set free. I feel incredibly blessed that I had the chance to know Oliver. And that we might always love one another. And I wonder what my destiny might be. Because though I finally showed up present and whole and ready to go, I grew up too late, and Oliver had already left. And if the universe has decided that they've got something for me that is bigger than that man, I can't help but look forward to how this sparkling ribbon of time pans out.

253

1 2 3 4 5 6 7 8 9 10 11 12 13 14 15 16 17 18 19 20 21 22
23 24 25 26 27 28 29 30 31 32 33 34 35 36 37
38 39 40 41 42 43 44 45 **46** 47 48 49 50 51

Date Forty-Six: Same Story, Different People

"Don't you miss it?" Mimi asks me as we stand, out of breath, at one of the highest peaks of our morning walk. We stare out at the sunrise view of the sloping hills and the Hollywood sign and that enigmatic Observatory. Mimi and I have been talking about romance.

"I do," I tell her. "I miss it all the time. I don't know. I think the hardest part is not being able to look forward to someone's call."

And it is. There is nothing more heart pumping than that little red light on my phone that tells me that someone has called or sent a text message. And I know that I am in a low point of romance when that light blinks, and there isn't even a shudder to be had that "he" might have called. Over the last few weeks, "he," as in Ben, has not been calling.

But ever since I met with Oliver, I just don't know that I need to be worried about that little red light. I kind of feel like love might be bigger than that. I can cry over losing that man for the rest of my life, or I can realize that he was the railroad switch that led me onto the next path. And maybe that's all relationships are really for: to teach us how to live in this world.

And so I am willing to bet that there will also be a lesson with Ben. It's like Mimi says, "That's a very interesting relationship you have there. I'm confused, but we'll just have to see."

And we will. We will just have to see.

On Saturday afternoon I am sitting in my bathroom, painting my toenails, getting ready to go out that night, when the phone rings.

"Hey, so how's the book coming?" Ben asks.

"Good. Amazing. I am in editing mania."

"I hear that."

"You too?" I ask.

"Yeah, I've just been polishing up some pieces."

"Oh." I get the feeling Ben does a lot of polishing, more than I am currently doing to my toes. That the polishing is better than actually going out there and making it happen. That it's safer that way.

"So I have an idea," Ben tells me. "I go to this writers' salon downtown every month, and they're having one tomorrow. You wanna come with me?" And that's how I go from not talking to Ben at all to sitting outside my apartment building, waiting for him to pick me up.

He pulls into the fire lane, and I bound down the stairs and into his car. I am tan. I have on makeup. My cleavage is obvious. But no compliments are coming from Ben. Instead, we laugh and joke and make a few nervous comments as we drive to the salon. We park across the street, and as we're making our way across the five-lane road that separates us from the studio, I watch Ben take off ahead of me. I want to tell him to slow down, to wait for me, but we're not there yet, and I know it.

We go inside and wait our turn to read. I look over to where Ben sits, and I try to figure out what I think of this strange man who keeps appearing in my life. He is wearing a ripped T-shirt and shorts and obviously has no interest in trying to impress me with how he is dressed. But again, I look at his tan calves, and his strong forearms, and I want to forget his dumb perverted jokes and the fact that he looks at me like I am just any other girl. Because I know he knows that I am not.

He gets up to read his piece, and he might as well be reading a chapter from this book. The story, the humor, the tempo, the loneliness. The looking for love in all the wrong places. Ben and I go out for coffee afterward. I am not sure if we are on a date, and when the bill comes, I pay for it because I get the feeling we're not. We talk about our work and our lives and our dreams and our childhoods and our families. I don't really go into the situation with my father, which is a clear sign to me that I am becoming a healthier individual. This night, I keep my big story to myself.

But it might just be that I really don't know what to say about him anyway. Because on Friday my father calls me to tell me that he is leaving Texas to go home to Connecticut for a couple of weeks. I am supposed to visit the following month. "I think I'm gonna try to stay there, K," he tells me.

"Why? What's wrong with Texas?"

"It's just really hard, Kris. They treat the animals so terrible, and the workers..."

"Last week you loved it. I don't understand. You have any other job offers?"

"I'll probably go back," he says, though I can hear the lie in his voice. "But I needed a vacation."

"Oh, okay, a vacation." The man has been playing handball in the federal pen for the last thirty years. I find a vacation laughable. But more than that, so much more than that, he is once again breaking the date that has been twenty-five years in the making. And though they are screaming in my head, I cannot say the words I most need to say: "But I have a ticket to come visit you."

He hears it in my voice, though, in the thick quiver I have put up to hold back the tears. "I'll probably still be there when you come to visit, K. And if not, you can just come to Connecticut."

"Mmm, well, we'll see. Nana and Uncle Tom and Vic are already expecting me to come to Texas. And that's why I bought the ticket..."

"Well, if it's about money, Kris..."

"No, Dad, it's not about money," I snap. I can't take this. I don't want to take this. I have lived my whole life being deceived and disappointed by this man. I am so tired of being promised that he is coming home, and then just when I finally decide to trust, when I finally buy the lie about my best date yet, he fucks me over. Again. He doesn't say anything because he knows what he has done, and there's just not much a parent can say to that.

"Yeah," I mutter. "Well, enjoy your vacation."

I hang up the phone, and I breathe in deep because I have spent too many tears crying over this man. And I have a job to go to, and a heart to heal, and I am too old to believe in some Santa Claus Daddy that doesn't know how to be a real father. I talk to my mom the next day, and I tell her that I think it is absolutely beautiful that since telling Nana that my dad might not be there, Uncle Tom and Uncle Vic have both called to let me know that they want to be my date for that weekend.

Two days later, Ben and I end up seeing each other at a meeting, and afterward, we talk again for an hour outside. About our work, our books, our feelings about romance. We have so much fun, and I wonder whether the long talks and shared beliefs are what is real—that they are the steel that creates those railroad switches, those points in the road that ask for us to change. And I know that as Ben tries to hide behind his walls of sarcasm and indifference that I can teach him as much as he can teach me. We agree to edit each other's work, and it is an intimacy that we breach. He will read all of this. And I am not scared. I am not scared to say that I do not know who this Ben character is, or what role he will play in my journey.

I know that we can only love as much as we are willing to be hurt. And so I must be open to that, as much as I need to protect myself from people who don't know how to love. Ben and I don't act like we might actually be attracted to each other, but I am okay with becoming friends and allowing the rest to happen as it should. Because as much as I like believing the fantasy, I know that it only leads to my disappointment. And I think I need to take my time to find out if a man is willing to show up when no one else will or run just when you let him in. And I can't go another twenty-five years not knowing the difference.

Date Forty-Seven: I Win

I don't win things. I just wasn't born with that kind of luck. I remember that by the end of elementary school everyone had won a school raffle or classroom toy giveaway or a game of bingo at least once. But not me, and by the time I was in high school, I would barely look at my ticket as they would call out the numbers to whatever raffle or drawing was being conducted. I know that there is a physical principle of luck and that it has as much to do with time and place as it actually has to do with fortune. But that's the thing—I have been ten minutes late my whole life, and so my little ticket would always flutter into the raffle bin at the wrong time. I would fail to show up for the writing contest, the big promotion, the man of my dreams. Until now. Because I feel like I might be more on time these days. Not perfect. Still a minute or two late, but close enough. Close enough that in the space of one week, I win thirty-three dollars and another shot at love.

On Friday night I am again set up by Mimi. I think she is giving up hope and is now just throwing darts aimlessly at the wall, hoping that something hits.

Joey is a graphic novelist with a forward-moving future in screenwriting. From the e-mail correspondence between him and Mimi, I pictured someone funny, with a good body, a slight Brooklyn accent, and a boyish face. I realized later that what I had pictured was actually Joey from *Friends*, but that's another issue.

Joey invites me to go to a Dodgers game with him, and I immediately accept. I like baseball, but even more than that, I like the fact that this guy is already asking me out for something more interesting than coffee. But then he starts sending me clips of Dodger games, and by the eleventh YouTube link, I find out that Joey is a Dodger fanatic. He has season tickets, goes to every game, and apparently I don't have much of a chance of seeing him anywhere else but there. But I'm okay with that because these dates have stopped being about finding love and have instead become a simple cure for loneliness.

Joey picks me up at work and drives me in my Dodger baseball cap with his Dodger-blue truck to Dodger Stadium. He leads me through the parking lot, past the concessions, and up into our seats, and I feel like I am in a movie. Because these are the kinds of seats that the main characters always have in the romantic comedies about baseball fans. These are Vince Vaughn/Tom Hanks/Jimmy Fallon kinds of seats. We are on the front row in left field, and the grass is bright green, and the sun is just going down, and the air is warm, and I feel like every kid at their first game—nervous and excited and proud to be there.

The field is so close I feel like I could touch it.

Later when I ask Joey if he brings friends to the games often he tells me, "All my friends are already at the game, so not really. Tonight was definitely the first time I brought a woman."

I get the feeling that as long as Joey is sitting at Dodger Stadium with a small group of primarily male Dodger fanatics, that statement probably won't be changing for some time. But he is great to go to a game with, and I think he feels the same way about me. I am up and down, screaming and hollering the entire game. I am asking questions and eating Dodger dogs and desperately trying to get Manny Ramirez to throw me his practice balls. As the game nears the finish we begin debating as to who is going to win the pool at the end of the night. There was a bet at the beginning of the game based on what time the game would end. It was a quarter per bet, and I put in a dollar. I chose four times, one of them being 10:32 p.m. As the game edged closer to 10:30 p.m., I began to get nervous. Sure we were in the top of the ninth and leading; sure we had one out—but two outs in two minutes? I didn't think it would happen. And then there was a man on first, and then there was a ball in the air. And then there was a catch, and one out became three outs. And we looked at the clock, and you got it. 10:32 p.m.

Joey tapes the whole thing and puts it on YouTube, so later I see what happens when someone spends thirty years waiting to win something. Thirty years of watching *The Price Is Right*, thirty years of school and workplace raffles, thirty years of always looking at my number and shrugging my shoulders.

"I WON!!! I WON!!!! I WON!!!" I am jumping in the air; I am screaming; I am high-fiving strangers and hugging Joey. I am handed all thirty-three dollars of my booty, and I am falling over myself. "I'm a Dodgers fan now!" I tell the camera as I spread out the cash in my hands.

The following week, I take my thirty-three dollars, fill my tank with gas, and drive to the new home of one Jimmy Voltage, knowing my luck has changed.

I am going on a three-day, horseback-riding trip into the mountains of the Sierra Nevadas over Labor Day weekend. We will be riding horses all day and camping at night and even getting the chance to fish. I haven't fished since I was fourteen, and fortune really didn't serve me there either. But I want to try again because, though it might have nothing to do with luck, that trip to the Sierras is one of the greatest prizes I have yet to receive in my life. As a bonus, Jimmy Voltage has offered to help me purchase my fishing tackle.

I meet him at his house. I get out of my car, and he is already standing on his porch, waiting for me. He is living in a beautiful two-bedroom home with a Jacuzzi and a backyard, and I can see that he too feels like a winner. He bounds down the stairs and nearly picks me up, and his hug is so big, I quickly find myself wrapped up in his warmth. We haven't spent time alone since we drove back together from Oxnard in November. And ten months later, I stand looking up at him, happy for his life.

"It's what I've always wanted," he tells me. "It's been my dream to have my own house, and now I do."

I smile as he squeezes me tighter and say, "You do."

We go to lunch, and we talk like we never have before. I tell him about my dates and my life and my firm belief that I am exactly where I am supposed to be. He tells me how he has had to let go of looking for the perfect partner. With being obsessed about finding just the right woman for the adventure. The conversation could get really thick here, but we are interrupted by a friend of Jimmy's, and so we let it go.

After our tackle buying trip, I drive Jimmy home, and he tells me about his own trials of online dating. He jokes, "I just get tired of sitting down with women who tell me, 'I drink an enormous of water.' I mean what am I supposed to say to that?"

"Oh, believe me, I get it," I tell him. "There is a point in every single one of my dates where it's just like 'Insert Obama conversation' here, and then we get in their Prius, and everyone's all smart and witty and aware."

"Except it's fake," he says. And I realize that Jimmy Voltage gets it a lot more than I've ever given him credit for.

I smile as I say, "Yes, it is."

We look at each other, and it's not fake—this energy sitting between us in the front seat of my car. Jimmy grabs me in a tight embrace, and I can feel us exhale, and I know that this is something we have both been missing.

"What are you doing this weekend?" he asks, holding onto my arm.

"A couple of things, but I have some time," I answer. He touches my face because we have been here before. And yet we haven't.

"How about I call you up and ask you out on a real date? I want to do it right this time," he says.

I don't hide my enthusiasm because I don't have to hide anything anymore. "I would love that."

"Good. Last year I don't know what happened. I know that there was something really strong between us physically, chemistry I guess, but..." he begins, but I don't let him. I don't know what to say either. Just that in this moment we are exactly where we are supposed to be. We are right on time.

He kisses me but just a nice soft kiss on the lips. Nothing sexual, just romantic. And he gets out of my car, and I drive off. Surprised that in one week I won thirty-three dollars at a Dodger game, but more than that, I won a date to find out who exactly this Jimmy Voltage guy is.

261

1 2 3 4 5 6 7 8 9 10 11 12 13 14 15 16 17 18 19 20 21 22
23 24 25 26 27 28 29 30 31 32 33 34 35 36 37
38 39 40 41 42 43 44 45 46 47 **48** 49 50 51

Date Forty-Eight: The Comedy Show of Errors

The last time I was at Lidia's house she joked as I was walking out, "You're gonna end up being friends with all of them." Though I laughed at the time, I secretly hoped she was wrong. I have enough friends.

Jimmy Voltage and I almost don't make it on what becomes the most highly anticipated date of the year. After our wonderful afternoon together, I wake up the next day, thrilled, excited, overjoyed. I keep checking my cell, waiting for the call, a text message, the red blinking light. But there is nothing. Jimmy had asked me what I was doing that weekend, so I figured he would want to call me by Friday. But he doesn't, and when Saturday rolls around, and I have made other plans, and my phone still hasn't rung, I am in shock. I have never been stood up before. Not like that. I leave Jimmy a message, giving him an opportunity to explain just in case there had been some confusion. And I hear nothing in return. That night I go to Sunset Junction, the annual street festival in our neighborhood. I walk around with friends; I watch a band; I eat a Philly Cheese Steak; we gather at Pazzo for gelato. And then I walk home alone. And I cry. I cry like I haven't in a long time. Because though I have been so happy recently, though I have been so at peace in being single, the reintroduction of Jimmy Voltage jump-started my heart. And now it hurts.

The streets are dark, so I don't hold back. People pass me as I walk, and I can tell they think I've been drinking. Because really, who cries like that so publicly without being drunk? I get home and stare up at the watercolor cheetah on my wall, the one that reminds so much of that magical Otorongo. I pray to that cat for the ability to see the truth in this one, and for the strength to follow it.

Two days later, Jimmy calls me back, filled with confusion and apologies. He says he never got my message; he had never planned for us to go out that weekend; he feels terrible. I don't think Jimmy Voltage is a bad man. I just think he is rather confused. And I think I am better off without him.

The next week I go to dinner with Ben again, and we talk about our books, and I feel pretty good that I have dropped the whole Jimmy Voltage thing. And then I go on the three-day, horseback-riding trip into the mountains, and I fuck it all up. Because while I am riding across desolate landscapes and lush meadows and up snarled mountaintops, while I sit on my mule, Dodger, and survey the beauty of this amazing earth, I realize that some of the most magnificent views are made not because of the world's perfection, but by its imperfections. It is not the pristine glass of the lakes that makes my heart lurch, but the burnt-out trees, the sliding rocks. The disproportionate jags of the cliffs, and my mule, who is the oldest steed in the bunch, and yet the most sure-footed. And then I sleep in near-freezing weather, and I wake up cold the next day, and I want for no one's arms but those of Jimmy Voltage.

So, I call him. Again. The night before my thirty-first birthday. I have just come home from the magical trip into the Sierras; I have just spent the day at work with my four-year-old Princess club; and I am soaring. My life is so perfect in this moment. I call Jimmy with an honesty I have never before expressed.

"I like you, Jimmy. I do. I don't know why. And I don't know if maybe all we're supposed to be is friends here, but I am willing to go on a date to find out," I explain.

There is silence for a moment, which is terrifying, and then he tells me, "I feel the exact same way."

I smile—what a great birthday present.

"Have you been to the Observatory lately?" he asks.

The next night is my birthday, and I go to the gun club with Mimi and Ivan and John and Nat and even my non-date Adam. It is such a gathering of characters that I feel like I am in a movie.

And then I get the message from Jimmy: "So I saw there's this comedy show for Obama on Wednesday night, and I really want to go to it, so let's do that instead of the Observatory."

I flip my phone closed and shake my head. Someone's been thinking. And he's not alone. Because I spent the better part of the weekend working on that script which I have suddenly become so sure of. The romantic points, the serious conversations, the jokes, the clothes, the setting, the choreography, the lighting, the cinematography. It was going to be perfect.

Jimmy was apparently doing his own future thinking, but his was more about how the Observatory was not such a good location after all. So in the space of one week, we go from a romantic night looking at the stars to a bad comedy show on Wilshire where the only redeeming factor is that we donate twenty bucks to Obama. Not what I had in mind.

Jimmy Voltage comes to pick me up, and I walk out my back door to find him standing by his truck, waiting to greet me, because he does have that part down. I expect some starstruck embrace that will make all the work that it took us to get on this date worth it. I expect some loving look that will make us ditch the comedy show and run off together. I expect some soft hand on my face and some loving compliment that washes away the last ten months and puts me firmly into his life.

Instead, I walk out to find my new neighbor flirting with him. When she sees me, I can tell she is embarrassed, and Jimmy and I hug briefly before we get in his truck. I ask Jimmy if he wants to hear one of the chapters about him because I am not very good with coming up with new tricks, and I figured if it were able to put Oliver and me in such an honest place, it might also do the same here. Jimmy crinkles up his face. "Really?"

"Why not? There's nothing bad. You're a good character, Jimmy."

"I know that." His confidence on the matter throws me. "But don't you think it will spoil the salad?" he adds.

I shrug and say, "It's no big deal. You don't have to read it."

I look over at him, and somehow he looks older. He is about to turn forty, and he is still smoking, and his face looks grayish, and his sideburns are too long, and in a quick flash, I realize: I might not actually be attracted to this man.

Jimmy just stares straight ahead. "Man, look at this traffic." And that's the end of that.

We go to the comedy show, which sucks. So we leave the comedy show and go to dinner instead. We talk about politics and our childhoods and the renovations recently completed at the Mexican restaurant where we are eating. Oddly enough, we go to the same place we did back when we were dating and thought we might be falling in love. That night we looked at each other all starry-eyed over the table, and Jimmy came and sat next to me at the end so we could continue kissing. This time we are both just a little bored. Halfway through my meal, I find myself desperately fighting off a number of yawns because here is what I always knew and forgot: though Jimmy and I have some amazing chemistry, though our bodies fit very nicely next to one another's, though our lives are similar and our passions not altogether different, we severely lack the ability to make easy conversation. It's like we're both working from the same symphony; we're both playing the same chords, but in completely different notes, with completely different tempos. And we just don't harmonize. And I don't know why. I wish I did. I couldn't tell you if you paid me a million dollars.

Jimmy drops me off, and though we have a tender, romantic moment with soft kisses and big hugs, I know as he says, "See you later, Kristen," that we won't try this again. It doesn't make sense to try this again. We have tried it enough, and we always ended up feeling the same way—that there is something missing.

The next night I go to the stables to work, and as I lean against Arrow, staring out at the amazing view, at the world's perfections and imperfections, I realize that because there is no man in my life, I have had to find new things to do to keep the loneliness at bay. And just like in high school, when the goal of meeting boys got me on the swim team and track team and debate club, now, not meeting boys has gotten me to the stables and into the Sierra Nevadas and on this intense, magical adventure I sent myself on almost a year ago when I decided that my life had to change.

1 2 3 4 5 6 7 8 9 10 11 12 13 14 15 16 17 18 19 20 21 22
23 24 25 26 27 28 29 30 31 32 33 34 35 36 37
38 39 40 41 42 43 44 45 46 47 48 **49** 50 51

Date Forty-Nine: The Stars and the Moon

The morning light guides me along the highway, through the city of Chatsworth, home of porn stars and horse farms, and then through Santa Susanna, where the rocks are stacked like children's toys, and the mountains overshadow the strip malls in their midst. I drive up through Box Canyon, and though there is a long, terrifying drop to the right of my car, I can't help but slow down and admire the great breathtaking golden bowl that is this Valley. With its weeping willows and isolated air, I love it immediately. As I drive up the rustic dirt road that leads to my shaman's new home my eyes fill with tears at the beautiful Spanish-tiled cottage that she now shares with Charles. Charles is not Lidia's husband. Charles is the shaman whom she met last January at a sweat lodge. Charles is the railroad switch and the catalyst for Lidia's divorce.

Two weeks ago, I drove up to the Ojai Valley to meet both Lidia and Charles at the sweat lodge they conduct together. I saw them talking, and I knew immediately that this was the man for whom she had been waiting. Charles went to stoke the fire, and Lidia walked up. She put her arm around me as we watched this grizzled, smoking man labor over the hot stones which were to make that day so special.

"So that's your bear?" I asked.

We both looked at Charles, so large and dark and beautiful. "Yes, he is."

Lidia told me that it wasn't easy. That she had been married to her husband for twenty years, and that in many ways, that man she just left was her best friend. She told me Charles was in a relationship too. But then she told me that once they knew they were in love with each other, there just weren't too many other options than to live that truth.

"You took the bold path," I said.

"Yes we did, honey. Sometimes life demands that we jump right in."

As I sit across from Lidia in her new home I know that as much as the choice was difficult, as much as it was bold, it was also right. Her home feels right. We sit in a different room now, but the couch is the same, and her chair is the same. The tea cups are also the same, and so it feels as comfortable as ever. She asks me if I liked the sweat.

"I did. It was a little hard. The first time doing this work, I think it's always a little removed. You have to get past the part where you think you're crazy."

"The hokeyness?" she asks.

And I love that she can see that, even in her life's work. I explain to her that I went in with the intention to let go of perfection and fantasy. To move past these concepts of movie-star love and scripted romances and what men are supposed to be in order to have a new experience in this world. I know that I cannot be open to my Charles if I am not willing to see him.

"Ho," Lidia says. I find out at the retreat that "ho" means a sort of "Right on" in the Native American culture.

And so I tell her. I tell her about Oliver. About Jimmy. About my father. And ultimately, about Ben.

I tell Lidia how the night before, I knew I was going to run into Ben at a meeting, and I knew that most likely we would hang out afterward to talk about our writing. We have been doing that more and more lately. Three times in the last week. We bring our work, sit down at coffee, and edit for each other. Last night, we were doing just that. Ben was talking about the chapter where I visit my dad in prison.

"I just don't think you're showing enough of you," he told me.

"Really, I feel like it's pretty honest."

"It's honest, but it's not the full story. I want to know all of you, Kristen, not just pieces."

"Okay," I said. And I tried to ignore that the comment on my work is the one thing I have been waiting years for a man to say.

I still can't figure out his intentions, but perhaps even more confusing, I can't figure out mine. I often ask my friends when they start dating someone, if they like the guy because they like the guy, or if they like him because they think he likes them. I am not sure if I want Ben in my life, or if I just want someone. But then I remember about giving up on these fantasies and these demands for romantic perfection. Maybe I just need be open to Ben—open to who he can be, open to what we might be. But that is also terrifying.

I explain to Lidia that I had wanted to invite Ben over to my house to work instead of going to a coffee shop, but then at the last minute, I just couldn't spit out the invitation.

"Why not?" Lidia asks me.

"Because I was worried he'd say no."

"What if he said yes?"

"Then I was worried he would be too hot. My apartment gets hot. I don't have air conditioning."

Lidia just looks at me. I am in the most honest room in my world, and I am trying to tell her that my fear of rejection comes down to AC.

"I think it's more than that, Kristen."

"It's the little girl."

When I don't invite Ben to my place, we get tea at a café up the street. We go over some of my work, and we talk about his, and we begin to ease into this new thing we're doing called flirting. But I am not entirely there, and I know it, and because Ben knows me rather well by now, he knows it too. By not speaking up and asking him over, I have in my own way checked out, and insecurity has shown up in the void.

Lidia and I stand up to begin the work. We stand with our arms raised as Lidia opens with a prayer, "Great mountains, great sky. Stars and moon and sun and the gravity which keeps us rooted in sweet mother earth, thank you for being the truth. You are the evidence of the Great Spirit. You are bigger than our fantasies. You are bigger than my sister's dreams. Please help her to have faith in the work of our ancestors. To believe in her own life, her paths, her truth."

We kneel down, and Lidia brings out her stones. She asks, "So tell me about the little girl? How old is she?"

I don't hesitate to say, "Ten."

"And what was happening when you were ten?"

I remember being that confused little girl, playing teacher by myself in our garage with the colored chalk I had stolen years before. I remember stinging from some insult my grandmother had just tossed at me—some question about why I wasn't more like Melanie, Missy, Sonia, or Sarah. And all I remember is thinking, "I wish I was someone else." I explain to Lidia that I used to fantasize about getting abducted. We would go to the mall, and I would try to wander off in the hopes that some man would steal me and take me away.

"Well, you were missing your dad," Lidia offers.

It's funny how it can takes decades to connect the obvious.

She smiles at me. "You're still missing your dad, Kristen."

And though I wish she was wrong, I know she is right. I am still missing my dad. Because after he moved back to Connecticut, it became clear that he is back in his old business. He has been running drugs in and out of Nogales, Mexico, and it doesn't take me long to figure out that he was doing that the whole time he was in Texas. That the farm and the Blue Tick hounds was all a front. That had I gone to visit him, I would have been going to visit a pot farm as much as a citrus one. And it hurts. It hurts that this man I was assigned as a father could be so untrustworthy.

We get on the floor, and when it comes time to pick out the stones, I reach for the big, shiny one that looks like a crystal ball. The one I wanted on my first visit. At first I hesitate, but then I tell Lidia, "The ten-year-old wanted the shiny one, but I wasn't going to let her have it."

"Why not?" Lidia asks, laughing.

"Because I always want the bright shiny one, and I used to take it without earning it."

She looks at me. "Kristen, you've earned it. She's earned it."

And we have. Nine months after that first visit with Lidia, I finally choose the crystal ball. Lidia decides where to place it, and I can feel the energy surge in my palm. It has craved that ball ever since we began here. As though she can hear my thoughts, I feel her place it in the palm of my left hand. I ask her, "What is the bright shiny one for?" And she tells me, "It is the source of femininity."

And we begin. I don't know what happens. It takes some time for me to settle into the spiritual netherworld that is this work. But then I can feel it. I can feel the energy flowing up through the ball, through my arms, through my body, and out through my open palm. I put it on my heart, and I go to meet that ten-year-old. And she wants nothing to do with me. She ignores my presence. She doesn't want this healing. But then as we continue, I enter into my childhood. I go back to the condominium complex where I grew up. I walk outside, along the creek bed where she used to play, and I watch my ten-year-old self. I can feel her. And I know she can feel me.

The energy is moving. And then it hits me. I will be in Dallas next weekend, and I can go to my childhood home, and I can meet that child for real. And together we can leave the past behind.

Date Fifty: La Cosa Nostra

It's a couple of days before my trip to Texas, and I am talking with Nana about whether Tom, Vic, and I should go boating. Three months ago, my uncle Vic's house was foreclosed on, he shuttered his business, and moved into my uncle Tom's house in Dallas. The Republican insurance agent and the gay florist might make for a great sitcom, but not for great roommates. They have been fighting ever since, and I am reasonably concerned about being on a boat all day with a cooler of beer and two hot Sicilian temperaments.

"Oh, God. Nana, I'm afraid Tom might throw Vic overboard."

"He does make Tom mad," she says, sounding disappointed.

"Well, Vic is kind of like Fredo."

Nana asks, "From *The Godfather*?"

"Yeah, I mean, he's cuter. But still. And Tom...Tom is just like Sonny. Good looking, charismatic." I think about it for a second. "Which makes me Michael."

"Yeah, you are Michael," she admits, which I'm pretty impressed she agrees with because Michael's kind of the star, and Nana normally likes being the star.

"And you, of course, are the Don," I tell her.

"I'm not fat," she argues.

"Well, you're not a man either, Nana. Come on, stick with the game."

"What about Mom, then?" she asks.

"Mom? Mom is Tom the Consigliere, the reliable one we all go to for counsel."

"She is reliable," Nana concedes, though I think she wants that title too.

And that is how I go to visit the Corleones in Dallas. Sonny, Fredo, and the Don want to take me on my fiftieth date, and I readily agree. I have the day off before I go and am house-sitting at Noelle's before I leave.

I am at work getting some last-minute things finished up before my trip when the phone rings. It is my father. The last time we spoke, my father attempted to send me money for my birthday. Money I ultimately declined. Because I didn't know the source, and it was too much, and sadly, I know that once my father gives you money, he thinks you're his. And $1,000 thirty-one years after the fact is just a little too late to claim this property overnight.

"Look, Dad, if you want to make things right, come and visit," I explain to him. "Take me to dinner. But I don't need this money. Not this way."

Five days later, I get that call at work, and I find out my dad is in Arizona.

"I'd like to come visit you," he tells me.

"Okay, I'd like that too," I reply because I need this date with my father.

"How about next week?" he asks.

"Okay, that works."

And then we get off the phone, and I realize that doesn't work at all. That we have spent our whole lives making plans for next week. I call him back and tell him, "Dad, every time we say next week, it never happens. How about you come tomorrow? I leave for Dallas on Saturday, but we can have dinner, spend some time together, and I'm afraid if we don't do it now, we'll never do it." I don't take a breath. I don't need one.

"Okay."

The next night I wait at Noelle's house for my father to arrive. I talk to Mom, and she asks me why it matters so much that I get to see him, and I know instantly that if I don't, I will regret it for the rest of my life. Because this will be the first time I have seen my father outside of prison walls since I was five years old. Because my dad is currently making bi-monthly trips to Nogales, one of the most dangerous cities in the world. Because though I find it terrifying that this man is in the middle of the double-crossing world of the Mexican drug trade, he is still my dad, and if he died, and I didn't get to have one dinner with him outside of prison walls, a part of me would die too.

I don't drink so I can't steady my nerves. I don't smoke, so that one is gone too. I eat a little bit of cookie dough, and I do the set of prayers I have learned from Lidia. I pray to Sach'amama that I might shed these scales of my old relationship with my dad, to let go of who my father is and who I am as his daughter. I pray to Otorongo that I am able to speak the truth tonight, to live the truths my father cannot. I pray to my ancestors that he and I are guided into a place of love and understanding. I pray to Lidia's great condor that I may be kept safe from his darker sides and see the big picture of who we are to one another. I pray to my mother Earth to keep me grounded in my flesh and in the present. And I pray to the universe, to the stars and the moon, that I be given the faith in this relationship, in my father's and my journey. I know that whatever happens, it is all part of that great plan of which I have very little knowledge. And by the time my father pulls up in his black Cadillac, I am calm.

My father gets out of the car, and I shocked again by how old he has become. I have my father's image embroidered in my mind from the photos I hold so dear from when I was young. Though skinny and short, my father cut a dashing figure. He had a wild mass of black curly hair, piercing hazel eyes, and the type of big nose that you just don't fight with. He wore beautiful Ralph Lauren clothes and though there were times he looked like the seventies drug smuggler he was, there was always an element of stylish class to his demeanor.

The man who gets out of the car is old. He has straight white hair and a busted-up nose, and he wears a Hawaiian shirt with shorts and a fleece vest. He is not the father I remember. He gets out and grabs me in a huge embrace, but it's awkward for me. I hug my uncles all the time because they are *mi famiglia*. But I realize in that moment, that though I know my father in many ways, I do not know him like this. I do not know him in the real world.

We go into Noelle's house, and we play with Rocky, who my father says looks a lot like Red Dog, and I warm a bit. He jokes, "Thank God we have this pup here; it certainly makes it less tense."

I laugh because it sounds like something I would say. Our similarities are real, and sometimes they're kind of nice. I drive my father to the stables because he was the man who introduced me to horses. He meets Arrow and as we walk away he grabs my hand and says, "Thank you, K, for bringing me here."

We go to my apartment before dinner so he can see where I live, and we look through old photo albums, and he touches these pictures of me growing up, of his parents who both died while he was still in prison, of the lives he never got the chance to be a part of, and he begins to cry. At one point in the night my father quips to me, when I press him about being back in the business, "That's just who I am, babe. No changing me."

But as he sits there, shaking over a photo of his own mother and father, I know there is a part of him that wishes he had gotten the chance to change. I bend down and hold him. This man who has offered me nothing but a fantastical love and many very real disappointments; this man who pretends that he is who he is, and we ought to just be fine with that; this man whose life is shot through with a thousand forms of fear and pain and loss; this man is real, and he hurts. He cries, and I whisper, "It's okay, Daddy," and I realize this night might not actually be about my closure. It's about his.

We go out to dinner, and he stares at me like I am the most beautiful woman he's ever seen. It makes me uncomfortable, but I also know my dad never quite knew who I was. We get gelato at Pazzo, and he puts his arm around me as we walk to the car. For all my family's jokes about being the Corleones, my father actually looks like a Mafioso, and I wonder what my friends would think if they ran into us. That I was using again, and this was my dealer. That my dad is creepy and cool, all at once. That I look rather awkward next to this man who is my blood, my love, and my oldest sorrow.

We drive down Sunset, and the opera Cavalleria Rusticana comes on. It is my favorite opera, so I turn the music up. The notes swell, and my father holds my hand. I look over at him and smile. And for a moment, for one brief moment, he is my dad, and I am his daughter, and the scales fall from my eyes, and the truth becomes clear, and I am guided back to him. And the big picture, and the present moment, and the faith that we are to each other exactly what we are supposed to be, fills my heart. Because as much as I know this will probably not happen again for a very long time, I am so glad it is happening now. Just this moment with each other, this things of ours, or as they say in Sicily, *la cosa nostra*. There is no fear or pain or loss. Just the two of us driving down Sunset Boulevard in my Honda Civic, listening to Cavalleria Rusticana, holding each other's hand.

I say goodbye to my father that night, and though it might not be the relationship for which I waited my whole life, I know that our lives are as they should be. And I do not question. I feel good. I feel blessed. And the next morning, I board a flight, and I walk into the loving arms of the Corleones.

Uncle Tom makes dinner, and I spend the evening lying on the shoulder of one uncle or another. And they both tell me consistently how much they love me, how proud they are of me, and I know that this is what I am looking for in a man. Someone who looks at me like I'm the most beautiful woman in the world but who also shows up time and time again to be there for me.

As I counsel Uncle Tom about his heartbreak and spend the next two days working with Uncle Vic on his depression, I know that I will be there for the right man too. Because I am for these men.

The next day, I walk from my grandmother's house to the condominium where I grew up. I skip along the railroad tracks that I wandered down so often when I was twelve and angry. I listen to The Velvet Underground, and I enter the world of my childhood. I am walking along the creek bed where I spent a good deal of my youth pouting when I see a tree house on the other side.

And the next thing I know, I am leaping from rock to rock to cross the creek, monkey-barring my way to the other side, and landing relatively gracefully on the opposite bed, after a swinging jump bigger than I have performed in years. I climb up into the tree house, lie down, and begin the energy work I know so well. I listen to the creek, and I reach out to the ten-year-old who gets scared inside. It doesn't take long as she is right there, and the fact that I have made this vision quest in her honor is almost enough to make her happy and whole. Because this is a little girl who just wanted to be loved. She wanted her daddy home; she wanted everything to be okay; and so I get to go to her, and I get to tell her that it is.

We go home and stop at our childhood McDonald's for an ice cream cone. We hug Don Corleone and know that as much as we wish we could change others, we cannot. And the only way out of our insecurities is to believe in change for ourselves. I can be confident. I can hold the gaze of a man and smile. But more than that, I can be the strong and loving woman, and the healing force my future partner will need. I don't need to turn into that little girl, but I don't need to ignore her either. Because she is the keeper of the light and the source of so much of my love, and she's on my side. She is on my side.

Date Fifty-One: The Sparkling Ribbon of Time, Act III

I find myself standing in the Griffith Observatory, reading again the passage about the Sparkling Ribbon of Time: "From the earliest moments of the universe, the pattern was set for the structure we see today, that structure is revealed by glowing galaxies of stars. Galaxies congregate in clusters which form webbing that extends throughout the universe. This webwork is the ultimate structure of reality."

This webwork is the ultimate structure of reality, and I am just one teeny little speck of dust in the infinite life of God. Just little ole me, looking for romance. I walk into Nat's bridal suite this morning wondering whether I will have gotten what I seek by the end of the night. Immediately I am greeted by the makeup artist Vincent, who asks me, "Which starlet are you?"

I smile and say, "I'm Grace Kelly." Nat asked all of us which Old Hollywood star we wanted to be styled like for her wedding, and I didn't even need to think about it. At first she protested, "You don't even look like Grace Kelly." But it didn't matter to me. I knew there was no one else I could be.

I tell Vincent this, and he laughs. "Honey, even Grace Kelly had to fight to be Grace Kelly." And I know he's right. Because I've had to fight to be me too. But then Vincent works his magic, and I slip on my bridesmaid dress, and I know my fight is over. I may not look like Grace Kelly, but I look like me, and I'm happy with that.

I saw Ben on Wednesday night after our meeting, and we were talking about the wedding when he realized that it would be occurring at the same time as one of the playoff games for the L.A. Dodgers. At first he was joking that if he got offered tickets, he might not be able to make it to the wedding. I laughed. "Well, I guess neither of us will be going then."

"I'm not kidding, Kristen. If someone gives me tickets, that's going to be a tough choice."

John is standing there, appalled. John is Reggie's sponsor and is also in the wedding party, so he's gotten a chance to see this burgeoning and questionable relationship up close.

"You can't cancel on Kristen," he tells Ben.

"For the Dodgers, I can," Ben shoots back.

John looks at me and back to Ben, "But *it's* Kristen."

Ben shrugs, "No. *It's* the Dodgers."

"Whatever," I say, turning around and walking off.

It doesn't take long for Ben to follow me and tell me he will be there. That he has made the commitment and that he won't ditch out. I try to be jokey and grab his arm. "It'll be fun, Ben. Besides, it's with me, and I'm actually quite charming."

We laugh, and he walks me to my car, and we say goodbye, and I wonder if that's what I want. Someone who isn't excited to hang out with me. I stand in the ladies' room, waiting for Ben to begrudgingly show at the wedding, and I wonder again whether romance will be mine by the end of the night. And if so, do I even want one with Ben?

I do a final primp and then go join the bride in her dressing room. She looks perfect, and she is so happy, and excited, and ready to go and embark on this adventure with her new husband, and I feel nothing but joy for her. We walk out to the sunroom, from which the procession will start. Everybody files out, and I am the last one standing with the bride.

She looks at me nervously, and I kiss her cheek. "You're going to have a beautiful marriage."

And I mean it.

The wedding is perfect. And the bride and groom are perfect. And I know that though I may not be ready to have one of these affairs right now in my life, I do look forward to having one someday. The bride and groom kiss, and we all head back inside for photos and mingling. I find Ben, and we get some coffee. The wedding is taking place in an old castle in which a wealthy family once lived, but like all great buildings too big for their ancestors, this one has now been converted into artists' residences above the spaces used for weddings and other receptions.

There is a staircase leading up to the rest of the building with a sign that clearly states, "Residents Only."

But Ben and I venture past the sign and up into the rest of the castle. The halls remind me so much of the Chelsea Hotel that it's a little eerie. I could spend hours looking at the art hanging in the hallways and listening into people's spaces, but Ben likes to cruise through. I lead us to the top floor because I think there might be something interesting up there, and Ben follows.

I like this. I like doing this with Ben. The fact that he instigated the expedition and is quick to follow my lead, makes me forget that he doesn't often seem so interested in doing so. And as I bound up the staircase, I lose sight of the fact that he doesn't open doors, that he failed to tell me that I looked pretty tonight, and that he seems to look at me only as a buddy.

"You're not a buddy," Mimi told me the other night when I explained Ben's and my relationship.

"Well, I am his, I guess," I replied.

"No, but Kristen. You shouldn't be. You're somebody's woman. That's the type of person you are."

"I don't know." I shrugged. "I used to be buddies with lots of guys. I was in a fraternity for Christ sake."

"Yeah, used to be. You're not anymore."

And she's right. I am somebody's woman. I am not their buddy. And as Ben and I go on our adventure through the Castle Green, I realize that I can do this as Ben's Grace Kelly, or I can do it as Ben's Girl Friday. So I lift up my head, toss my shawl across my shoulders, and float back down the staircase like my girl Grace.

Ben and I sit down at our table, and after the food and toasts, people get up to go dance. I lean over and tell Ben, "So I need to leave here at eight."

"At eight?" He looks at his watch. It's 7:05 p.m.

"Yeah. For whatever reason, I have found myself at the Observatory with almost every important date. And every time I am there, I see people in line for the show at the Planetarium. I keep waiting for the person I am with to say, "Hey, let's catch the show," but no one ever has. So tonight, I want to catch the show. It's at 8:45. And either I will go alone, or you will come with me."

"I already know the answer to that," Ben says, smiling. But it's a Cheshire grin, and I can't really tell which way he is leaning. I'm not really sure that I know which way I am leaning either, but I know that this is how the chess game works.

I remind Ben that when we were talking the other night, we talked about how exciting it is when you meet someone you like and then you go traveling on your own right afterward. Ben had told me how he always fantasizes that the new love interest is sitting next to him on the plane. And he imagines what the trip would be like together.

He laughs. "Yeah, I can't believe I told you that."

"I know," I say. "And that's why I also know that you're secretly a romantic."

"So?"

"So then, why don't you do romantic things?" I ask him.

"Because if you do romantic things with a girl," he tells me, "she will immediately begin to think that you want some long-term thing with her. She'll start hoping for the future."

"So you just lock up all the romance. Keep it in the garage?"

"Sure do," he says, feigning a Texas accent.

I shake my head again because though we're joking, it's all so damn true. John and Teresa Tull show up at the table, and they drag us off to dance. I hit the dance floor with my usual maniacal, white-girl moves, but Ben just stands off to the side. He doesn't like to dance. After the first song, I join him because I feel bad.

"Aren't people strange?" I say. Because I always say that.

"How so?"

"I don't know. Whenever they dance, I just get this feeling that we're still so primitive, all participating in our weird funny tribal rituals."

"Well, isn't that your whole thing? The ritual of romance and mating," Ben asks.

"Yeah, I don't get that as much on the dance floor though. I'm kind of a solo dancer."

"Aha," Ben says. "There's your problem."

I smile sadly. "No, that's the thing. Every guy I ever loved knew how to move with me. They just came in and molded me into dancing with them."

Ben looks at the dance floor, and I know he has no clue how to do that.

Cradle of Love comes on. Originally Natalie had tried to choreograph a routine to the Billy Idol hit for the bridal party to perform as the first dance. But there was no time, and no one was that interested. Except for John and I. We hear the first two chords and see each other across the dance floor. Teresa nods for him to go for it, and he and I lead the bridal party in whatever parts we can remember from the dance. Nat and Reggie join in, and we're all jumping around and yelling and laughing. I am falling over myself and having a blast. Ben watches from the side, and though it is a perfect opportunity for him to join in, he just sips his coffee and nods in my direction.

The dance ends, and I rush up to Ben. "What time is it?"

He looks at his phone. "7:53 p.m."

I grab my purse and say goodbye to the bride and groom and walk up to Ben at 7:58 p.m. We leave the Castle Green and are standing on the sidewalk in front of it.

"Well, are you supposed to make a formal request?" Ben asks.

"Sure. Ben, would you like to come with me on an adventure to the Observatory Planetarium tonight, right now, at eight o'clock?"

He smiles. "I can't."

And I smile back and say, "Garage door...shut." And then I turn around.

And I leave. Just like that.

No more conversation. No more easy jokes. Because I am done waiting around for men who don't know how or don't want to be there.

I get in my car, and *Love Will Tear Us Apart* comes on. I drive down the 134, the highway under which I go horseback riding into the mountains. La Cañada sits to my North, and the lights of Jimmy's new neighborhood Eagle Rock glow to the South. I move onto the 5, one of Los Angeles's most notoriously crowded highways, but it is wide open for me, and I drive with the window down, through Burbank, past the Equestrian Center and my wonderful Arrow. The Dodgers played tonight, but I have missed their traffic too as I exit onto Sunset Boulevard and drive through Echo Park, past the Mexican restaurants and hipster bars, through Silver Lake, past Pazzo gelato and my studio apartment and my great, big, magical life. I turn onto Vermont, and I drive up toward Griffith Park. I can see the hills rise up before me. The bright light of the Observatory beckoning me home.

Winter is on its way, and the night smells of it. Even though it would be considered warm in any other part of the country, I can tell that people have lit their fireplaces tonight. They are settled into Sunday evenings at home with their husbands, their wives, their lovely smiling children. As I pull into the lot of the Observatory, I know, that just like winter, my partner is on his way too.

And when he arrives, there will be no closed doors. Because love doesn't happen like that. Love happens when the door is open. When the romance is real. When the faith is bigger than the fear. And I am ready. Ready to go on the adventure with someone who is excited to be on it with me.

I rush up to the Observatory as eager as I have ever been, excited, finally, to see the show at the Planetarium, whether I have a date or not. My dress flutters behind me, and my hair looks perfect as I take the steps two at a time. I hit the box office with all the excitement and quiver on my lips as though a man is standing there.

And then I see it.

The sign.

The sign on the window of the box office. It reads: "Due to technical difficulties, the Planetarium is closed today."

And I burst out laughing. I don't care that I am standing by myself in the Observatory wearing a bridesmaid dress and hair and lipstick reminiscent of an Old-Hollywood star. I don't care that there are people looking at me and that a small group of Japanese tourists have just taken a picture. I stand there, and I laugh, and I say quite out loud, "Perfect. It's perfect." Because it is.

I walk downstairs past the Sparkling Ribbon of Time, past the history of our universe, and our destinies and our legacies and our smallness in the great vastness of God. And I go outside to where I once stood with Oliver, and I look out at Los Angeles, at the big, lighted grid that is this city I love, and I know that they are out there. Ben, Jimmy, Arrow, my next magical man, my railroad switch, my soul mate, and I know that the inscription on my favorite Observatory exhibit makes us all seem so moot: "We are connected to the origin of the universe by the sparkling ribbon of time, that reaches from the Big Bang to today, and we observe what the universe is, understand what it is doing, and appreciate how long all of this has been going on."

Because that sign at the Observatory box office says something far more than "Due to technical difficulties, the Planetarium is closed today." It says, "Not yet, Kristen. Not this way."

The city sparkles below me.

My home. My love.

And like all great loves, this city has taught me so much. Because I came to Los Angeles looking for a life that shone like the Hollywood sign, and I found something quite different.

I found rose gardens and kind people who just want to make the world a better place. I found sobriety and spirit guides that have shown that faith is in me. And in that magic, I have no doubt that the chess game is being played exactly as it should.

I can get on my horse and ride into the hills, and I can create any kind of story I want. Because life can be just a series of ice cream sandwiches eaten while watching TV, or it can be the ultimate adventure into who we are and where we want to go.

And one day, there will be a man who enters into that life and fits just right. I know he's out there. In that big, sparkling grid, in that big, sparkling world, he is there.

But for tonight, and for now, I get to do this part of the adventure on my own.

Acknowledgments

I never understood why people always thanked their agents first until I had one myself. Michael Broussard: you are so much more than my agent. You are my friend, brother, and biggest cheerleader. Many thanks to you, and Dino, for always believing in me.

To Dan Smetanka—for believing in this project from beginning to end to end. You've become my family, and I am truly sorry for that. Thank you for making this an exceedingly better book as well as making it a reality. If only you could edit everything I say, I would be a much better person for it. To all the people at Counterpoint/Soft Skull Press, thank you for giving me a new home and this book, a new life.

Gregg Sullivan for being the only ex-boyfriend not named in this book, and instead, becoming my publicist. Thank you, Gregg, for always supporting me—in our last chapters and our latest one.

If I could dedicate this to someone who wasn't my family (which they would never allow), it would be to the amazing support system of friends who listened to each date as they were being written and who showed up to star in the book, even if they weren't too sure they wanted to: Annathena Grigclevich, Michelle Chaplin, Gavril Lourie, MJ Offen, Maureen Williams, Susan Burnett, Jennifer Sullivan, Lucy Madeline, Cathlyn Lang, Jennifer Hallock, Maggie Brown, Jesse Marrero, Michelle Matheson, and Eilene Walsh.

And to my professional friends who helped me to believe that a good story is always worth being told (and who gave me the time to tell it): Kiwi Smith, Neil Strauss, Deanna Kizis, Dominick Anfuso, Judith Regan, Lee Cohen, Andrea Chu, Julia Gaskill, Avery Bell, and Alex Lopez.

This would have been a really boring book if not for the spiritual guides who helped to make this story what it is and to make me who I am. My heart is forever connected to yours: Gisselle Acevedo, Elissa Zimmerman, Paul Perrotta, Carla Moore, Noelle Franco, Suzanne Curtis, Eddie, Arrow, and Rocky.

To the men: the dates, the exes, my great, wonderful (and otherwise) lovers. Thank you for letting me tell your stories. And ours.

And finally, to the people this book is actually dedicated to: mi famiglia. Mom: there are no words to describe my love for you. I won the day I was born by getting you as my mom. Nana: thank you for loving this book and for being my soul mate and my swipey. Uncle Tom: Thank you for taking on the starring role as dad. And for being so cute and single. Uncle Vic: I would never have known to believe in art without you—or designer labels.

Daddy: thank you for the dream. The next one is for you.

photo by Gavril Lourie

Kristen McGuiness was born in Easton, Connecticut, but spent her formative years amongst the horse stables and shopping malls of Dallas, Texas. She left the Lone Star State at seventeen to attend Hamilton College in Clinton, New York, where she studied government and partying.

After college, she spent years working in the book industry in both publicity (at St. Martin's Press) and editorial (at Free Press/Simon & Schuster and for Judith Regan at HarperCollins). Upon moving to Los Angeles, Kristen worked in film development for Spring Creek Productions, and also as an assistant to a top Hollywood agent. The last few years, she has worked as a fundraising manager for a Los Angeles–based nonprofit which provides educational and social services to low-income children, youth, and families.

In addition to her passion for child advocacy, Kristen has been a dedicated writer since the age of five, when she won first place for her short story, "Run Sally Run." Since that time, she has had her first screenplay, *The Betty*, optioned by an independent film producer, and is currently hard at work on her second book.

When she is not hanging out with the children at her work, the horses at her stables, or the sober people and shamans who have helped to make it all possible, she likes to go on magical adventures throughout Los Angeles.